A suitable Snubnose Morris rolling chassis and parts, originally registered in Cornwall in June 1930, has formed the foundation for the recreation of one of Michelin's fleet of Technical Service vans, in use between 1930 and 1932 (see pages 73-75). This picture was taken in early April 2005 at a time when the major restoration work had been completed in readiness for the van's first public appearance on 11 May 2005.

ISBN 2 06 711495 6

Published by Michelin Travel Publications
Hannay House, 39 Clarendon Road,
Watford, Hertfordshire WD17 1JA
Tel: 01923 205 240 Fax: 01923 205 241
Int. tel: +44 1923 205 240 Int. fax: +44 1923 205 241
E-mail: travelpubsales@uk.michelin.com
Website: www.ViaMichelin.com

Michelin Tyre PLC
Campbell Road, Stoke-on-Trent ST4 4EY
Tel: 01782 402000 Fax: 01782 402011
Website: www.michelin.co.uk

Edited by Louise McIntyre
Designed by Richard Parsons
Printed and bound in Great Britain
by J. H. Haynes & Co. Ltd, Sparkford

MICHELIN

Centenary

1905-2005

A CELEBRATION OF MICHELIN'S FIRST HUNDRED YEARS IN THE BRITISH ISLES

Acknowledgements and picture credits

The pictures and photographs that illustrate this book were sourced from Michelin's archives in the UK and France, from Automobiles Citroën and Automobiles Renault in France, and from the John Reynolds Collection.

Many of the drawings and cartoons of Monsieur Bibendum reproduced here were created by Ernie Sherry during his time as an employee of Michelin at Stoke-on-Trent. They originally appeared in the company's house magazine, *Bibendum*, during the 1960s and 1970s.

All reproduction of these copyright images is strictly forbidden without the prior written permission of the publishers.

The assistance of the following individuals and libraries is also gratefully acknowledged:

Malcolm Bobbitt
Bryan Goodman
Chris Marshall
Peter Rowley OBE
Tony Stokoe
Dr Charles Veys OBE
Jean Roberts
John Walker
The British Rubber Manufacturers Association
Christie's, South Kensington
Edinburgh Central Library
The Imperial War Museum
Kensington Central Library
The London Borough of Barking & Dagenham
The Ludvigsen Library
The National Archives, Kew
The Society of Motor Manufacturers and Traders

Plus many Michelin employees, current and retired.

This project has opened up new avenues of research and Michelin takes this opportunity to thank John Reynolds warmly for his guidance, knowledge and contribution to this publication.

Contents

Foreword

One hundred years at the forefront of progress

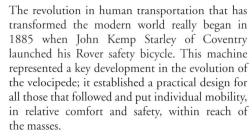

The revolution in human transportation that has transformed the modern world really began in 1885 when John Kemp Starley of Coventry launched his Rover safety bicycle. This machine represented a key development in the evolution of the velocipede; it established a practical design for all those that followed and put individual mobility, in relative comfort and safety, within reach of the masses.

My great-grandfather Édouard and his brother André also had the foresight to realise that efficient personal mobility using machines was a goal worth pursuing. It presented a commercial opportunity from which a healthy business could be developed. They took that opportunity in 1891 when a cyclist, thought to be an Englishman, presented himself at the gates of their rubber factory in Clermont-Ferrand looking for someone who could repair the punctures in his new-fangled air-filled tyres. Within months, Michelin tyres, of a novel detachable design which had only just been patented, were put on display at London's Stanley Bicycle Show where orders were taken for 2,000 pairs.

André and Édouard had tremendous faith in their cycle tyres but realised that the future lay in products for the automobile, primitive examples of which were already taking to the roads by the mid-1890s. Their thoughts were translated into reality with their success in the 1895 Paris-Bordeaux race when they competed in a vehicle they had created themselves and which was equipped with Michelin pneumatic tyres – the first time that air-filled tyres had ever been used on an automobile. As Édouard Michelin's direct descendent, I am proud to be able to say that, thanks to the brothers' pioneering efforts, the mobility which we all enjoy today is a direct consequence of the outcome of that race. At last, pneumatic tyres could be used not just for bicycles but also for heavy vehicles, and the way was opened for the huge advances in travel and transport that have changed society and brought freedom to the masses.

Once the notorious Red Flag Act had been repealed, the flood gates opened for the rapid development of the British automobile industry. We knew such progress was important for us and our famous Bibendum building in London heralded, in no uncertain terms, our desire to be a major part of it. Michelin Tyre Co. Ltd was one of our earliest subsidiaries outside France and we had both British and French directors, even then.

During the course of the past 100 years, the Michelin name has become a familiar household word for the inhabitants of the British Isles. Bibendum, the Michelin Man, has always been a great ambassador for us and I know he holds a place of great affection in British hearts. But Bibendum can only deserve such a place if our customers are satisfied with our products. In this respect, our commercial success reflects a high level of user satisfaction, whether in tyre related products or in travel publications. I therefore take this opportunity to thank all our British and Irish customers for the support given to us since 1891.

The development of a strong manufacturing base, begun in Stoke-on-Trent in 1927, and extended considerably with the opening of five more production sites between 1960 and 1973, resulted in Michelin contributing significantly to the UK's export activity. Gaining two Queen's Awards for Export Achievement was a pleasing reflection on the efforts of all our employees who made it possible. We have also been honoured to receive recognition for training excellence and in technical matters, with the Prince Philip Medal presented to my father François Michelin at Buckingham Palace in 1983.

I take great pride in knowing that my forefathers, at both a personal and at a Company level, have contributed constructively to the daily life of the British Isles. In 1920, André Michelin assisted in the British government's enquiries about road numbering schemes. Marcel Michelin was keenly interested in sports and he was instrumental in developing a tradition of sporting excellence at the Stoke factory in the 1930s. His work lived on after the war when Michelin hosted annual Sports Days in which thousands saw national and international athletes competing. My great uncle Robert Puiseux was a regular visitor to Stoke, even taking time to play tennis with fellow Michelin employees!

A centenary is a time for celebration and for acknowledging the people who have made it possible. I therefore thank all our English, Irish, Scottish and Welsh employees for their contribution towards Michelin's growth over the years. Now that the Michelin brand-name has been present in the British Isles for ten decades, I feel confident in looking forward to a continued presence in these islands, lasting equally as long, if not longer still. I hope that in the future, as in the past, we can continue to make a positive contribution to the mobility of people, goods and services throughout Great Britain and Ireland, thereby satisfying the expectations of our many customers and partners. We have achieved a great deal together so far and I am pleased to be able to add my name to this publication which records those achievements.

Édouard Michelin

March 2005

Introduction
Pioneers of automotive excellence

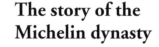

The story of the Michelin dynasty

Early in May 1889, two brothers from Clermont-Ferrand, then a small town in the remote and mountainous Auvergne region of central France, journeyed to Paris to attend the Grande Exposition Universelle. This was a great international trade and industrial fair which had just been opened to commemorate the 100th anniversary of the French Revolution and to celebrate the achievements of French science and technology. The brothers' mission was to exhibit the 'Silent' range of rubber brake blocks for horse-drawn carriages and wagons that they had recently developed at their factory at Clermont. There, they specialised in manufacturing agricultural machinery and rubber goods, such as drive-belts and hoses. Located on the Champ de Mars on the left bank of the Seine, under the shadow of the gigantic tower designed by Gustave Eiffel, which had been constructed specifically to mark the event, the Grande Exposition drew exhibitors from all over Europe and North America, and attracted enormous crowds of visitors from all over France and beyond. More than 15 million people passed through its portals within six months.

The exhibition's organisers hoped that by displaying the French Republic's engineering and manufacturing abilities alongside its accomplishments in the visual arts, they would encourage a

1886 The first self-propelled automobiles built for sale to paying customers are produced by Karl Benz in Germany, but they are no more than motorised tricycles.

1889 The Michelin company is founded, as Michelin & Cie, on 28 May, at Clermont-Ferrand in the Auvergne region of central France.

1891 In May, Michelin perfects its first detachable pneumatic bicycle tyre. In June, an application for a French patent is made and granted. This is followed by the award of a British patent on 18 September.

That month also, a bicycle equipped with Michelin's tyres, and ridden by Charles Terront, wins the 750-mile long Paris-Brest-Paris cycle race, organised by the newspaper *Le Petit Journal.*

In October, the first Michelin bicycle tyres go on general sale and are immediately imported into the UK.

1892 By the end of the year, more than 10,000 French cyclists have equipped their machines with Michelin pneumatic tyres, to replace the sold rubber tyres or iron bands used previously.

1893 In November, Michelin is again represented at the Stanley Show, an annual indoor exhibition held in London. First staged in 1877, up to 1900 the show was devoted exclusively to bicycles.

1894 In July, the first trial of 'horseless carriages' is staged by Comte Albert de Dion, in which 25 vehicles followed a 78-mile route between Paris and Rouen. André Michelin rides as a passenger in the car built – and driven – by Léon Serpollet.

1895 In June, the Michelin brothers enter the Paris-Bordeaux automobile race driving l'Éclair, a vehicle which they have built themselves (using a Peugeot chassis and a 4HP Daimler engine) to demonstrate the advantages of their pneumatic tyres which are patented in May 1896.

In 1895 also, Panhard & Levassor define the 'in-line' anatomy of the modern car by introducing a new four-wheeled model, having the engine at the front, the driving axle at the rear and the steering axle (still controlled by a tiller rather than a steering wheel) at the front. The wheels were shod with solid tyres, however.

The Automobile Club de France is founded by Comte Albert de Dion.

In the UK, in October, the first-ever exhibition of motor vehicles is held, at an open-air event staged at Tunbridge Wells. The following month, five cars are displayed at the Stanley Cycle Show, an indoor event held at the Agricultural Hall in London.

In December, the first issue of *The Autocar* is published – the first British magazine to be devoted exclusively to motoring – it has appeared on a weekly basis ever since. In due course, Michelin becomes a major advertiser in its pages.

Frederick Lanchester produces the first British four-wheeled, petrol-engined automobile. It is the first in the world to be designed from scratch on first principles as a total, integrated concept, rather than as merely a collection of available components obtained from elsewhere. It is designed to be equipped with pneumatic tyres.

1896 The first five Fiacres or horse-drawn cabs to be equipped with Michelin pneumatic tyres appear on the streets of Paris, where a total of 8,000 cabs were then circulating. Within a year three hundred more have joined them.

André and Édouard Michelin, the patriarchs of the Michelin company. By pioneering the pneumatic tyre for cycles and motor cars, the brothers transformed a modest French rubberware firm into a major international business.

marriage between artistic creativity and industrial skill that would guarantee the nation's prosperity over the next one hundred years. Clearly, they were entirely successful in this lofty aim, for the Exhibition resulted in many of the industrial innovations and commercial initiatives that were to transform France (and the world in general) over the coming century and, most especially, in the field of transport. For example, prominently displayed in the Galerie des Machines and the Palais des Industries, were several primitive automobiles and internal combustion engines, exhibited by such pioneering firms or inventors as Peugeot (then principally a bicycle-maker), Serpollet, de Dion, Benz and Otto.

Indeed, the exhibition's Gold Medal was won by the German firm of Otto & Langen for its low-speed, four-stroke internal combustion engine designed by Nikolaus Otto for stationary power-production duties, and later built by the Deutz

Motorenwerk. Also, Karl Benz might never have found commercial success had he not attended the exhibition, for it was here in Paris that he attracted the interest and support of the French entrepreneur, Emile Roger, who signed an agreement to become his French concessionaire and placed an order for several vehicles. The exhibition also resulted in the meeting of Gottlieb Daimler (Otto & Langen's technical director) and Emile Levassor, who arranged for Daimler's new high-speed internal combustion engine (the first engine really suitable for mobile use in propelling an automobile) to be manufactured by Levassor's engineering firm, which led to the founding of France's oldest automobile marque, Panhard & Levassor.

It has often been said that while Germany fathered the motor car, France was its mother country. If so, it was at the Grande Exposition Universelle that the fruitful union was consummated. Besides Benz, Daimler and Levassor, the list of motoring

1896 In February, the first Michelin automobile tyres go on sale in France.

In the UK, in November, the first London to Brighton run is staged, to mark the increase in the permitted speed limit for automobiles, from 4mph to 12mph.

1897 The first official meeting of the Automobile Club of Great Britain and Ireland (from 1907, the Royal Automobile Club) takes place in August.

1898 The first Paris Motor Show is staged. Michelin is a major exhibitor.

Louis Renault introduces the universal-jointed shaft drive to transmit power from the engine to the rear axle, replacing the belt or chain drives used until then.

Monsieur Bibendum, Michelin's world-famous mascot and trademark, makes his debut in a poster that appears in April.

1899 An electric-powered car – la Jamais Contente, driven by Camille Jenatzy – becomes the first vehicle to break the 100km/h (62mph) barrier. Naturally, it is fitted with Michelin tyres.

1900 The first edition of the Guide Michelin or Red Guide is published in France with 35,000 copies printed and given away free up to 1919, to promote tourism by automobile.

In the UK, the Prince of Wales, later King Edward VII, takes delivery of his first motor car, a Daimler built at Coventry.

1901 The first of the great international capital-to-capital automobile races, the 687-mile Paris-Berlin event, is won by a Mors car fitted with Michelin tyres. These are now capable of lasting for 1,250 miles.

In the USA, the world's first mass-produced automobile, constructed from standardised parts, is built by Ransome Olds.

1902 The expatriate English racing driver Henry Farman wins the next great international motor race, run between Paris and Vienna. Piloting a Panhard fitted with Michelin pneumatic tyres, he averages 38.4mph for the 615-mile course, run through the most treacherous parts of the French, Swiss and Austrian Alps.

In the UK, the Society of Motor Manufacturers and Traders (the SMMT) is founded. Michelin is an early member, joining in 1906.

1903 The Michelin brothers introduce their first beaded-edge, or Clincher, tyre for automobiles. In this arrangement, the rubber outer cover fits into a recess in the rim and is held in place by air-pressure alone, thus dispensing with the need for clamps, nuts and bolts.

The third and last of the great international automobile races, the Paris-Madrid event, is stopped at Bordeaux after a number of fatal accidents. Marcel Renault (co-founder of the Renault marque, with his brother Louis, who also competed in the race), is among those killed. The leading car at this stage, running on Michelin tyres, had averaged 65mph over 342 miles!

The Tour de France cycle race is held for the first time – Michelin tyres are much in evidence.

In the UK during February, the SMMT holds its first motor show, at the Crystal Palace. Naturally, Clincher-Michelin tyres are on show.

1904 In April, the patent litigation brought by Dunlop collapses and Michelin is able to market its car tyres in the UK under its own name. Consequently, in November, the company opens its first sales office in the UK, at 49/50 Sussex Place, South Kensington, London.

Also in the UK, the Motor Car Act is passed by parliament that August, requiring motor cars to carry numberplates and for drivers to have licences. The speed limit is raised from 12mph to 20mph.

The 'Silent' brake shoes made from rubber by Michelin & Cie in the 1890s sold well in the UK. They were used on horse-drawn carriages and wagons.

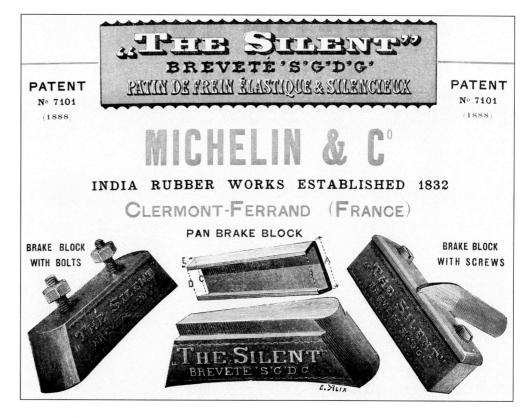

pioneers who are known to have attended the event included the Comte Albert de Dion, Alexandre Darracq, Louis Delage, René Panhard, Armand Peugeot and even André Citroën and Louis Renault, although these two were only boys, aged 11 and 12, at the time.

The Grande Exposition also provided inspiration and encouragement for two other vitally important figures in the history of motoring – the two artist-engineer exhibitors from the Auvergne, whose names were André and Édouard Michelin. Although their 'Silent' brake-block products had won a Bronze Medal at the Paris show, that achievement alone was not enough for the ambitious and enterprising pair. Convinced that the days of the horse-drawn carriage and wagon were coming to an end, and that the future of human mobility lay initially with the bicycle, but ultimately, with the motor car, bus and lorry, they vowed to take immediate steps to reorganise, revitalise and rename their company, ready to meet the new challenges of the automotive era that lay ahead.

So it was that, just a few days after their return from Paris, on 28 May 1889, the firm of Michelin & Cie was formed, thus founding one of France's greatest industrial dynasties and creating an enterprise that was destined, over the following 116 years, to become one of the most widely recognised and trusted brandnames in the world.

The bride from Scotland

It is surely one of the strangest facts of industrial history that the major international company which now dominates the manufacture and marketing of tyres world-wide – for aircraft, trucks, buses, cycles, motorcycles, tractors and earthmoving machinery as well as automobiles – had its origins not in rubber products but in sugar and candy.

The story really began in 1830 when Édouard Daubrée, an ex-army officer from Paris, bought a small sugar refinery at Lavort, about ten miles south-east of Clermont-Ferrand, on the banks of the Allier river. The Daubrée family had made its fortune by importing and refining sugar from the West Indies during the 18th century, but the trade had collapsed as a result of the blockade imposed on French shipping by the Royal Navy during the Napoleonic Wars. This had led to a boom in homegrown sugar-beet production in France, which Daubrée was intent on exploiting, using his family connections and expertise. The reason for his choice of the Auvergne region, where he had once studied, seems to have been influenced by the availability of government grants and the abundance of water-power in that mountainous region.

In October 1829, Édouard Daubrée had married a young Scotswoman, Elizabeth Pugh-Barker, whom he had met in Paris, where she was a pupil at

the finishing school run by his mother. Their marriage took place at St Marylebone parish church in London. Elizabeth, then aged 20, just happened to be a niece of the pharmacist Charles MacIntosh, who had been the first person to discover the secret of dissolving natural rubber in benzine, knowledge which he employed to waterproof fabric and clothing. He founded a company in 1824 to produce the range of patented rain-wear and other outdoor garments that bore his name, corrupted to Mackintosh; this firm survived until 1925 when it was taken over by Dunlop.

Elizabeth (who died in 1858) took with her to the Auvergne, the know-how for making toy rubber balls and other domestic items, which she developed as a side-line to her husband's sugar-refining and confectionary business. This diversification helped the couple to survive the disaster that occurred during the winter of 1831, when following a flash-flood, the River Allier overflowed its banks destroying the buildings in which the sugar-refining firm was located.

Faced with ruin, Édouard Daubrée invited his cousin Aristide Barbier (originally a Paris-based lawyer) to join him in partnership and introduce further capital to relaunch the business, which was to be relocated at Clermont-Ferrand. Fortunately, the partnership flourished and, in 1863, it was formally established as a *société commandite* (private limited company) registered as Barbier, Daubrée & Cie. By then, its activities extended well beyond its principal original purpose, and included the manufacturing of farm machinery and equipment such as pumps and boilers. Its products are known to have won many medals and prizes at industrial fairs and exhibitions, including two gained in London in 1862. In 1836, it supported over 100 employees and by 1890 had expanded way beyond its agricultural beginnings to become a major industrial concern, manufacturing a wide variety of vulcanised rubber articles for domestic, industrial and agricultural uses, such as flexible hoses, drive belts and, of course, the 'Silent' brake-blocks which were exhibited at the 1889 Paris exhibition.

By that time, the management of the family-owned firm had passed into the hands of Aristide Barbier's two grandsons, the Michelin brothers. Messrs Barbier and Daubrée had died in 1863 and 1864 respectively, Daubrée leaving two sons of whom the eldest, Ernest, succeeded his father as managing director, while Barbier left two daughters, Emilie and Adèle. Emilie married a certain Jacques Mage but was widowed, childless, in middle age, but, in 1852, Adèle found a husband in Jules Michelin, a government official in the French customs and excise service who was also an accomplished amateur watercolour artist. She had set up home with him at Clermont-Ferrand where they soon produced three children, a girl, Marie, and two boys, André Jules Aristide (born 16 January

Elizabeth Pugh-Barker (1809-1858), the niece of Charles MacIntosh and wife of Édouard Daubrée. It was she who took the know-how of rubber-goods manufacturing to Clermont-Ferrand from Scotland.

BARBIER ET DAUBRÉE
CONSTRUCTEURS.

EXTRAIT DE L'ALBUM GÉNÉRAL.

CLERMONT-FERRAND
(PUY-DE-DÔME).

POMPES D'ÉPUISEMENT ET D'IRRIGATION

I. SYSTÈME DENIZOT

BREVETÉ S. G. D. G.

POMPE N° 3, AVEC SA TRANSMISSION DE MOUVEMENT.

PRIX : FR. 1,750

TARIF

Pompe n° 1. — 8 mètres cubes à l'heure. Prix : avec balancier à bras, f. 850 » ; — avec transmission de mouvement, f. 1,150 »
Pompe n° 2. — 18 — — Prix : — — » 1,150 » : — — — » 1,450 »
Pompe n° 3. — 50 — — Prix : — — » 1,450 » : — — — » 1,750 »

A LA DEMANDE DES ACHETEURS, LES POMPES SONT, OU A DÉVERSOIR, OU A REFOULEMENT.

Paris. — Imp. FÉLIX MALTESTE et Cie, rue des Deux-Portes-Saint-Sauveur, 22.

The precursor of the Michelin company was the firm of Barbier & Daubrée, makers of pumps and agricultural equipment. Founded in 1832, it was reorganised as Michelin & Cie in May 1889.

1853) and Édouard Etienne (born 23 June 1859). Jules Michelin died in 1870, and Adèle Michelin (née Barbier) in 1898, so it was their sons who became the true founding-fathers of the present-day Michelin industrial dynasty. The elder, André Michelin (1853-1931), trained as a civil engineer at the École Centrale in Paris, graduating in 1877, after which he entered the École des Beaux-Arts to study architecture. Following these studies, for the next five years he became involved in map-making and cartographical design at the French Ministry of the Interior in Paris. Eventually, his interest in maps and guides led him to join the family firm to take charge of its public relations and advertising affairs, and also to develop its publishing activities, including its famous series of road maps and touring guides for motorists, which were launched in 1900. At the same time, he continued to be actively concerned with running a metal-working business, designing and making ornamental wrought-iron gates. He had opened this in rue Bagnolet, on the outskirts of Paris in 1883, dividing his time between Clermont-Ferrand and the capital city, where he owned a large house on the boulevard Péreire, which served as the Michelin company's Paris embassy.

The younger son, Édouard Michelin (1859-1940), set out in life by studying law, but then took up painting at the École des Beaux-Arts in Paris where his tutor and mentor was the academic painter William Bouguereau, the master of conventional or 'official' art. By 1888, at the age of 29, he had set himself up in a studio in Montmartre intending to become a professional artist, although there is no suggestion he would ever have followed in the path of the Impressionists such as Monet, Manet, Pissaro and Degas whose avant-garde work was currently revolutionising the Parisian artistic scene. Before long, however, he was forced to abandon this ambition and embark instead on a remarkable career as an engineer, administrator and entrepreneur, running the family business at Clermont-Ferrand.

The crisis that provoked the Michelin brothers' change of career-plans occurred as a direct result of the death, in 1878, of the family firm's current owner-manager Ernest Daubrée, aged only 48 and the eldest son of Édouard Daubrée. Ernest had proved to be a competent leader. By expanding the business he had provided the other family shareholders with ample private incomes and thus enabled André and Édouard to follow their own personal business interests in Paris. Unfortunately, Ernest was succeeded as managing director by his lawyer and accountant, Jean-Gilbert Bideau, who had become a partner in the firm in 1867, since the obvious heir, Ernest's son Adolphe, was then only 14. Bideau proved incapable as an entrepreneur, so much so that the company soon went into a steep decline; the payroll, which had once totalled as many as 320 employees fell to 30 and even then, their wages were not always paid regularly and promptly. In fact, within ten years of Ernest Daubrée's demise, the situation had deteriorated to such an extent that it threatened the financial security of the entire extended Michelin family, severely reducing the dividends upon which the Michelin brothers and their close relations depended.

Consequently, when Bideau retired in 1886 at the age of 75, André and Édouard Michelin were invited by the then head of the family, their aunt Emilie Mage (*née* Barbier), to take the firm in hand and to reorganise and refinance it. Following a request from the brothers, she provided the necessary funds. Under these circumstances, Édouard had little alternative but to close his studio in Paris and return to Clermont-Ferrand, eventually assuming full control of the company's affairs on a full-time basis, as managing director. Luckily for all concerned, his gift for business was such that, although he had received no commercial or engineering training whatsoever, in the course of the following fifty years he transformed a modest rural

André and Édouard Michelin competed in the 1895 Paris-Bordeaux-Paris race in l'Éclair, the vehicle they had designed themselves to demonstrate their new detachable pneumatic tyres for automobiles – the first to be suitable for fitting on a car.

business into a substantial international organisation employing over 25,000 people. Later, on 28 May 1889, the firm, (which was then trading as Jean-Gilbert Bideau & Cie) was reformed, recapitalised and renamed as Michelin & Cie. Remarkably, even today, the Michelin organisation retains a family-owned strength which is rare in international enterprises.

Interestingly also, both the two artistically gifted Michelin brothers, André and Édouard, found their wives among the same Parisian family, by marrying three daughters of their piano tutor, Auguste Desiré Wolff, who had 12 children. A.D. Wolff was the former professor of music at the Paris Conservatoire who became head of the Pleyel piano business. André married the second eldest daughter Sophie and, later, following her early death, her sister Jeanne, while Édouard married the fifth daughter, Marie Thérèse.

Enterprising and astute, the Michelin brothers prospered greatly in the bicycle and motorcar booms which took place before and after the First World War and soon became figures of great importance in the French economy. Despite being

cunning and secretive (so much so that they were known in Paris as the 'old foxes of the Auvergne') they were certainly not backward or old-fashioned in their outlook. On the contrary, like a good many other entrepreneurs from a rural or provincial background, they proved to be extremely go-ahead in their business methods and embraced modern technology with enthusiasm. Although they were undoubtedly secretive to the point of paranoia, they also possessed a flair for publicity, notably by the creation of their famous and ubiquitous Michelin Man trademark, Monsieur Bibendum, regarded as one of the world's most widely recognised brand symbols.

The creation of the detachable pneumatic tyre

At the outset of the Michelin brothers' involvement with the Clermont-Ferrand rubber firm, their activities had had little connection with wheels, tyres or transport matters, except for the manufacture of brake-blocks. However, shortly after Édouard's return from Paris to take charge of the

enterprise, an event took place that brought about a complete change of direction for the business. This eventually produced a spectacular transformation in the fortunes of the Michelin family as a whole.

The invention in the mid-1880s of the chain-driven safety bicycle equipped with a metal frame, two equal-sized wheels, brakes, pedals and ball-bearing hubs, brought with it a craze for bicycling that swept across England, France and the USA in the last decade of the 19th century. Unlike the penny-farthing and bone-shaker that had preceded it, almost anyone could ride one with ease, although not necessarily in comfort. So for countless middle and upper-class young men and women (who lacked the means or inclination to travel on horseback) its arrival brought freedom and mobility and the urge to escape from the towns to explore the countryside. It also brought prosperity to the many manufacturers which entered the bicycle market at this time, among them such famous names as Rover, Humber, Clement and Peugeot, whose badges would later adorn the earliest automobiles.

As more and more producers joined the business, prices dropped and a bicycle boom ensued – a process that was accelerated yet further by another important innovation: pneumatic rubber tyres which soon began to supersede the solid rubber tyres used hitherto. Patented by John Boyd Dunlop in the United Kingdom in 1888, these comprised an inflatable inner tube surrounded by an outer cover of hard rubber, which was actually bonded

semi-permanently to the wheel by glue, and thus could not easily be detached, repaired and refixed in the frequent event of a puncture. After making the necessary repairs to the tube, the cyclist had to re-unite the outer casing with the wheel using an adhesive which took several hours to set. Normally, he or she would have to wait until the following day before being able to resume the journey.

In 1891, a cyclist on a tour of the Auvergne called at the Michelin factory, seeking assistance. His machine, most likely a Humber (British in name but probably French-made) had suffered a puncture to the novel Dunlop tyres with which it was equipped. He had been carried to the rubber works in a farmer's ox-cart. After struggling for more than three hours in various attempts to repair the tyres and put the bicycle and its rider back on the road, Édouard Michelin had the visionary idea that led to one of the world's earliest detachable pneumatic tyres for bicycles, an invention, which in due course, he repeated for automobiles.

Even at this very early stage in events, he was convinced that, given the rough gravel or cobbled roads of that era, such an innovation could hardly fail to transform road transport. The comfortable ride produced by the pneumatic tyre would guarantee its success – providing the problem of punctures could be overcome. He therefore began a series of experiments to work out a system of repair that would enable a cyclist to 'replace an inner tube within a quarter of an hour by a simple means, and without the need for a specialist …' In other words,

The 'Jamais Contente' – the first car to exceed 100 kilometres per hour, as photographed just after the event in 1899. It was fitted with Michelin tyres.

Although not competitors
as such, the Michelin
brothers were among the
earliest promoters and
pioneers of motor racing.
Here, André Michelin is
seen with Louis Renault
at the 1905 Gordon
Bennett Cup race, held
on the Circuit
d'Auvergne, near
Clermont-Ferrand.

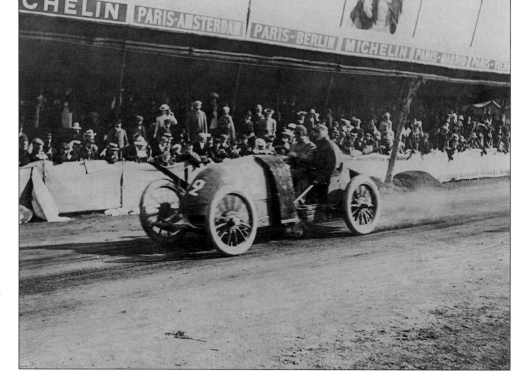

This sixth and last
Gordon Bennett Cup
race of 1905 (also known
as the Grand Prix
d'Auvergne) was won by
Théry in a Richard-
Brasier car running on
Michelin's Semelle tyres.

a detachable tyre which the layperson could repair on his or her own and without fuss.

Creating an easily repairable pneumatic tyre became the Michelin brothers' top priority, a crusade in which they began to invest all the time, effort and money they could spare. Nevertheless, it took much painstaking work by trial and error before Édouard's idea bore fruit and a truly practical, marketable solution was found. From then on, it was possible for cyclists to ride in comfort on a cushion of air and, when experiencing the inevitable puncture, to overcome the difficulty at the road-side by rapidly removing and repairing the tyre, patching the inner tube with the kit that Michelin provided, and then re-inflating it with a portable pump, ultimately also supplied by Michelin.

Patented in France in the summer of 1891, the first Michelin detachable pneumatic tyre for bicycles comprised a flexible rubber inner tube containing air held under high pressure by a valve and protected by an outer cover of canvas coated with a layer of vulcanised rubber, moulded with a smooth finish and lacking an indented tread. Unlike the Dunlop version, which relied on glue, this cover could be clamped securely, but not permanently, to the wooden wheel rims of contemporary cycles by a series of 17 nuts and bolts located on its circumference. In short, the Michelin invention offered three vital advantages over the solid rubber tyres then generally fitted to bicycles. Firstly, the elasticity provided by the pressurised air acted as a spring to absorb the shocks and vibration transmitted by the wheel and frame to the saddle. Secondly, it also served to reduce rolling resistance, which meant that the effort involved in pedalling the bike was reduced and its speed increased. And thirdly, it also acted to reduce the weight of the machine itself, making it more controllable. Now that Édouard Michelin had solved the problem of damage caused by any debris that might lie in the cyclist's path, there was nothing to prevent its widespread public acceptance and rapid commercial success. The rusty horseshoe nails that littered the highways and bye-ways of that era were a particular hazard, as were the sharp flint-stones and gravel from which the roads were constructed.

Indeed, all these benefits were proven convincingly by the victory of a Michelin-shod machine in the famous Paris-Brest-Paris cycle race run in September that same year, when the winner, Charles Terront, covered the 750-mile course non-stop at an average speed of 10mph. On crossing the finishing line he had built up an eight hour lead, after riding for three whole days and nights without sleep, an extraordinary feat of athleticism. Thanks also to the barrage of publicity immediately fired-off by André Michelin, within twelve months or so,

After their victory in the 1905 Gordon Bennett Cup race, the two 9.8-litre Richard Brasier cars were sold off to private owners. This example came to England where in October 1908 it lapped the Brooklands circuit ten times at an average speed of 101mph with the French driver Bablot at the wheel. Shown here in this 1908 photo from The Autocar *is the then British owner, Clement Hobson.*

more than 10,000 French cyclists were using Michelin tyres. However, even though the first detachable tyre marked a huge advance on what had gone before, heralding the age of the practical inflatable tyre, there was still considerable scope for improvement. As Terront had discovered, the lengthy and laborious procedure of undoing and refastening 17 screws when repairing a puncture still took up far too much time. Within three months of Terront's victory, Édouard Michelin had perfected a new version of his detachable tyre which reduced puncture repair times to levels comparable with those prevailing today. When it was exhibited at the Stanley Show in London in December 1891, visitors saw how the new tyre could be removed at will in under two minutes – and orders for over 4,000 tyres were taken within the day. Moreover, a distributor, Paul Hardy of Tottenham Court Road, London, was appointed to market Michelin's bicycle tyres in England at this time.

By then, the Michelin brothers had become convinced that the comfort provided by the air-filled tyre would transform road transport in all its forms and, indeed, that the development of the horseless carriage could not proceed without it. So, over the next four years they turned their attention to applying the principle of the detachable pneumatic tyre to the automobile, realising that therein lay the greater commercial opportunity. In 1895, they demonstrated the results of their labours by competing in the first great automobile race, run from Paris to Bordeaux and back, driving l'Éclair, a vehicle they had built themselves using a Daimler engine and a Peugeot chassis. Although they finished last (having consumed their entire stock of 22 prototype tyres, none of which lasted much more than 100 miles) the experiment proved the value of their creation beyond doubt. Despite being the only car in the race to be fitted with pneumatic tyres, l'Éclair's performance proved that the comfort conferred by this invention would inevitably make it an inseparable and indispensable feature of motoring, as vital perhaps to the progress of road transport as the contributions made by Daimler and Benz. It only remained for the numbers of automobiles on the roads of France to increase sufficiently to provide as commercially a viable market as was the case with bicycle tyres, though at that time, there were probably less than 300 horseless carriages running in the whole of Europe.

Nevertheless, the following year, in February 1896 to be precise, the Michelins introduced their first detachable pneumatic tyres specifically designed and manufactured for use on automobiles – the earliest examples of true air-filled tyres for

In 1913, Michelin came up with the idea of the detachable solid steel disc wheel, which made the spare wheel possible for the very first time. The company has been involved with wheel manufacture ever since.

motor vehicles to be commercially available. By the turn of the century, they had virtually abandoned their agricultural machinery activities to concentrate on the refinement of their car and bicycle tyres and the expansion of their rubber-goods interests, which still included toys and sports equipment. By dint of their vigorous and enterprising marketing methods, including the persuasive promotional and public relations campaigns devised and written by André Michelin himself, for publication in the cycling and motoring press, both domestic and export sales rose substantially year by year, especially in the United Kingdom. Here, following the repeal of the notorious Red Flag Act in 1896, interest in the horseless carriage began to catch up with, and even overtake, the enthusiasm shown by automobilistes in France. Thanks to the relative affluence of the British upper classes, by 1907 this market had become the largest in Europe with over 53,000 motor vehicles registered in the UK, well ahead of France with 31,000 cars and Germany, with 16,000.

Following the resounding success of the range of bicycle tyres exhibited at the 1891 Stanley Show (an annual event that had been running since the 1870s) at which 2,000 pairs of tyres were sold, Michelin's business and reputation in the United Kingdom increased by leaps and bounds. But then,

just five years later, the firm experienced a set-back that put a stop to its expansion in the UK for several years. The cause of these difficulties involved the name that was destined to become Michelin's major rival for the next half century or more: Dunlop.

John Boyd Dunlop, the person who is generally, but wrongly, acknowledged to be the inventor of the pneumatic tyre, was a Scots-born veterinary surgeon who lived in Ireland, first in Belfast then later, in Dublin. In 1889, he had floated a company, named the Pneumatic Tyre and Booths Cycle Agency Limited, to commercialise the patent that he had taken out the previous year in both England and France. Among the directors was the buccaneering Irish entrepreneur and financier, William Harvey du Cros, who very soon began to play an important part in establishing the British motor industry; later he was instrumental in backing Herbert Austin's attempts to set up an automobile factory in Birmingham.

Unknown to Dunlop and du Cros though, Dunlop's French and British tyre patents (the only two he had taken out) were both invalid and never conferred the slightest protection upon their owners. In fact, the world's first pneumatic tyre had actually been invented and patented by a Scotsman, Robert William Thomson, as early as

Michelin was also the first to provide double rear tyres and wheels for trucks, which they called the Jumelé, as seen here on this right-hand-drive Renault lorry, photographed in Great Britain around the time of the First World War.

1845. Thomson's Aerial Wheels for carriages and wagons were ahead of their time, however, and did not catch on. Production lapsed, the patent expired and the inventor was soon forgotten until the existence of his patent was discovered in France by patent agents working for a consortium of French industrialists including the Michelins. The Dunlop patent – at least as registered in France – was therefore deemed invalid by the French courts in 1896, on the grounds that Thomson's prior claim had expired in 1860, so that Michelin's freedom to continue manufacturing car tyres in its own home country was unrestricted.

However, on this side of the Channel, despite the *Entente Cordiale* eventually established in 1904 the situation was rather more complicated. Undeterred by the patent revelation, in 1895 Harvey du Cros bought out Dunlop's interest in the Pneumatic Tyre company, formed the Dunlop Tyre Company Ltd and moved the manufacturing operations from Dublin to Coventry, intent on aggressively promoting the Dunlop name and entering the fast-growing and already very lucrative market for automobile tyres, by then dominated by Michelin. It is generally acknowledged that, around this time, the life of a set of pneumatic tyres was unlikely to extend beyond 1,000 miles, or at best, 2,000 miles in the case of a light vehicle driven carefully – so as each set cost at least £500 (about £25,000 in today's money), it can be seen that the comfort they afforded was indeed a luxury!

In October 1896, together with a syndicate of British investors including Ernest Hooley and Harry Lawson, du Cros had bought-up the old-established French bicycle making firm of Clement, together with its rival Gladiator (owned by Alexandre Darracq) and the French branch of the English Humber firm, merging them into a single concern. Adolphe Clement (who went on to found the Clement-Bayard automobile marque) had acquired the French manufacturing rights to Dunlop's patents, and in 1893, had started-up a company to market bicycle tyres under the Dunlop name in France, in direct competition with the Michelins, who objected vigorously to this enterprise. In a series of patriotically worded advertisements published in 1900, intended to protect the French tyre industry, they pointed out that the products of the Compagnie Française des Pneumatiques Dunlop were not French at all, but had been made in England.

Meanwhile, in his efforts to uphold the reputa-

> Around this time, the life of a set of pneumatic tyres was unlikely to extend beyond 1,000 miles, or at best 2,000 miles in the case of a light vehicle driven carefully

tion of the Dunlop name and develop a British car tyre industry, du Cros had already attempted to establish a monopoly in the United Kingdom by purchasing all the relevant competing patents that he could acquire. By virtue of the far greater weight and speed of automobiles compared with bicycles, the key patents governing the making and marketing of automobile tyres at that time were not merely those relating to the principle of the air-filled tyre itself, but those concerning the system used to fix detachable tyres to a car's wheels in such a way that they would not come off when punctured, so causing an accident.

By this time, two fundamentally different, rival methods had been invented. The first, the so-called wired-on method of fastening the outer casing to the wheel, had been patented by Charles Kingston Welch of Tottenham, in September 1890, for use on bicycles. In this system, used on the first Dunlop automobile tyres introduced in July 1901, a ring of steel wires wound into a strong cable was embedded in each outer edge of the tyre casing so that it sat firmly against the outer rim of the wheel when the inner tube was inflated. The circumference of the edges was just large enough to allow the casing to be slipped over the well-based wheel rims to facilitate quick and easy removal. This principle is in essence that which is in common use today.

The rival system of fixing had also been patented in 1890, this one by William Erskine Bartlett of the North British Rubber Company, located in Edinburgh, just one month after Welch's. Known as the Clincher or beaded-edge fastening, this had no wire rings to hold the tyre on the wheel. Instead, it allowed the cover to be secured in place by a lip or flange of rubber formed around the rim, retained solely by the pressure of the air present in the inner tube. In 1896, du Cros had acquired this patent also, at great expense, although in this case, his rights did not extend to Scotland.

Possessing the English rights to both systems, du Cros claimed that, without exception, all the other pneumatic tyres then competing on the British market – be they for automobile or bicycle use – contravened the patents he had bought-up, and he began litigation to prevent infringement. It is hardly surprising then that a bitter legal battle ensued. Throughout this long contest with du Cros in the courts, the Michelin brothers were prevented from manufacturing or marketing their products in Great Britain, except under licence from Dunlop. This situation meant that between April 1896 and September 1904 Michelin car or bicycle tyres were only permitted to enter the country if fitted as original equipment on an imported machine constructed in France, but their use as replacements was prohibited.

In practice, however, Michelin overcame this restriction by a convenient arrangement with the North British Rubber Company, which remained the legitimate holder in Scotland of the Bartlett patent. As du Cros had been unable to cancel these Scottish rights, the result was a range of fully detachable automobile tyres employing the same beaded-edge or constrictor fastening technique pioneered by Bartlett, branded as Clincher-Michelin tyres and manufactured by Michelin at Clermont-Ferrand. Not surprisingly, du Cros also contested the validity of Michelin's sub-licence to the Bartlett patent, but the Court of Appeal affirmed that the head-licence had not been violated and that Michelin was acting merely as an agent of the North British firm.

The matter was finally resolved in September 1904, when the rival Welch patent, owned by Dunlop, expired and Harvey du Cros was obliged to set fire to the document ceremoniously. Thereafter, Michelin adopted this type of fastening also, together with the many other contemporary tyre makers currently supplying the British market, such as Avon, Firestone, Goodrich, Goodyear, India and John Bull. Eventually, during the 1920s, this system was standardised by all manufacturers world-wide, so that, in principle, any make of tyre could be used with any make of wheel, providing their sizes matched.

With the legal position settled at last, the way was now open for Monsieur Bibendum to lead a massive expansion of Michelin's activities on this side of the Channel. Almost immediately, a temporary sales and distribution office was established in London, in rented premises located at 49/50 Sussex Place, South Kensington, a street name which has long since vanished from the map having now been incorporated into Old Brompton Road. A works and depot at Barking was also created in association with the old-established rubber-ware firm of William Warne & Company Ltd through which supplies of tyres arriving from France by sea and along the River Thames were imported. Machinery was also installed in these premises, and from 1905 to 1911, many Michelin products were actually manufactured there. Tyre repairing, a common practice by all manufacturers at the time, was also undertaken by Warne's until this activity was set up in Fulham Road in 1911.

By 1905, there were no less than 58 officially approved and appointed distributors of Michelin products located in 53 towns across Great Britain. Michelin was represented for the first time by its own stand at that year's SMMT Olympia Motor Show. By 1906, there were 179 distributors in 155 towns, in 1908 there were 460 distributors in 371 towns, and by 1911, this nationwide coverage had increased to 834 distributors in 590 towns.

The birth of Monsieur Bibendum

Michelin's world-famous mascot and trademark, the jovial, amiable Monsieur Bibendum, the Michelin Man, was actually conceived in 1894, when Édouard and André Michelin exhibited their pneumatic tyres at the Universal and Colonial Exhibition held in Lyon. Observing a stack of tyres of different diameters, piled high to decorate their stand, Édouard Michelin remarked to his brother: 'With arms and legs added, that pile of tyres would look just like a man!'

Within a matter of weeks, the pair had commissioned the artist and cartoonist Marius Rossillon (who worked under the pseudonym of O'Galop) to produce a poster featuring the rotund, pneumatic personality

In 1914, Michelin published this extraordinary poster, advocating the creation of the Channel Tunnel. It took another 80 years for the link with France to be built.

Monsieur Bibendum comes to Britain, on one of the first Michelin posters to be published here, circa 1912.

Opposite: The 1905 victory of the studded Semelle tyres was aggressively publicised and promoted in another famous Bibendum poster drawn by O'Galop.

Below: Monsieur Bibendum, the Michelin Man, as seen in one of his first appearances, in a poster published circa 1901.

of Édouard's imagination. The idea was that, with a body seemingly formed entirely from tyres of various sizes, this comic character would be able to demonstrate the virtues of their products pictorially, by being depicted in posters and advertisements, rolling down the road and consuming any rusty nails or broken glass strewn in his path, with no apparent ill-effect.

So it was that O'Galop's famous poster – first displayed in April 1898 – showed Édouard Michelin's creation as a bucolic, roly-poly creature drinking-up road debris as if it were wine and raising a glass in a bacchanalian toast. The Latin caption read: 'Nunc est Bibendum – Now is the time to drink', a quotation from the Roman poet, Horace, which emphasised the proposition that Michelin tyres could be relied upon to swallow up all

obstacles with impunity, thus preventing punctures.

In the space of just a few months, Monsieur Bibendum had captured public affection and achieved celebrity status throughout France and beyond. At a bicycle trade fair held in Paris in December 1898, a man dressed as M. Bibendum attracted huge crowds to the Michelin stand and created a sensation. More public appearances at races, fairs and exhibitions followed, and the Michelin Man was soon on his way to becoming one of the most popular advertising characters of all time.

For almost a century, Monsieur Bibendum continued to serve as Michelin's omni-present emblem and talisman, his appearance evolving in tune with tyre fashion, but fundamentally unchanged. Invariably depicted clutching an over-brimming wine-glass while smoking a huge Havana cigar, he epitomised good-living and conviviality. Possessing an undeflatable sense of optimism, he was adopted by international *routiers* or truck drivers as an alternative to Saint Christopher, the patron saint of travellers, and thus his ebullient figure was often to be seen riding high on the roofs of their lorry cabs, swaying along the world's highways.

But, inevitably, by the 1970s, his bibulous appearance and personality had begun to be toned-down, in tune with changing social attitudes. Drinking, smoking and over-eating were no longer considered appropriate conduct for a motoring hero, and so Monsieur Bibendum has curtailed his epicurean pleasures and gone on a diet, in order to lose a few 'spare tyres'. Today, having bowed somewhat to the pressures of political correctness, he is a reformed character, energy-conscious, environmentally responsible and abstemious. Yet, despite having lost so much in weight and girth, he is still just as solid an embodiment of automotive progress as he has always been, as bouncy and cheerful as ever, and full of his usual bonhomie and savoir faire!

Indeed, well over 100 years since his first appearance on the motoring scene, Monsieur Bibendum remains an international cult figure, at home in over 170 countries and numbered among the ten most widely recognised and best-loved brand symbols in the world. This feat of enduring popularity is all the more remarkable since, until relatively recently, no advertising agency or publicity consultancy was ever employed by Michelin to enhance his image or boost his career!

1905–1914
Bibendum arrives in the British Isles

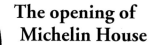

The opening of Michelin House

By the end of 1906, some 15 years after the first Michelin tyres had been imported into the UK, the French firm's British subsidiary, the Michelin Tyre Company Ltd, had outgrown its first London offices and depot, located at 49/50 Sussex Place, South Kensington. The staff now numbered over 50, compared with the 17 employed at the time of the company's formal incorporation in May 1905, and it was evident that much larger, more ambitious premises would soon be required to serve as its headquarters and distribution centre.

It appears the Michelin brothers decided at the outset that they would prefer to design and build a completely new headquarters building which they would own outright, rather than to continue making do with rented accommodation, so a search began for a suitable site. A number of different London locations were investigated, including Broad Street, Shaftesbury Avenue and Vauxhall Bridge Road. Indeed, plans for a two-storey building to be erected at the latter address, drawn up by Michelin's architectural department at Clermont-Ferrand in 1907, still survive in the company's archives.

These drawings were never submitted to London County Council for planning permission, however,

1905 On 11 May, the Michelin Tyre Company Ltd is incorporated in the United Kingdom, based at premises in South Kensington, London SW3. André Michelin is appointed Chairman and his brother-in-law, Marc Wolff, Managing Director.

A Panhard & Levassor car equipped with Michelin tyres beats the Paris-Calais Express (then the fastest railway train in the world) by covering the round trip of 370 miles in 6hr 50min.

In the UK, the first general meeting of the Automobile Association is held at London's Trocadero restaurant, and the SMMT holds its third and fourth London Motor Shows, this time at Olympia, in February and November. Michelin is among the leading exhibitors.

The last of the Gordon Bennett series of races is run on a circuit in the Auvergne proposed by the Michelin brothers.

Michelin introduces the Semelle, the world's first successful non-skid tyre. Unlike the smooth, untreaded surface of other contemporary tyres (including those from Michelin), its circumference comprised a bonded leather belt studded with small steel rivets to improve grip and prevent skidding.

1906 Michelin builds its first foreign factory, in Turin, Italy.

Michelin introduces the Miracle detachable rim, which makes its competition debut at the first ever Grand Prix race. Organised by the Automobile Club de France (the ACF), this is held on a closed dirt-track circuit at Le Mans. The winning car, a 90hp Renault, driven by Ferenc Szisz is equipped with the new Michelin wheels and tyres. The detachable rim is a split, two-part device with a detachable outer half fastened to a fixed inner part by bolts, so enabling a damaged tyre and its deflated inner tube to be removed and replaced with a spare in a matter of minutes, saving vital time in races. The Renault was also equipped with Semelle studded tyres, another Michelin innovation, introduced the previous year.

In the UK, Rolls-Royce launch the 40/50 six-cylinder Silver Ghost.

1907 Michelin opens its first factory in the USA, at Milltown, New Jersey.

The first motor taxi cabs appear on the streets of London. The majority are made by Renault and Unic and feature Michelin pneumatic tyres.

Brooklands Motor Racing Circuit is opened near Weybridge, Surrey. Until this time, motor racing had been banned in the United Kingdom. (It closed in 1939.)

1908 The Michelin Tyre Company Ltd is awarded the Royal Warrant by King Edward VII, which remained in force until 1927.

To help get aviation off the ground, the Michelin brothers propose their Aero Cup and Prize to be awarded to the first aircraft to fly from Paris to Clermont-Ferrand and land on the summit of the Puy-de-Dome. This feat is accomplished three years later by the pioneering aviators, Renaux and Senouque.

The first English-language edition of the Michelin Guide to France is published.

Michelin introduces the twin-tyre concept.

1909 Louis Blériot becomes the first man to fly across the English Channel.

Michelin launches its British Empire Cup aviation competition in Great Britain.

An excise duty on petrol is introduced for the first time in the UK.

1910 The first Michelin road maps are published in France.

British car registrations exceed 100,000 vehicles. The number of motor cars on the streets of London exceeds that of horse-drawn vehicles for the first time.

1911 Michelin House in South Kensington, London is inaugurated on 20 January.

The first Michelin Guide to the British Isles is launched.

1912 The Michelin brothers launch a petition demanding that all roads in France should be numbered and signposted. Eight years later, with support from Michelin, the idea is subsequently adopted in the UK.

1913 Michelin introduces the detachable pressed-steel disc wheel, the ancestor of all the car and truck wheels used today.

Henry Ford produces his Model T 'Tin Lizzie' on a moving assembly line.

The first roadside petrol pump appears in the UK, although these devices do not come into general use until 1921. In the meanwhile petrol is normally sold in cans.

1914 The First World War breaks out in August when Germany invades Belgium and France. Michelin places its factories at the disposal of the French government for the construction of aircraft.

A Renault taxi wearing Michelin tyres, seen in London in 1905.

Opposite: Bibendum appeared 'in the rubber' at countless shows and events in England in those early days of motoring. This photograph is believed to have been taken at the Olympia Exhibition in 1908.

because the project was abandoned when, in June 1909, the site on which the new Michelin building was eventually to be erected became available. This, of course, was the large plot of land in Chelsea, bounded by Fulham Road, Sloane Avenue, Lucan Place and Ixworth Place. Today, this is a fashionable shopping and residential location known as Brompton Cross, but which was then a purely commercial district. It offered all the advantages the Michelin brothers were looking for – a place that would be prominent, prestigious, spacious and easily accessible for both passing customers and the large fleet of delivery vans needed to distribute all over Britain, the huge quantities of tyres that had to be stocked at the premises. Here, automobile owners would be able to have their tyres checked, changed or repaired as well as to purchase all the other many motoring items and accessories the Michelins intended to offer, including the famous range of maps and guides, which were to be published in English, from 1911 onwards.

The first set of plans for the Fulham Road site were drawn up in France in August 1909, but these were not adopted. Instead, a much larger, grander

and far more imaginative scheme, dating from October 1909, was chosen.

The architect was François Espinasse, born in August 1880 in Vic le Comte, deep in the Auvergne region about 50 miles from Clermont-Ferrand. Epinasse had joined Michelin's civil engineeing department in 1906. This was an important part of the Michelin organisation since the company's rapid expansion had required substantial building work, not only to provide sufficient factory buildings, but also to construct the subsidised residential accommodation needed to house the many employees who were recruited from all over France, there being a general shortage of labour in the area.

Espinasse continued to be employed by Michelin until his early death, at the age of 44, in May 1925. Although he was normally resident in Clermont-Ferrand he spent some time in Paris in 1908 (where he was responsible for the design and construction of the company's headquarters at 97 boulevard Péreire) and paid regular visits to London between 1907 and 1912. Apart from these two major building achievements, very little else is known about his otherwise uneventful career. As he was

*Opposite: In 1911,
M Bibendum announced
a move to his newly
completed home,
Michelin House in
Fulham Road, South
Kensington. The building
still stands today, little
changed after almost 100
years. It remained
Michelin's London base
for 75 years.*

*Monsieur Bibendum
lectures British
colleagues on the virtues
of the pneumatic tyre,
on the cover of an
instruction booklet
produced in 1911.*

not a trained and qualified architect, the French Order of Architects has no record of him, and no obituary was ever published in either the French architectural press or the local Clermont newspaper, *La Montagne*.

This obscurity makes Espinasse's work at South Kensington all the more remarkable since, by common consent, his design for Monsieur Bibendum's new London home, Michelin House, was (and remains today) an extraordinarily imaginative and inventive achievement. Conceived in a uniquely original and individualistic style that anticipated the Art Deco movement of the 1920s, it was a radical departure from contemporary architectural ideas and practices which was never to be copied or repeated anywhere else in the world. Among its novel features were the use of glistening white or vividly coloured encaustic tiles for the cladding of the façade and some interior surfaces, the inclusion of ceramic-tile panels depicting scenes from the Michelin

firm's already eventful history and three enormous stained-glass windows on the front elevation portraying Monsieur Bibendum in various poses. Espinasse's original drawings – which have survived in the Michelin archives – indicate that the building was also to have included two spherical cupolas, made from glass and illuminated from within, resting on the turrets located at the corners of the narrow Fulham Road frontage. It was intended that these cupolas would provide a convenient perch for a pair of huge Bibendum figures, but in the event these bizarre but amusing adornments were not included in the final design eventually passed by the town planning office of London County Council in October 1910.

The Michelin building was completed in little more than a year, and opened on Friday, 20 January 1911 by Edward Manville, President of the Society of Motor Manufacturers and Traders in the presence of André Michelin, and a host of distinguished guests including the French Ambassador M. Paul Cambon. In his inaugural speech Mr Manville stated that 'In regard to our own particular automobile industry, there is no man who has done more to render it practicable than M. Michelin. He was the first man to make tyres for automobiles which were sufficiently reliable to enable the use of them on vehicles to progress, and although it is undoubtedly true today that there are many other tyre makers who also make excellent tyres, I think I may truly say that M. Michelin's tyre has never been surpassed.'

Clearly, Espinasse's design received widespread acclaim in the motoring and architectural press. Indeed, its extravagant and audacious visual detailing must have had an enormous impact on spectators, stunning local residents and passers by alike. Nothing remotely like it had ever been seen in the Capital before – or since – and it remains a unique landmark in London, even today. Its combination of stylish modernity and unabashed opulence must have seemed extremely impressive, even to those sceptics who were not entirely convinced of the desirability or future prospects of the automobile. Above all, it served as a permanent expression of *les Michelins'* vigorous though witty propaganda machine which seized upon every opportunity to publicise the company's brand-name, and proclaim the virtues of its products before the eyes and ears of their fast-expanding

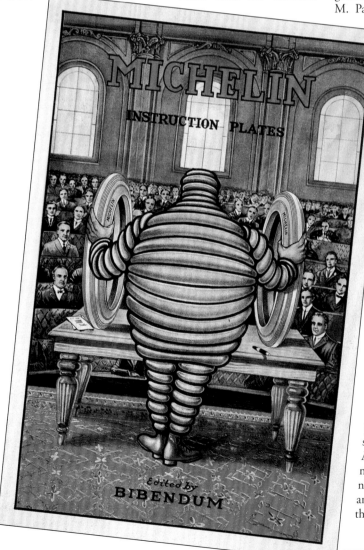

The exterior of Michelin House photographed in 1911. It was later extended by the addition of upper storeys at the rear.

Opposite: The plans for Michelin House have survived in the Michelin archives. François Espinasse was responsible for the majority of them.

motoring and cycling clientele. Certainly, it seems safe to conclude that the artistic brothers, one of them actually a trained architect, would have played a large and influential part in its conception, making innumerable suggestions to guide and inspire François Espinasse through every stage of the design process, from the first rough sketches through to the final triumphant realisation of his plans.

Yet this powerful visual impact concealed the fact that underneath the building's bold exterior there lay an impressively rational and functional structure, well suited to its commercial purpose. Actually, it was the first in London to be built from ferro-concrete, a technique which made possible large unobstructed interior spaces laid out on a semi-open-plan arrangement across all three floors. It also permitted very rapid construction; from start to finish the building work took only six months. Apart from the ample office accommodation required for the normal managerial, administrative and clerical functions of the business, generous space for the storage and distribution of tyres to be

despatched all over Great Britain was also provided. An inventory of more than 25,000 tyres and 30,000 inner tubes was held continually in the basement, and there was also a garage housing and maintaining the firm's large fleet of delivery vans.

Described by *The Motor* as 'commodious, well-lit and well-aired, with everything throughout the premises telling its own tale of efficiency,' Michelin House also acted as a retail centre where customers could purchase tyres over the counter and, if necessary, have them fitted in a purpose-built bay. Petrol and other motoring sundries and supplies were also available. An equally important innovation was the opening of a touring office where Michelin's new range of maps and guidebooks, recently introduced in English and covering the British Isles as well as France and the Continent, could be obtained or consulted 'in quiet and comfort' according to *The Motor* report. There was even an early example of the telephone kiosk provided solely for the convenience of customers. It all demonstrated the Michelin brothers' interest in every aspect of motoring and transport, and exemplified their

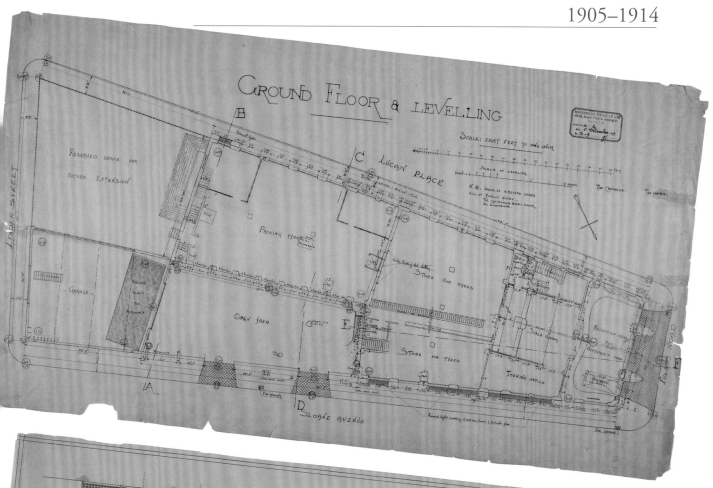

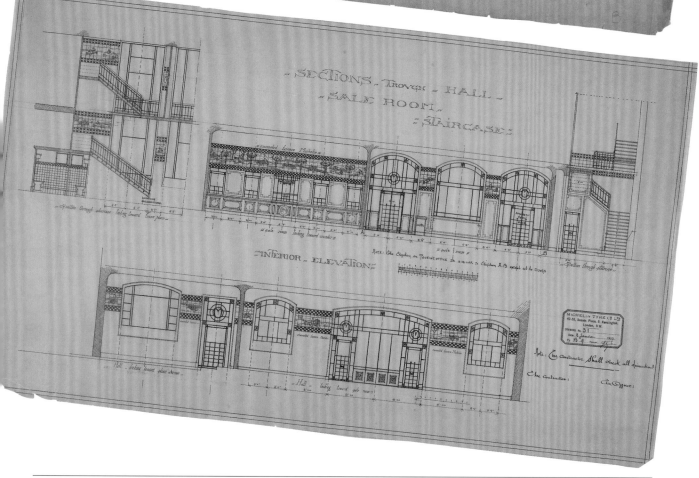

A parade of Michelin Men passes 81 Fulham Road in a typical Michelin promotion of the period. This particular publicity stunt was probably staged to coincide with the opening of the London Olympia Motor Show in October 1911.

determination to foster the development of travel by motor car with every means at their disposal.

In 1912, the facilities were substantially expanded by the erection of a three-storey extension located behind the original building and fronting on to Lucan Place and Ixworth Place. Once again the design and construction methods used were unconventional, although not quite as radically innovative and decorative as before. The extension was used primarily for additional storage space although extra offices and a vehicle and tyre repair shop were also included in the scheme, largely the work of François Espinasse again. Another major extension took place in 1922, which completed the original site's total coverage by buildings. Following the opening of Michelin's first British tyre factory at Stoke-on-Trent in 1927, the importance of Michelin House as a distribution and administrative centre was reduced; in fact, the UK company's headquarters were transferred entirely to Stoke in 1930. It was not until 1947 that the South Kensington establishment was again to

see Michelin personnel other than those involved in distribution, Until then, it served solely as a retail outlet leaving two thirds of the building unoccupied; the surplus space left vacant was let out for use as a furniture warehouse. Sales and advertising personnel progressively returned from Stoke in the late 1940s/early 1950s such that Michelin House evolved into the company's UK commercial headquarters for the next 30 years, while manufacturing and finance remained at Stoke. In 1972, a comprehensive redevelopment of the site was proposed, involving the demolition of all but the original 1911 building, which had already been protected by a Grade II listing in 1969. The intention was that a ten-storey office block would replace the 1912 extension, but fortunately, due to more pressing building requirements elsewhere, which assumed a higher priority in the company's financial plans, the scheme was soon abandoned. Eventually, as we shall see later, in 1985, the building was sold to Sir Terence Conran and Paul Hamlyn of the Conran Octopus publishing

A view of the delivery and despatch bay at Michelin House, taken between 1912 and 1914, when horse-drawn carriers' carts and drays had not yet been completely superseded by motor vehicles.

A Renault delivery van as used by Michelin in London around 1904, ferrying tyres between its depot at Barking and its retail premises in South Kensington.

Two views of the original interior of Michelin House, as it was in Edwardian times: above, the Reception and Sales Room and, below, the Touring Office.

One of the tyre-fitting workshops located at Michelin House, as it looked circa 1912.

company, which after renovating and restoring it as closely as possible to its original design, occupied it as offices until 1996. The Conran Shop and Bibendum Restaurant created there by Terence Conran remain in place, however.

The pictorial tile panels at Michelin House

Perhaps the best-known surviving architectural feature of the Michelin building as it exists today is the series of 34 pictorial tile-work panels which decorate the exterior surface of the building and the walls of the former entrance hall and tyre-fitting bay, which nowadays serve as a reception area and oyster bar. Each rectangular panel comprises, on average, 24 individual glazed ceramic tiles, hand-painted in the Art Nouveau style, and assembled to form scenes from the early history of cycle and motor racing or other events in which the Michelin firm played an important part. In reality, these panels are replicas of a similar set originally commissioned for the Michelin firm's Paris head-quarters in the boulevard Péreire. Based on a series of drawings executed earlier by the artist Ernest Montaut (who, in 1905, had produced the famous poster entitled 'The Rail Vanquished by Michelin Tyres') they were manufactured in 1910 by the ceramics and glassware specialists Gilardoni Fils & Cie, located in the rue Paradis in Paris.

Not unnaturally, the first plaque in the series depicts the Michelin brothers' first great competition success, when their detachable pneumatic bicycle tyre helped the veteran ace rider Charles Terront to win first prize in the Paris-Brest-Paris cycling race, held in September 1891. This marathon event, which was organised by the popular Paris daily newspaper *Le Petit Journal* (boasting a circulation of more than a million regular readers) was billed as a trial of strength that would prove the mettle of both riders and bicycles alike, as the 750-mile round trip had to be covered by the same man on the same machine. No fewer than 206 entrants crossed the starting line outside the newspaper's offices in the rue Lafayette, at 5am on Sunday, 6 September. They represented at least 59 different makes of cycle and tyres, very few of them

Overleaf: Four of the series of 34 tiled wall panels that adorn the exterior of Michelin House, to illustrate the company's achievements in the earliest days of racing and manned flight.

PARIS-BREST
1891

CH. TERRONT

PARIS-BORDEAUX
1895

1ᴱᴿᴱ VOITURE sur
PNEUS MICHELIN

COUPE GORDON-BENNETT 1904

Gillardoni fils et Cie
38. rue de Paradis-Paris

THÉRY sur **RICHARD-BRASIER**

GRAND-PRIX A·C·F 1906 Sarthe

SZISZ sur **RENAULT**

pneumatic, but all competing for the commercial recognition and reward that a victory would bring.

The Michelin brothers had realised right from the start that the rigorous test of quality involved in racing would be the ideal way to promote and publicise their products. But since the favourite among this large field of competitors, Joseph Laval, had already been signed-up by Dunlop, they had to persuade the highly experienced champion rider Terront to postpone his retirement and compete under their banner, riding on a Humber. This was indeed a bold and risky step for the fledgling entrepreneurs to take. Their new detachable tyre had only just been perfected and patented a few weeks previously, and stocks were extremely low – perhaps as few as twelve examples.

Fortunately, the result exceeded their wildest expectations. When Terront crossed the finishing line on the boulevard Maillot in Paris, at 6.35am on Wednesday, 9 September, he had built up a lead of almost nine hours over Laval and the rest of the field, having completed the course non-stop in just 71 hours, 18 minutes. In other words, he had cycled for almost three days and nights with scarcely a break, never once pausing for rest or sleep. It was a truly extraordinary achievement of stamina, athleticism and sheer determination.

Of course, Terront had experienced numerous punctures en route, but thanks to the virtues of the Michelin detachable tyre (and the support provided by a mobile team of Michelin mechanics) he had been able to overcome them without suffering serious delays. He later blamed these stoppages on the rusty nails and shards of broken glass which, he believed, had been strewn in his path by saboteurs acting in the pay of his opponents. Doubtless, it was this experience which, following the creation of Monsieur Bibendum seven years later, led to the advertising claim that 'le pneu Michelin boit l'obstacle', meaning that Michelin pneumatic tyres could be relied upon to swallow-up any sharp objects or other minor obstructions littering the road ahead without suffering ill-effects.

Naturally, the Michelin brothers lost no time in proclaiming Terront's triumph. In fact, they had even gone so far as to anticipate the victory by printing a leaflet for distribution among the crowds gathered at the finishing line. 'The air-filled tyre is and always will be faster than other tyres' it announced, pressing home its point with a humorous anecdote typical of the advertising copy of that era, of which André Michelin soon became a master:

King Louis XVI, on being informed by the Marquis de La Fayette that the Bastille had fallen to the insurgents exclaimed: 'Good heavens, is this a revolt?' 'No Sire,' the Marquis replied, 'it is a revolution.' To this André Michelin had added:

The British patent for the detachable pneumatic tyre was registered by Michelin on 18 September 1891.

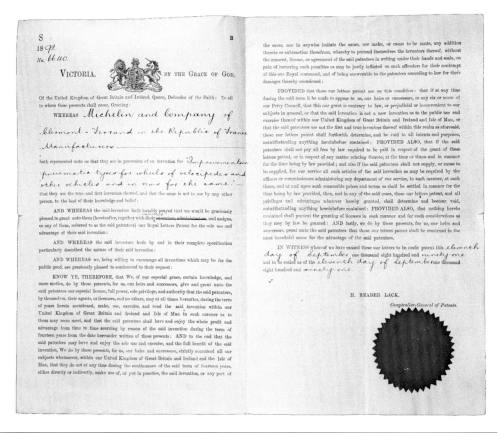

An elaborately crafted ceramic panel from the interior of Michelin House, celebrating the custom of HM King Edward VII, and depicting him riding in the royal Daimler limousine.

'In the event that the bicycling public on learning of our new tyre should exclaim "Good heavens, is this an improvement?" we have no hesitation in replying: 'No – it is a revolution.'

Next, to capitalise on this success and gain further publicity, while public interest in their new product was at its height, they immediately organised another race themselves. Announced as the International Michelin Competition, this was held on a course between Paris and Clermont-Ferrand at the end of October 1891. The only entry restriction was that all the contestants had to use Michelin tyres. To demonstrate how easy it was to remove and repair these tyres, the Michelins themselves actually scattered nails on the road before the approaching riders, as had happened to Terront. Sixty-one of the 73 competitors reached their destination, all having suffered at least one flat tyre which they were able to mend quite easily along the way.

The response to the enthusiastic reports that ensued in the cycling press was phenomenal, and at first the Clermont factory could scarcely keep up with demand. Yet little by little, and by all manner of means, over the following twelve months production was increased substantially. By the end of the following year more than 10,000 French cyclists had been able to equip their machines with Michelin pneumatic tyres, to replace the solid rubber tyres or iron bands used previously. The comfort and convenience of the bicycle – and with that the scale of the Michelin company's prospects and profits – had been transformed beyond belief, just as Édouard Michelin had predicted. In the years 1891 to 1900, sales revenue soared from 460,000 to 6 million francs – and the surplus was re-invested not just in improving production facilities but also in research and development. The next step would be to produce a detachable pneumatic tyre for automobiles.

Consequently, the second of the ceramic tile panels at Michelin House commemorates an event that occurred four years later, when André and Édouard took part in the first ever automobile race staged in France. Organised by the aristocratic playboy-entrepreneur, the Comte (later Marquis) de Dion, this was run in June 1895 along a 720-mile course from Paris to Bordeaux and back again. Driving l'Éclair, a vehicle that they had built themselves, employing a Peugeot chassis and a Daimler engine, the Michelin brothers came last among the nine cars that actually finished the race, there being 23 starters. The name l'Éclair means forked-lightning, but this was not intended as an allusion to speed. On the contrary, it evoked the erratic zig-zag course that the primitive vehicle followed as it travelled along at an average speed of just 12mph, due

The Three Leaders Of The Country.

to its rudimentary tiller-type steering gear and its lack of a differential.

L'Éclair failed to complete the course within the 100-hour time limit set by the Comte de Dion. Nevertheless, despite its lack of pace, and the time spent changing its tyres to mend the frequent punctures encountered en-route, the brothers were well satisfied with the result. Doubtless they were also proud to go down in motoring history as the first persons to fit pneumatic tyres to an automobile. Although none of the other competitors (including the winner, Emile Levassor) would agree to try out their prototype product, they had succeeded in demonstrating that this important technical innovation could withstand the heavy demands of motor vehicle use, even along rough unpaved roads. Clearly, the prospects for the Michelin detachable pneumatic tyre would not depend merely on bicycles and tricycles, which were far less heavily built and carried a much lighter load than any car. Although there were probably no more than 400 motor vehicles in use throughout the whole of France at that time, already the visionary pair had realised that the future of road transport lay with the automobile. 'In ten years' time all vehicles will be fitted with pneumatic tyres – the automobile will never succeed without them' wrote André in his weekly newspaper column, a prediction that aroused a certain scepticism in the light of l'Éclair's crab-like performance in the race. But as events turned out, a mere five years were sufficient to fulfil his prophesy, and by the turn of the century inflatable tyres had become an essential component of the motor car.

Indeed, by February 1896, the first Michelin pneumatic car tyre as tested on l'Éclair had been perfected and put on sale in France, to immediate acclaim, so much so that they were swiftly adopted by the leading manufacturers of the day, such as Panhard & Levassor, de Dion & Bouton, Mors, and Renault, for use on the cars that these famous firms entered in the long string of great inter-city marathon races that shortly followed the Paris-Bordeaux event. The first of these, that same year, was run between Paris and Marseille and back in 1896, followed by others between Marseille and Nice in 1897 and between Paris and Amsterdam in 1898. In 1899, a Tour of France took place, then, in 1900 there was a race from Paris to Toulouse and back. Next, came the series of international long-distance marathons, beginning with the race between Paris and Berlin in 1901, and Paris and Vienna in 1902. Michelin tyres were a principal factor in the success of the majority of the prize winners.

Most of these events are depicted in the ceramic tiles at Michelin House, as is the very last of these capital-to-capital runs, the ill-fated Paris-Madrid race of 1903. Now known as the Race of Death, this marked the end of an era in early motor racing. Planned to take place in three stages, from Versailles to Bordeaux, from Pessac to Vittoria, and from Vittoria to Madrid, it began on a Sunday in order to attract the largest possible crowds. The 275 competing cars set off at one-minute intervals to chase each other at speeds of over 65mph along open unfenced roads thronged with spectators who surged ever closer to the roadway to gain a better view. As each car passed by, the excited crowd parted just wide enough to let it hurtle through before closing up the gap again. Not surprisingly, accidents began to happen as one car crashed into the next before hurtling out of control into the tightly-packed hordes of bystanders. By the end of the day, between 300 and 400 drivers and

The Michelin brothers employed Monsieur Bibendum as their spokesman and political propagandist in England too. These cartoons showing him in action at the Houses of Parliament appeared as adverts in London newspapers just before the First World War. Opposite, Bibendum is seen between the two leading politicians of the day, Herbert Asquith (Prime Minister) and David Lloyd George (Chancellor of the Exchequer).

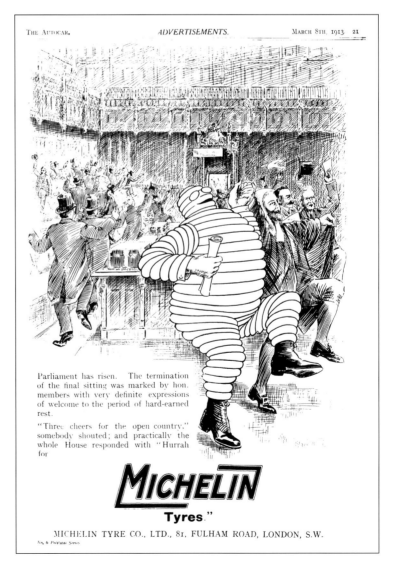

spectators had been killed outright. Among the fatalities was Marcel Renault, brother of Louis Renault, who had won the previous year's race between Paris and Vienna, on Michelin tyres.

Thereafter, motor racing in Europe was confined to closed-circuit events such as the Gordon Bennett International Cup and the various Grands Prix organised by the Automobile Club de France, where dangers to competitors could be minimised and the crowds kept safely behind barriers. Named after the prize offered by the American newspaper tycoon, James Gordon Bennett, owner of the *New York Herald*, the sixth and last Gordon Bennett Cup race, held in 1905, was actually organised by the Michelin brothers in conjunction with the Automobile Club de France. It was run on an 85-mile long dirt-track circuit laid out through mountainous terrain in the Clermont-Ferrand area.

This event, which attracted 18 entrants from six countries and over 80,000 spectators, was notable for the first appearance of a completely new type of tyre invented by Michelin and fitted to the winning car, a Richard-Brasier. Called the Semelle, this was in effect

In 1908, the Michelin Tyre Co. Ltd received the Royal Warrant as suppliers of motor car tyres to His Majesty King Edward VII.

the world's first non-skid tyre. Unlike the smooth, untreaded surface of other contemporary tyres (including those from Michelin), its circumference was reinforced by a leather band studded with small steel rivets to improve grip and prevent skidding. To celebrate this victory, the Michelins commissioned O'Galop to produce another of his Monsieur Bibendum posters showing the pneumatic hero in a kick-boxing pose, revealing the studded soles of his shoes. Entitled 'le Coup de la Semelle' (the sole scores a big hit), this became one of the most popular of all the Bibendum images and was used time and time again until the mid-1920s. A version in the form of a stained-glass window was included in the exterior decoration of Michelin House, and also on the front of the Michelin building in Paris.

The decade between 1895 and 1906 had witnessed a massive improvement in the performance of the automobile, at least in its racing and sporting forms. Whereas the average speed of the winner in the Paris-Bordeaux race was no more than 15mph, that of the victor in the Paris-Berlin race in June 1901 was 44mph. Even the 615-mile long Paris-Vienna endurance race the following year, run through the toughest mountain passes of the French, Swiss and Austrian Alps, had an average speed in excess of 38 mph. Moreover, these surprisingly high speeds – 97mph was often exceeded on the straight – were maintained for very long periods, often in the most arduous of conditions, making gruelling demands on both men and machines alike. For example, when winning the 1908 Grand Prix of the ACF held at Dieppe, the German driver Lautenschlager wrestled with the steering wheel of his monster Mercedes for over nine hours virtually non-stop, to complete ten circuits of the 47-mile long course at an average speed of 75mph. This was another famous victory, achieved on Michelin tyres, which is recorded in a tiled panel on the walls of Michelin House.

Clearly, the rapid development of the Michelin detachable pneumatic tyre had contributed immeasurably to this progress, not just through the extra margins of comfort, economy, safety and reliability that it offered touring motorists or their chauffeurs, but it also made possible the outright top speeds of these few brave racing aces. The advertising and marketing strategy adopted so brilliantly by André and Édouard exploited with unashamed vigour the prestige to be gained from their

MOTOR CAR TYRE MANUFACTURERS

BY APPOINTMENT
TO
HIS MAJESTY THE KING

MICHELIN

participation in all the major motorsport events of that golden era. Not only that, but as well as supporting and sponsoring motor racing, they saw to it that the ubiquitous presence of Monsieur Bibendum in the press and upon poster hoardings would serve to publicise the brand and kindle enthusiasm for Michelin products among the wider travelling public, by promoting automobile ownership and motoring in general.

Only three of the tiled panels on the walls at Michelin House do not show aspects of the company's early racing exploits. One of these exceptions portrays the first horse-drawn cab (Fiacres) in Paris to run on Michelin pneumatic tyres, in 1896. At the start of that year just five examples were introduced, a tiny fraction of the total of 8,000 such Fiacres then circulating in the French capital. However, thanks to André Michelin's untiring efforts, within two years there were over three hundred and by 1903, some 6,000 cabs were shod with silent-running pneumatic tyres. Another tile panel depicts the aircraft piloted by Hubert Latham, a Frenchman of British parentage, who was the first aviator to attempt to fly across the English Channel, in July 1909, just ten days before Louis Bleriot made his successful flight. The wooden frame of Latham's plane was covered with a skin of Michelin aeroplane sheeting, a rubberised fabric that was specially devised for aeronautical construction in the years before the First World War. The final image celebrates the Royal Warrant granted by King Edward VII to Marc Wolff, Managing Director of the Michelin Tyre Company Ltd, in February 1908. It shows the King and the Prince of Wales riding in a Daimler Sedanca de Ville equipped with Michelin tyres.

None of these Michelin House panels features motor racing in a British situation, of course. Motorsport of any type or description was banned in Great Britain during the Edwardian age, due to the speed limits then in force. It was not until the opening of the dedicated Brooklands circuit in 1907 (just 3.7 miles long and provided with specially banked curves in the interest of safety), that competitive events such as those seen on the Continent or in the USA could take place legitimately in the United Kingdom.

In 1905, the Michelin Man appeared on a British poster once again, this time dressed as Sir Bibendum, a truly parfait knight.

1915–1924
Roaring through the 1920s

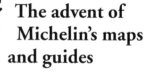

The advent of Michelin's maps and guides

In 1898, there were still only about 500 private cars circulating on the roads of France, a total that hardly presented the Michelin firm with a huge demand for replacement tyres, although they were then an extremely expensive luxury product with a very limited life. Even bicycle tyres cost about 90 francs a pair, at a time when the average workman's wage was just six francs a day, or less than 40 francs a week. So to develop a thriving and profitable market, the Michelin brothers had little alternative but to deal with the automobile manufacturers directly, in the hope that their tyres would be adopted as the specified original equipment. At this time, when ordering a car, a private customer had to purchase its wheels and tyres separately, on the maker's recommendation, as was the case with the luxurious and expensive coachbuilt bodies with which these earliest cars were generally equipped.

As we have seen, this strategy led to a close collaboration with these car makers through their joint participation in motorsport and other competitive events. The many spectacular victories achieved by the racing cars equipped with Michelin pneumatic tyres served to boost the reputation and prestige of both parties, so that by the turn of the century, the company had become the exclusive or preferred supplier of tyres to virtually all the major French car makers of that era, including Panhard & Levassor, Peugeot, de Dion-Bouton, Darracq, Delage, Delahaye, Mors and Renault. Thus the period between 1895 and 1905 was one of rapid expansion. Constant growth in sales of both bicycle and automobile tyres alike meant that the number of workers at Clermont-Ferrand rapidly increased from under 300 to more than 3,000.

Even so, the brothers refused to rest on their laurels and redoubled their efforts to attract potential customers, by demonstrating the superiority of the air-filled tyre over the solid rubber article at every possible opportunity. In 1901, they began a long-running series of brilliant advertising campaigns designed to popularise the automobile and promote motoring in general. By devising all manner of imaginative displays and entertaining stunts (usually involving their rotund mascot Monsieur Bibendum) they succeeded in establishing the Michelin name as a permanent feature in the public consciousness, so fostering a widespread loyalty and affection for their brand. Despite the fact that at this point in transport history car ownership remained the privilege of a small elite of aristocrats and plutocrats, the Michelins were convinced that, inevitably, these small numbers would soon be greatly magnified by the inclusion of the bourgeoisie. They also reasoned that, providing greater numbers of motoring enthusiasts could be recruited and then encouraged to drive longer distances, the greater would be the number of tyres that they could ultimately sell. And so, almost single-handedly, they invented the idea of tourism by motor car.

As promoted by the Michelin brothers, *tourisme par l'automobile* was an entirely new leisure activity, at first pursued only by the idle rich, but later by the middle classes too. By travelling in their luxurious Mors, Delaunay-Belleville or Rolls-Royce vehicles (usually with their chauffeurs at the wheel) these affluent automobile owners of the Belle Epoque and Edwardian era could escape the inconveniencies of railway timetables and travel from place to place at will, often for no greater purpose than to enjoy the scenery. So, to direct and encourage them in their travels through unfamiliar territory, André Michelin came up with yet another remarkable innovation, the series of Michelin guides and maps which still endure today.

In his early career, André had worked as a cartographer at the Ministry of the Interior, and remained fascinated by the whole process of map-making. Recognising that there was currently no range of maps or guides covering France that was really

1915 The first 100 examples of the Michelin-Breguet bombers, powered by Renault engines, are constructed at Clermont-Ferrand at Michelin's expense.

1917 Michelin buys BF Goodrich's patent for incorporating carbon black in the rubber mixes used in tyres. Michelin uses this innovation in conjunction with an anti-skid tread design to produce its RU (roulement universel) tyre.

1919 André Citroën introduces France's first mass-produced, mass-marketed car, the Type A. It is equipped with Michelin wheels and tyres, including a spare.

In the UK, the Ministry of Transport is established.

1920 The 1920 Finance Act in the UK requires an annual road tax to be paid, initially at the rate of £1 per unit of the vehicle's rated RAC horsepower. The Act also requires the issuing of tax discs and log books.

No fewer than 177 different manufacturers exhibit their wares at the Olympia Motor Show, the largest collection ever; so great, that an overflow is accommodated at the White City.

1922 The Lancia Lambda is introduced, featuring chassisless monocoque construction and independent front suspension.

1923 Michelin produces the first low-pressure balloon tyres for cars, marketed under the Comfort name.

In the UK, Henry Segrave exceeds 200mph in a Sunbeam racing car.

There are now more than a million motor vehicles on British roads.

1924 The 1915 McKenna Duties are repealed. As a result, motor vehicle imports soar to over 47,000 units, a figure which is not exceeded until 1960.

Another typical Bibendum poster, this time from the 1920s. He has changed his appearance slightly and no longer smokes a fat cigar!

precisely. This diversification into a second, subsidiary business field led the brothers to adopt a curious division of labour. André, from his base in Paris, dealt with the travel publications and all the other myriad aspects of publicity and propaganda, while Édouard remained in Clermont-Ferrand, responsible for manufacturing and product development. In other words, the engineer had become the publisher and advertising man, and the artist had become the engineer.

No fewer than 35,000 copies of the first edition guide were printed and issued free to all comers by Michelin's sales agents. By later standards, it was a rudimentary affair, no more than a pocket-sized brochure/handbook, but the following year the content and presentation were greatly improved and expanded to make it an essential reference book. The 1901 edition numbered 577 pages and was bound in hard covers like a proper book, thus beginning a tradition that, with minimal interruptions, has endured for well over a century. The 600 pages of the 1902 version were packed with information about garages, motor repairers, hotels, inns, restaurants, museums, chateaux and other sight-seeing possibilities, and also included 100 small-scale maps of city centres and a large detachable road map covering the whole of France. The hotels (but not the restaurants – these came later) were rated by stars, good and bad roads were differentiated, and the choice of an alternative picturesque scenic route was provided, indicated by symbols, to help the motorist choose the most pleasant itinerary. Naturally, the addresses of Michelin distributors (together with details of the sizes and prices of the tyres) were also provided, as well as the location of fuel supplies, there being no petrol stations with pumps in those far off days. Even postal, telegraph and telephone offices were included.

The 1903 edition ran to 60,500 copies, and this time a questionnaire was included, inviting the public to verify the fairness or accuracy of the star ratings awarded to the listed hostelries, as well as to

suitable for use by motorists, he decided that customers should be provided with a reliable means of navigating their way around unfamiliar territory and of identifying the best hotels and restaurants en route. The result was the first edition of the famous Michelin Red Guide which appeared in 1900, when the number of cars in France had climbed to just 2,897

supply further information of use to motorists and tourists. 'The success of our Guide has exceeded our expectations' wrote André in the unsigned preface, 'and one can say without exaggeration that one finds it nowadays in the hands of all drivers, and all over France.'

In fact, the Michelin Guide proved such a success that in 1908, the brothers opened a touring office located at their Paris headquarters on the boulevard Péreire, with the specific task of answering motorists' requests for information on how to get from A to B across France or Northern Europe in the shortest possible time. Presented as written reports, these individual itineraries were provided free of charge as a form of public service, just like the Guide itself. Before very long, requests were flooding in at the rate of over 5,000 every month, although at that time there were still hardly more than 12,000 voitures de tourisme, or private cars, registered in France.

It goes without saying, that when the Michelin Tyre Company's British headquarters opened for business in 1911, the Michelin House building contained a touring office providing route information, just as in Paris. It also distributed the very first Michelin travel publication to be printed entirely in English, *The Michelin Guide to the British Isles*, which contained the same helpful mixture of facts and figures as could be found in the Michelin Guide to France. English versions of the French book had started in 1908, as were English adaptations of the recently introduced guides for Germany, Spain and Portugal, and various other counties where Michelin tyres were sold. Two other specialist guides covering The Sunny Countries (the French Riviera, Southern Italy and North Africa) and The Alps and Rhineland were also published. 'The Michelin Guides, distributed gratis every year would, if placed one upon another, make a pile sixty times as high as St Paul's Cathedral', announced the new British Isles guide book, described as 'The Motorist's Vade-Mecum'.

Earlier, in 1910, André Michelin had produced the first of the company's road maps proper, drawn with exemplary accuracy on a 1:200,000 scale with each separate sheet measuring 420 x 1,000mm. Featuring the inevitable presence of Monsieur Bibendum and printed in four colours, the first of these large-scale folding route maps covered Clermont-Ferrand and its surrounding area, but two more on the Paris region and the Côte d'Azur (Mediterranean coast) between Marseille and Nice quickly followed. By 1914, the number of sheets available had risen to 45, covering the

entire territory of France. Later, of course, the series was extended to cover the rest of Europe including, from 1914, the British Isles. Further, improved and revised, editions followed periodically, now printed in full colour, with some maps being dedicated to specialist leisure or travel activities such as camping and skiing. These early Michelin road maps were the first to recognise landscapes and give an indication of steep upward gradients or descents. Indeed, their cartographical quality was such that during the Second World War they were used by the military in preference to the official government alternatives, first by the French Army in 1940, and then after the Allied invasion of June 1944, by the British and American armies too. To assist in the Liberation, over two million copies were printed in secret by Michelin here in the UK for use by the Allies and the Resistance. During the war also, Michelin embarked on its series of town plans and guides beginning with locations in the unoccupied zones such as Vichy, Toulouse and Montpellier, but eventually covering all

The first Michelin Guide to France dates back to 1900. The earliest English language edition was published in 1908. The first Michelin Guide to Great Britain and Ireland was published in 1911.

**THE TYRE AND THE
TELL - TALE CAMERA**
Remarkable experiments
filmed by the
MICHELIN RESEARCH DEP^T

This Bibendum poster image drawn by an unknown artist was published in England in 1926 to advertise his appearance in a promotional film.

the major towns and cities of France.

During the 1920s, the number of cars circulating in Western Europe increased three-fold as more and more motorists took to the roads. So it is not surprising that Michelin's *bureaux de tourisme* in Paris and London soon developed into sophisticated two-way information exchanges dedicated not only to collecting, checking, collating and disseminating travel-related facts and figures but also to improving urban and rural traffic systems and promoting motoring activities of every kind. Moreover, as car ownership expanded downwards to include the middle classes, holiday travel by automobile became the favourite recreation of the bourgeoisie, although not as yet the masses in general. The result was that in 1926, the company launched its range of highly detailed regional guides for tourists, the precursors of the present-day Green Guides. For the benefit of sightseers, these listed the places of historical interest or scenic beauty to be explored throughout specific areas of France. The first region to be covered was Brittany, closely followed in successive years by the French Alps, the Pyrenees, the Chateaux of the Loire, the

Auvergne, the Gorges du Tarn, the Côte d'Azur, the Vosges mountains and lastly, by 1933, Provence and Normandy also.

One of the greatest difficulties experienced by these pioneering motorists, as revealed by numerous reports and complaints received by Michelin's *bureaux de tourisme*, was that it was all too easy to get lost on the roads of France in those days, even when equipped with a Michelin map. The problem was that although the road network was classified into various different grades, dating from the Napoleonic era – routes nationales, routes departmentales etc – none was given individual numbers by which it could be identified from way-side sign posts. With no proper markings on the milestones, all too often drivers had no indication at all of which road they were actually travelling on, or of exactly what distance they had covered or had yet to cover to reach their destination. The whole situation was confused, to say the least.

'There is a total lack of method' commented André Michelin in one of his regular Michelin Monday columns in *La Vie de l'Automobile*. 'Something is needed to revolutionise automobile tourism. We suggest that all roads be given a number that is indicated on road maps and on the roads themselves.' The issue came to a head when, in October 1912, he launched a petition demanding that all French roads be systematically numbered. Within a month, 200,000 signatures had been collected, including that of the French President, Armand Fallières. So it happened, that four months later, in March 1913, the Minister of Public Works signed a decree ordering that a system of road numbering be established. It is known that a similar system of route numbering and signposting did not start to come into general use throughout the United Kingdom until 1921, so it is not unreasonable to suggest that the example set by Michelin in France may well have inspired this important development here – a document dated 18 November 1920 at the National Archives at Kew shows that André Michelin offered helpful suggestions to the Ministry of Transport during the deliberations regarding a road numbering system. One thing is sure – Michelin set to work on revising and updating its British Isles' maps and quickly produced a road map with numbers in 1921, almost certainly the very first of its kind.

Pioneers of flight

Following this successful exercise in lobbying, André Michelin began a series of campaigns of a more overtly political nature, in which he sought to impress his views on the authorities and influence decisions on public spending, especially with regard to matters of national defence and, in particular, aviation. Witnessing the very beginnings of manned flight by heavier-than-air machines, as evidenced by the exploits of Wilbur and Orville Wright in the USA in 1903, and later by Alberto Santos-Dumont, Louis Blériot and Gabriel Voisin in France, he and his brother had reached a firm conclusion about the coming importance of air travel and air warfare. However, their views were both optimistic and pessimistic simultaneously. By 1912, the pair had become convinced that a war with Germany was inevitable, and were alarmed and frustrated at the lack of preparations being made to equip France with an air force. With typical foresight, they realised that in the conflict that lay ahead, aircraft would have a military potential far greater than merely as instruments of aerial reconnaissance. Indeed, they had already envisaged the necessity of a fleet of bombers that could actually strike at the foe deep within enemy territory.

Doubtless, too, they had been mightily impressed by the achievements of Henry Farman (an Englishman born in France of a British father and brought up in Paris), the very same sportsman who had won their Paris to Clermont cycle race in 1892, but who had long since abandoned bicycles in favour of automobiles and aircraft. In January 1908, Farman had become the first man to fly a distance of one kilometre around a measured circuit, to win the huge prize of 50,000 francs (around £100,000 in today's money) offered by the wealthy

The cover of a folder produced circa 1921, designed to hold a Michelin Travel Itinerary, available from the Touring Office at Michelin House.

¶ It does not matter whether you are contemplating a trip merely from London to Brighton, or from Edinburgh to Rome.

¶ We recently supplied an itinerary from London to Pekin.

¶ Our services for which we make no charge, are at your entire disposal irrespective of the make of tyre you use.

MICHELIN TOURING OFFICE.
81, Fulham Road, LONDON, S.W.3.

TELEPHONE | TELEGRAMS
4400 Kensington. | Pneumiclin, London.

Your next Motor Tour

¶ Do you realise how much more enjoyable a well prepared tour can be?

¶ Our touring Office will send you, free of charge, an itinerary as complete as the specimen page overleaf.

¶ A rough draft of your proposed tour sent to us with approximate date of departure brings the detailed itinerary to you within a few days.

The first Michelin maps of the British Isles appeared as early as 1914.

entrepreneur Ernest Archdeacon. This feat – truly the first sustained, fully controlled, mechanically propelled flight in which an aircraft took off, made a round journey and returned to land in the same place – was followed three years later when, at the Grande Semaine d'Aviation at Reims in August 1910, Farman flew round a circular course for more than three hours, covering 11 miles at an average speed of 45mph to win the Grand Prix and a further purse of 60,000 francs. Much of this prize money was invested by Henry Farman in the aircraft construction firm that he founded with his brother Maurice, and which later provided many of the aircraft designs used by the Allies in the First World War, including the Royal Flying Corps and its successor, the Royal Air Force.

Evidently, Farman's first triumph inspired André and Édouard to offer an even greater prize of their own, to help get aviation off the ground. Announced in March 1908, the Michelin Grand Prix, worth 100,000 francs, was to be awarded to the first pilot who could fly the 250 miles from Paris to Clermont-Ferrand carrying a passenger, and then land his aircraft on the summit of a nearby mountain, the Puy-de-Dome, an extinct volcano. In the event, the prize was not claimed until three years later when, in March 1911, the pilot Eugène Renaux and his passenger Albert Senouque, succeeded in accomplishing the Michelin challenge, covering the distance in five hours and ten minutes in an aircraft designed and built by Farman, and powered by a 50hp Renault engine. 'This new industry will revolutionise the world, don't doubt that for a minute', said André Michelin at a banquet held to welcome the aviators.

No sooner had Renaux collected his trophy than the brothers returned to their aeronautical campaign with renewed vigour. In a letter addressed to the President of the Aéro Club de France and dated 22 August 1911, André Michelin proposed yet another contest, the Michelin Air Target Competition with prizes totalling 150,000 francs. The top prize would go to the pilot who, within a year, could place the greatest number of 20 kilogramme bombs within a circle of 33ft radius while flying at a height of at least 650ft. 'Our aim is to demonstrate the power of aeroplanes with facts', wrote André in the letter. 'We hope that once we have proved these facts, public opinion and the government won't hesitate to accept the need to order aircraft from French industry – not some

dozens of planes but five or six thousand which, after all, will cost no more than a battleship.'

Next, in February 1912, the Michelins produced a prophetic, but highly controversial brochure entitled 'Notre Avenir est dans l'Air – Our Future lies in the Air'. Over a million copies were printed and distributed free of charge. 'The empire of the air is there for the taking', it proclaimed. 'Whoever gains supremacy in the air comparable to Britain's supremacy over the seas will have nothing to fear from invasion.'

It seems that this serious form of propaganda had little effect in changing the uncomprehending attitude of the War Ministry towards creating a state of military preparedness, so André Michelin returned to the humorous approach that had served him so well in the past. At the annual Aeronautical Exhibition held at the Grand Palais in Paris that autumn, visitors to the Michelin stand were regaled by the sight of the Bibendum plane, a comic mock-up of an aircraft piloted by the larger-than-life-size representation of Monsieur Bibendum which straddled its fuselage. At intervals two human-sized Bibendums, one dressed as a soldier, the other as a sailor, bombarded the crowd with coloured

postcards carrying the message of Michelin's campaign calling for the immediate creation of a force of 5,000 bombers.

It was all to no avail, however, for when war broke out two years later – exactly as the Michelins had predicted – France had no more than 120 military aircraft in service, and these were a motley collection of different types and makes. So in August 1914, scarcely two weeks after the Germans had commenced hostilities, they informed the government that they were prepared to donate 100 bombers, to be manufactured entirely at their own expense at Clermont-Ferrand. And more than that, they also volunteered to go on to produce, at cost, as many aircraft as were needed, forgoing the profit. Their offer was accepted, and by July 1915 production was well underway. The aircraft in question was a biplane powered by a 200hp Renault engine and based on the prototype, first flown at Clermont-Ferrand in June 1915, which the Michelins themselves had helped to design in collaboration with Louis Breguet. The first 100 of these Michelin-Breguet aircraft – the ones provided free of charge – comprised a formation known as the Michelin squadron.

A Michelin-Breguet bomber of the type that served with the French Armée de l'Air during the First World War, and powered by a Renault engine. The first 100 aircraft were built by Michelin at Clermont-Ferrand and presented to the French government, free of charge.

Above and Opposite: The two British Empire Cups presented by Michelin between 1910 and 1913 to encourage the development of aviation in the UK, the winged Blacksmith and Pegasus Trophies.

By the time of the Armistice in November 1918, the Michelin factory was turning out seven planes a day. In all, it produced 1,884 Michelin-Breguet bombers for service with the French Armée de l'Air and the air arm of the American Expeditionary Force, plus 342,000 bombs of various types, and 8,600 bomb launchers.

The Michelin British Empire Cup

The Michelin brothers' generosity in encouraging and promoting the development of aviation was not confined to France where, in 1908, they had inaugurated their famous annual Michelin Cup competition, the first winner being Wilbur Wright with Henry Farman the second. The following

year, under the auspices of the recently formed Michelin Tyre Company Ltd, they announced the inauguration of the British Empire Cup contest, open only to British and Colonial aviators, flying British-made aircraft powered by British-made engines.

Eventually, there were two contests, with separate prizes and trophies. The first, the original No. 1 or Pegasus Cup of 1909, was offered for the longest endurance flight on a straight-line course, while the later No. 2, or Winged Blacksmith Cup, was to be awarded to the aviator who completed a flight around a circular course of about 125 miles in the fastest time. The total prize purse of £3,600, was to be competed for in increments of £400, £600 and £800 spread over three years.

The first award and its accompanying Pegasus trophy was won in March 1910 by J. T. C. Moore-Brabazon who flew 19 miles in a Short No. 2 biplane, powered by a 60hp Green engine. The next winner, in December 1910, was the American, S. F. Cody (whose real name was Cowdery) who achieved a flight of 185 miles in 4hr 47min in an aircraft of his own design and manufacture, also powered by a 60hp Green engine. The following year, in October 1911, Cody repeated the feat when he made a flight of 261 miles around a closed, seven-mile circuit at Aldershot, in 5hr 21min.

From 1911 onwards, the contest was revised and held under the rules of the Royal Aero Club. Two prizes were offered, the first trophy, the original Pegasus Cup, was to be won by the British aviator who could stay in the air the longest without touching down. The second, the Winged Blacksmith Cup, was to go to the British aviator who could cover at least 186 miles (300km) in the air, both feats to be achieved before 31 October each year.

The first of the new contests, for the Pegasus Cup, was won in October 1912 by Harry G. Hawker with a flight lasting 8hr 23min. The new Winged Blacksmith trophy was won in September 1911 by S. F. Cody who covered a 125-mile circuit from Farnborough to Andover, Hendon, Brooklands and back to Farnborough, in his Cody MkIII in a little over three hours. In 1912, Cody won the Winged Blacksmith trophy once again when he made a 186-mile circular flight from Farnborough to Farnborough via Larkhill, Newhaven and Brooklands, accomplished in 3hr 45min. As he became lost in fog during the fight and passed over Southampton, he probably covered more like 220 miles.

For 1913, the cups were to be awarded to the two pilots who flew, either for the longest time, or for the greatest distance, within the hours of daylight around the 125-mile long circuit covering Brooklands, Hendon, Farnborough and

Brooklands, taking off at sunrise and landing before sunset. Cup No. 1 (the greatest time in the air, with a prize of £500) was won by R. H. Carr who flew back and forth from Brooklands to Hendon, covering the 60-mile trip five times, to reach a total of 315 miles, in a Grahame-White Type 10 aircraft, but Cup No. 2 was not awarded that year.

With the outbreak of the Great War in August 1914, all further activities in the British Empire Michelin Cup competitions were cancelled, and the contest was never revived. Nevertheless, the principal prize-winners were sufficiently encouraged by their successes to continue their pioneering work, just as the Michelin brothers had intended, and in due course they all became founding figures of the British aircraft construction industry.

Most notable among the four prize winners was the first, John T. C. Moore-Brabazon, later ennobled as the First Baron Brabazon of Tara. Having served as an apprentice at the Darracq Works in Paris, his earliest achievements were as a motor racing driver, when he won the Circuit d'Auvergne race in 1907, driving a Mors. In November 1908, at Issy-les-Moulineaux in France, he became the first Englishman to pilot a heavier-than-air machine, a French-built Voisin biplane. A year later, in October 1909, he made the first all-British circular flight around a one-mile long course at the Isle of Sheppey, in a Short No. 2 machine. The following year, he gained Pilot's Certificate No. 1, awarded by the Royal Aero Club, making him the first-ever person to be licensed to pilot an aeroplane in the UK. Eventually, he entered politics and was appointed Minister of Transport in 1940 and then Minister of Aircraft Production from 1941 to '42.

Samuel Franklin Cody (aka Cowdery), who won the Michelin contest four times, was born in the USA in 1867. He started out in life as a circus stunt man and as a Wild West music-hall artiste before beginning his flying career in the UK as a maker of man-carrying kites and observation balloons. In 1904, he became the chief instructor at the British Army's Balloon Factory and School at Farnborough (later the Royal Aircraft Establishment). In 1908, he made his first powered flight in an aircraft that he had designed himself and which was later adopted as British Army Aeroplane No. 1. The following year, he adopted British citizenship in order to be eligible for the Michelin prizes. He was killed in a flying accident in 1913.

Born in Australia in 1889, Harry Hawker came to England in 1912 and very soon became the chief engineer and test pilot of the Sopwith Aviation Company, the makers of many famous First World War aircraft such as the Pup and Camel. He died in an air crash in 1921, shortly after the formation, with Tommy Sopwith, of the Hawker Aviation

Company, which was ultimately responsible for the Hurricane fighters that played an important part in the Battle of Britain during the Second World War.

The all-steel wheel and the Cable tyre

Naturally, during the Great War, the Michelin firm continued the production of its tyres and other rubber products. It also began the manufacture of another important Michelin innovation, the detachable all-metal wheel, which was introduced in 1913 for military use. The forerunner of all the car and truck wheels used today, this superseded the detachable rim and was made available for the civilian market as early as 1917. Formed from a disc of pressed steel and fastened to the vehicle's hubs by six

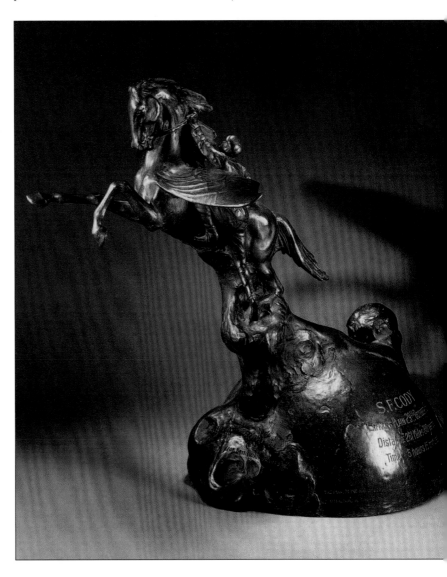

A winner of the Michelin British Empire Cup on two separate occasions was Samuel F. Cody, a noted pioneer of heavier-than-air flying machines. He began his short career as an aviator as the designer and builder of man-carrying kites.

to its rubber compound. This substance was found to conduct heat away from the tread and so to double or even treble tyre life. Previous Michelin tyres had not been black in colour, but red, white, green or even yellow! The Cable was followed in 1923 by the Cable Comfort, the first low-pressure balloon tyre for cars. Larger, wider and more flexible than the old high-pressure tyres, it was far less prone to bursting and rolled more smoothly over obstacles and rough surfaces. Running at 34psi rather than the 50psi that was normal previously, the Cable Comfort served not only to extend tyre life to 9,000 miles or more, but also to increase vehicle speeds and permit heavier kerb weights. Not surprisingly, it was soon adopted by all the major French car makers including an important new player in the field, the industrialist André Citroën who created, in 1919, France's first mass-produced, mass-marketed automobile.

Enter the 'Henry Ford of France'

It is estimated that by the eve of the Great War in 1913, there were 125,000 cars on the roads in France – about one for every 318 inhabitants – compared with 250,000 in the UK. However, French automobile production was by far the greater, totalling 45,000 vehicles, compared with the 34,000 which rolled out of British factories in 1913. This French output was shared among approximately 30 firms, only two of which (Peugeot and Renault) were large enough to construct more than 4,500 cars in a year. Yet, on the basis of a survey carried out on the exhibits at the 1913 Paris Motor Show, Michelin enjoyed at least 65 per cent of the French market for tyres supplied as original equipment, as compared with 50 per cent in 1910. Put another way, this meant that of any 25 automobiles seen travelling on the roads of France, running on a total of 100 tyres, between 60 and 70 of those tyres would have been made by Michelin. The same was true right across Europe and in South America, North Africa and Indo-China too. On top of this, Michelin was also enjoying the lion's share of a vast and highly profitable market for bicycle tyres. It has been estimated that in 1914 there were at least 3.5 million *vélocipèdes* in France – approximately one for every 11 persons, or one for every four males over 12 years of age. A similar situation would surely have existed in Great Britain.

The arrival of André Citroën not only transformed the French automobile construction industry, but it also increased the Michelin brother's dominance of their market yet further, making their Clermont-Ferrand firm the largest tyre and

bolts, this strong and robust improvement soon replaced the fragile wooden-spoked artillery wheels used hitherto. In England, however, another innovation of that era, the wire-spoked Rudge-Whitworth wheel, secured to the hub by splines and a quick-release nut, remained more popular with sporting motorists throughout the 1920s and 1930s.

Immediately after the war, Michelin introduced its first car tyre constructed with a casing reinforced by several overlapping plies of woven cotton cord fabric, a material invented by Palmer and developed by B.F. Goodrich in 1910. Called the Cable, Michelin's tyre used the Roulement Universel tread pattern first seen in 1917. Versions of the Cable tyre for bicycles and motorcycles followed in 1921 and 1922. It is interesting to note that in 1917 also, Michelin began using carbon black as an additive

wheel maker in Europe by a very wide margin. The Michelins had known Citroën well for many years, originally through his helical gear-cutting business founded in 1902, but then latterly in connection with one of their customers, the old-established car makers Automobiles Mors. In 1908, Citroën had assumed responsibility for reorganising the failing Mors firm and by trebling production he had rescued it from bankruptcy. More recently, during the war, the Michelins had further frequent contact with Citroën on account of their mutual interest in armaments and military matters. Without doubt, they would have visited the munitions factory that he had built at the Quai de Javel in Paris to produce artillery shells for the French army, using the latest methods and machinery from the USA. By the end of the war, over 28 million shells had been produced there at the rate of up to 55,000 a day by a labour force of 12,000 workers, most of them female.

In 1919, Citroën entered the motor industry on a very grand scale, by converting his munitions factory to produce automobiles. What is more, he chose not to produce expensive luxury models intended for the elite, like those he had made at Mors, but instead, to construct in large numbers a range of relatively inexpensive popular cars designed

and built in the American style, to suit the purposes and pockets of the middle classes. His first car, the Type A, manufactured between June 1919 and December 1921, was the first in Europe to come ready for the road, complete with electric lights and an electric self-starter together with five wheels and tyres including a spare, supplied, of course, by Michelin. In 1920, no fewer than 12,224 examples were sold, a total previously unheard of in Europe.

By 1925, André Citroën had introduced two new models and built an American-style moving assembly line at the Quai de Javel, capable of turning out more than 60,000 cars a year, as many as Renault and Peugeot combined. By 1927 when more than 76,000 vehicles were produced there, he had overtaken his competitors completely to become the largest car maker in Europe. In 1929, only ten years after starting his automobile manufacturing business, he made over 102,000 cars (a figure not to be exceeded for another 30 years) to win his reputation as the 'Henry Ford of France' and to consolidate his position as Michelin's biggest and most important customer by far. As we shall see, it was a relationship that was destined to have far-reaching consequences for both parties, to say the very least…

Cody became a leading figure in the development of British military aircraft, working at a base at Farnborough, Hampshire which eventually became the Royal Aircraft Factory/Establishment. He died in a flying accident in 1913.

1925–1934

British production starts at Stoke-on-Trent

The Battlefield Guides

As can be seen from their contribution to the war effort during the conflict of 1914-1918, members of the Michelin family were both fervently patriotic and devoutly Catholic. Not only did they help to establish a French Air Force by building and maintaining a squadron of bombers, but they also provided a military hospital at Clermont-Ferrand at their own expense, as well as paying generous allowances and pensions to the wives and children of all their employees who had been called up for service during the war, or had died in action. Of the 8,410,000 Frenchmen mobilised, casualties totalled an horrific 73 per cent, so that three out of ten males between the ages of 18 and 28 were lost.

After the Armistice the Michelins continued to uphold what they regarded as their patriotic duty, by publishing, in 1920, a remarkable series of Illustrated Guides to the Battlefields of the Great War, dedicated to the remembrance of the conflict in which the lives of 1,357,000 French, 908,000 British and Empire, and 1,800,000 German troops had been sacrificed. Produced in English as well as in French, this series of panoramic guides and histories was actually compiled during the course of the war and

1925 Michelin introduces the star system to grade and recommend the restaurants listed in its Great Britain Guide for tourists. In 1925 there are three categories, in 1927 five, from Simple to High Class.

To protect British automobile manufacturers, the McKenna Duties are reintroduced in the United Kingdom.

In France, André Citroën introduces the first all-steel bodied cars to be built in Europe.

1926 The first of the Michelin regional Green Guides appears.

André Citroën opens a factory at Slough to produce right-hand drive cars for the British and Commonwealth markets. Louis Renault follows suit the following year with a plant at Acton. Michelin is the sole supplier of tyres to both firms.

1927 To supply Citroën and its other customers in the British Isles, Michelin opens its first factory in the UK, located at Stoke-on-Trent. By now, the company's French factories employ more than 10,000 people.

1928 The first fully automatic traffic lights go into action at Wolverhampton. The first manually operated lights had already appeared in Piccadilly, London, in 1926.

1929 The Micheline rubber-tyred motorised trains are introduced in France.

1930 The number of private cars on British roads exceeds one million for the first time.

Michelin files a patent for a tyre with a built-in tube, ancestor to the tubeless tyre.

1931 André Michelin dies at the age of 78.

In the UK, the Highway Code is introduced while the Motor Vehicles Construction and Use Regulations come into effect, making the fitting of pneumatic tyres compulsory on all new cars and commercial vehicles in the UK.

The first cross-Channel car ferry enters service between Dover and Calais. It can carry 35 cars and 120 passengers.

1932 The low-pressure Michelin Super Comfort tyre is introduced, with a service life of over 30,000km (18,500 miles).

The heir apparent of the Michelin dynasty, Édouard Michelin's eldest son Étienne Michelin, is killed in a flying accident when attempting to land his plane on the Puy-de-Dome mountain near Clermont-Ferrand.

1933 The tally of deaths on British roads reaches an all-time high of 7,203 persons, although there are only 1½ million vehicles registered.

1934 André Citroën introduces the Type 7 Traction Avant, the world's first mass-produced front-wheel-drive car, featuring monocoque construction and hydraulic brakes. However, the enormous expense involved in this innovation leads to his bankruptcy and premature death. As his largest creditor, Michelin takes over the Citroën firm.

The Michelin Stop anti-skid tyre with zig-zag tread arrives on the market. The very first 'rain tyre', it features special sipes in its tread, to improve adhesion on wet and slippery roads.

In the UK, the Vintage Sports Car Club is formed, while standardised road signs are introduced.

Michelin Tyre Co. launches its house magazine *Bibendum*.

The Citroën 12-20hp de Luxe saloon as built at Slough in 1926. Its Michelin tyres and wheels can be clearly seen.

recorded events as they unfolded. Aimed at encouraging motorists and cyclists to make patriotic pilgrimages to the scenes of the most important battles such as the Marne, Verdun, le Chemin des Dames, Ypres and the Somme, the series eventually totalled 34 volumes. There was also a further series that chronicled the role of the Americans during the Great War.

Conquering the British market

In September 1915, the British government had introduced an import duty of 33⅓ per cent on motor vehicles and components such as tyres, to reduce the demand for private cars of overseas origin. Named the McKenna Duties after the current Chancellor of the Exchequer, Reginald McKenna, these taxes were intended as a temporary wartime measure and were repealed in 1924. The effect of this relaxation, however, was to stimulate a very large increase in imports at the expense of the British motor industry and so the protectionist duties were re-introduced in 1925, remaining in force until the UK joined the Common Market in 1973.

For those foreign producers such as Ford, Citroën, Renault – and Michelin too – who had already succeeded in establishing a toe-hold in the British and Commonwealth markets, there was only one option. If they were to avoid the McKenna Duties and gain access to these right-hand-drive markets on preferential terms they would have to establish their own manufacturing or assembly facilities in the UK. Henry Ford had been the first to do so, at Trafford Park near Manchester, as early as 1911. His example was followed by André Citroën, who opened his British factory at Slough in 1926 and by Louis Renault who set up a similar, but much smaller, establishment at Acton the following year. To qualify for export to the Commonwealth countries such as Australia, New Zealand and South Africa under preferential terms, 51 per cent of the invoiced value of each completed item from these foreign-owned assembly plants had to be of UK origin, including an allowance for the cost of labour and administrative overheads.

Initially, Citroën's British factory was extremely successful, producing almost 6,000 cars in 1927, its second year of operations, which represented sales of over 30,000 wheel and tyre sets for Michelin, although later the wheels of the Slough-assembled cars were of British origin. Therefore, to supply this captive market, as well as to cater for Michelin's many other British and Irish customers and outlets, the Michelin brothers decided, in 1926, to open a

An aerial view of the Stoke-on-Trent factory in 1929, just a few years after it had been completed. The first tyre was made there in November 1927.

incognito visits by Michelin staff to locations in various parts of England, and an initial shortlist of eleven towns was drawn up. In order of merit, these were London (where potential sites were identified at East Ham, West Ham, Barking and Woolwich), Manchester, Leeds, Nottingham, Derby, Bristol, Reading, Northampton, Lincoln, Luton and Crewe. Yet by mid-December, the shortlist had been whittled down to just two candidates – Nottingham and a newcomer, Stoke-on-Trent in North Staffordshire. Lying on the River Trent, Stoke was noted mainly for its dependence on the pottery industry that had been established in the area during the 18th century, but which was now in decline.

Stoke must have produced a very attractive proposition indeed, and in double-quick time, for on Christmas Eve 1925, the Town Clerk presented Michelin's Fulham Road London office with an Agreement and Plan detailing the financial incentives that the Council (a local authority with appropriate independent powers) had agreed to provide.

Besides the freehold of the site itself, these included concessions on rates and electricity supplies, the provision of a rail link with sidings (for which a Parliamentary Bill, hotly contested by Dunlop, was passed) and housing for the specialist senior personnel who would be moving to the town, from London or Clermont-Ferrand. On 28 January 1926, the *Staffordshire Sentinel* published a report about Stoke-on-Trent City Council's most recent meeting which had just approved the outline plans. *'The Michelin factory – Terms approved – Unanimous Decision'* its headline proclaimed. Similarly, the following day, the *Nottingham Journal* reported Michelin's decision to favour the rival location by itemising the offer, stating that 'It must be presumed that Nottingham's terms did not range on such generous lines.'

The site chosen was an 80-acre area of open fields at Campbell Road in the Boothen district of Stoke-on-Trent, which was a marshy area that was part of the alluvial plain of the River Trent which rises some ten miles to the north. Previously, it had been

factory in the UK at the earliest opportunity. This would add to the foreign and overseas production facilities that had already been set up in Italy and the USA (in 1907), and which would later be established in Germany (1931), Argentina (1933), Czechoslovakia (1934), Spain (1934), and Belgium (1937).

Archive documents show that exploratory work to locate a suitable site had actually begun as early as June 1923, when a fact-finding team from Michelin's *Service Bâtiments* (Building and Construction Department) at Clermont-Ferrand visited England to consult leading figures in the British motor industry, among them Sir Percival Perry, Henry Ford's representative in this country. Perry provided information on the American's activities in England and Ireland, notably the factory in Manchester, so that a detailed study of the industrial operations of a major automotive manufacturer (perhaps the largest then operating in the UK) was formed. Even then, Michelin's commercial objectives were two-fold, as was plainly stated in an internal note.

First, the company planned to be able to sell Michelin tyres of English origin and hence free of import tariffs. Secondly, it sought to produce these tyres in a sufficiently large quantity to be able to contest a price war with its UK competitors such as Dunlop. It was planned that only the essential workshops and production facilities would be created in England and that the Clermont-Ferrand headquarters would provide and fund the cost of all other necessary services and overheads.

Michelin also consulted French firms with established UK operations, in order to get a clearer view on how best to establish and operate a British factory, and to compile a dossier on matters such as employment regulations, working conditions and tax obligations.

The search for a suitable location, either greenfield or with existing buildings, began in earnest on 11 May 1925. There were many obvious key issues to consider, for example, proximity to ports and the railway network, adequate electrical power supplies and a sufficient availability of labour, particularly female. Other factors were more specific and mostly concerned a wish to avoid remote locations with little industrial activity or infrastructure and which would therefore require the construction of substantial housing facilities to accommodate migrant workers, as had been the problematic case at Clermont-Ferrand.

A specification for the ideal site was completed by October of that year, following numerous

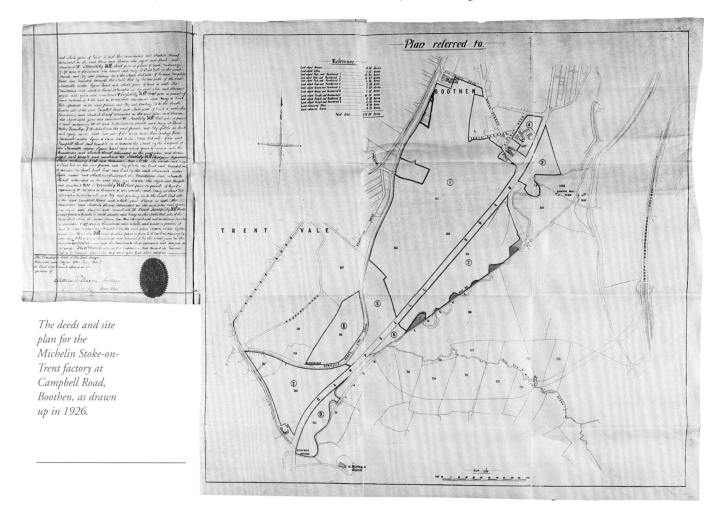

The deeds and site plan for the Michelin Stoke-on-Trent factory at Campbell Road, Boothen, as drawn up in 1926.

noted only as the location regularly used by Barnum & Bailey's Circus when visiting the town. Construction of the factory complex, enclosed by a boundary wall 1³/₄ miles long, got under way almost immediately, with the British contractors, Peter Lind & Co. acting closely with Michelin's design team at Clermont-Ferrand. Work on building and equipping the production facilities took about 100 weeks, so that the first Staffordshire-made Michelin tyre was produced in November 1927. During this building process, over 2,200 architectural drawings were produced at Clermont-Ferrand, the first on 27 January 1926. All of them used metric dimensions, which must have created certain problems for the British contractors at a time when imperial measurements were the norm in the UK.

The British journal, *Engineering*, of 11 January, carried an article attempting to 'give some idea of the buildings of an interesting modern factory… one that offers an indication of the imposing proportions that the manufacture of motor cars and allied equipment is attaining in this country.' The magazine's extensive report detailed the construction methods and materials used and gave an appreciation of the statistics involved. In its first year of operation the factory had three major production buildings together with five support workshops, covering a total floor area of more than 500,000ft². The plant used almost 10 million kW of electricity, 130 million gallons of canal water, 8 million gallons of fresh mains water and burnt

9,000 tons of coal to generate 88,000 tons of steam in the boilers. Tyre production requires a great deal of water, and so a prominent feature of the original works (like all other early Michelin industrial sites) was a large water storage tower, over 100ft high, The first all-reinforced concrete water tower to be built in England, it had a capacity of 43,700 gallons, sufficient to maintain an essential supply in the event of an emergency. Although demolished in 1967, the tower was a local landmark for over forty years, especially when it was later adorned by a floodlit sign, visible for miles around, showing M Bibendum running around its circumference.

The Stoke-on-Trent factory also boasted extensive railway facilities for the transport of the many thousands of tons of raw materials it regularly required, as well as for the despatch of finished products. In the 1920s and early '30s the

For much of its early life the Stoke factory was reliant on the railways, not the roads, for deliveries of supplies. This Fowler diesel shunting locomotive worked in the sidings there from 1948 to 1961.

road transport network in the region was far from being what it is today. With a general lack of good roads and most certainly no dual carriageways or motorways, a fleet of trucks and lorries would have been inadequate. Ironically for a maker of tyres, therefore, rail freight was the only answer, particularly when communicating with the sea ports through which material from France was imported. Construction of a railway connection, which involved building bridges over the Trent & Mersey Canal and the River Trent began in July 1926. Ultimately, over three miles of track were laid, half within the works and half outside, to join the sidings to the main line of the London, Midland & Scottish Railway.

The first shunting locomotive on the site was a petrol-electric loco-tractor, built in 1927 by the Parisian firm of Gaston Moyes and costing £2,026. It was unusual for its day in that it was powered by a four-cylinder Panhard & Levassor petrol engine which drove an electric generator of Thomson-Houston construction; this delivered direct current to operate the two electric motors connected to the axles. The Moyes engine remained in use until 1948 when it was replaced by a new diesel locomotive of conventional design purchased from John Fowler of Leeds.

As the 1950s and '60s progressed, however, so did the efficiency and cost-effectiveness of road transport and thus Michelin's reliance on rail freight declined year by year. By 1961, traffic on the sidings had ceased altogether, so it was decided to close the line and remove the track. By 1964, all

trace of Michelin's private railway had disappeared, ending 35 years of association between the company and the LMS and its successor, British Railways. Ironically, when the track and sleepers were torn up for scrap, the shunting locomotive was left stranded on the site and had to be taken away by road.

From the outset, the construction of the factory required the recruitment of a great many employees as, progressively, the buildings were completed and the machinery installed. On 1 January 1927, the company's payroll numbered 435, but within two years this had risen to 2,342. Ultimately, as increased production and new processes evolved, many thousands of employees were recruited and by the early 1970s, Stoke's workforce totalled more than 9,000, making Michelin the largest single-site employer in the district.

The Church of Saint Teresa

It is interesting to note that the Michelin family's concern for the welfare of its employees extended to matters spiritual as well as temporal, by providing an appropriate place of worship on the Stoke factory site. A drawing in the company's archives, dated 12 April 1927, shows that the church, consecrated as St Teresa's, was planned right at the outset of the Stoke construction project, a reflection of the strong commitment to the Roman Catholic faith which has been in the Michelin family's blood for generations.

The original building was a private chapel, intended not merely for the French employees who had come to Stoke-on-Trent from Clermont-Ferrand but also for Michelin employees in general, although the religion typically followed in the North Staffordshire region is Methodism. Father Denis was the original priest, replaced by Father Humphrey Bright in around 1936 when Michelin gave the chapel to the diocese. St Teresa's became a parish in its own right and in subsequent years has developed a thriving presence in the local community in conjunction with its adjacent primary school.

Today, externally, the original rectangular brick structure, 9½m wide by 28m long, can be easily identified but its enhancements are also evident. Various external changes have taken place, such as extending the nave, but it is the interior which has undergone an impressive transformation. Very recently, the whole of the inside has been remodelled giving now, at one and the same time, a feeling of both spaciousness and intimacy.

One of the first British-made cars known to have been equipped with Michelin tyres – a Straker-Squire of 1909, as exhibited at the London Motor Show that year.

The Micheline railcars arrive in England

Although the Michelin private rail system was designed for the use of freight trains, there was at least one occasion on which it played host to passenger traffic. This occurred with the arrival from France in 1932 of an example of the light-weight, high-speed, diesel-engined Micheline railcar pioneered by Michelin. Running on wheels shod with pneumatic rubber tyres, the Michelines had just been adopted for regular public service on the French rural railway system. Later, they were used in Belgium, Italy and the Netherlands too.

Having successfully completed their in-service trials the previous year, on the line between Paris and Deauville, the Michelines had already attracted world-wide attention within the railway industry. A 24-seater unit was then brought over the Channel to stage a series of demonstration runs for the benefit of officials from the LMS and the Southern Railway, who were possibly interested in acquiring a fleet. The journeys known to have been made by the Micheline unit while at Stoke included trips to Ascot via Birmingham, Bletchley to Oxford, Ascot to Alton and Wellington to Crewe via Wolverhampton.

In 1936, two prototype 56-seater railcars were built at Coventry to Michelin designs for extended experimental trials by the LMS. Contemporary reports indicate that they were 'beautifully made

and sumptuously upholstered.' Little is known about their fate but it seems that they were taken out of service well before the war, stored at the Stoke-on-Trent factory for the duration and subsequently broken up, probably in the late 1940s as a result of the nationalisation of the railways. It had become apparent that they would never be adopted for service in this country. Yet by 1939, no fewer than 140 Micheline units were in regular scheduled use in other parts of the world.

The idea for these rubber-tyred trains was originally suggested by André Michelin in 1928. After spending a sleepless night in a conventional *Wagons-Lits* sleeping car, he mentioned to his brother Édouard that they should work out a way to put trains on pneumatic tyres so that passengers could get a good night's rest. It was thus a desire for silence and comfort that motivated the initial research, in the course of which Michelin's engineers developed the use of high-tensile steel cords for the reinforcement of the tyre casing. The same technique was later used in the Metallic tyre for trucks, introduced in 1937.

Although the Micheline railcars have long since been withdrawn from the French railway network, the concept of the quiet-running, pneumatically-cushioned rubber-tyred train remains alive today in numerous urban transit railway systems around the world, including certain lines on the Paris Metro where it has been employed since April 1952.

The experimental Micheline diesel railcar, with rubber-tyred wheels, was evaluated by the LMS railway in England in 1936/37.

1935–1944

On the road to victory

Michelin at war, 1939-1945

For several months following the declaration of war against Germany by Great Britain and France in September 1939, the Michelin organisation in the United Kingdom remained in normal daily contact with its parent company in Paris and at Clermont-Ferrand. The Stoke-on-Trent factory continued with the production of tyres for the civilian market. However, in May 1940 the Wehrmacht invaded France and the Low Countries, bringing to an end the Phoney war and changing this situation most abruptly. Under the terms of the Franco-German armistice signed in June, the country was divided into two parts, the northern or Occupied Zone including Paris, controlled by the Germans, and the southern or Free Zone controlled from Vichy by a nominally independent French administration led by Marshal Pétain. Henceforth, until the liberation of France in August 1944, Michelin's interests in the UK (including the Citroën factory at Slough) were regarded by the British government as being under German control and were placed under the supervision of the Official Custodian of Enemy Property. In fact, under the provisions of the Trading with the Enemy Act of 1939, all communication with France was forbidden.

Although the production of private cars and commercial vehicles for the civilian market was suspended throughout the British motor industry in October 1940, the assembly of military vehicles was given top priority, in order to replace the huge motor transport losses suffered during the evacuation of the British Expeditionary Force at Dunkirk. Over 63,000 military vehicles had been abandoned on French soil, plus 2,472 tanks and self-propelled guns, leaving only 10,000 lorries and personnel carriers in service throughout the UK. As a first step towards replacing these losses, the government promptly requisitioned all the civilian goods vehicles in the country that could be spared from normal work, and introduced petrol rationing to curb all but essential private motoring. At the same time, it made an appeal to all manufacturers having the engineering skills and capacity to assist in the production of wheeled military vehicles and the heavy-duty tyres on which these many different types of four-wheel-drive lorries or amphibious and armoured fighting vehicles were reliant.

In common with the entire British tyre industry, Michelin answered the call with 'blood, sweat and tears'. Over the next four years a labour force of 2,000, chiefly at Stoke, the majority of them female, worked round the clock, three shifts a day, seven days a week, in conditions of the highest secrecy, undertaking numerous vital contracts

1935 Michelin Tyre Company Ltd joins The Tyre Manufacturers' Conference, a body set up in 1929 to provide a forum for tyre manufacturers to discuss issues of the industry. The Conference played an important part in maintaining tyre supplies during the Second World War.

Pedestrian crossings signposted by Belisha Beacons are introduced, a 30mph speed limit is imposed in urban areas and driving tests are made compulsory.

The London Motor Show moves to Earls Court from Olympia where it had been held since 1905.

Citroën produce the world's first diesel-engined passenger car, closely followed by Mercedes-Benz.

Édouard Michelin's surviving son Pierre is named president of Citroën with Pierre Boulanger as vice-president. Together, they authorise studies for a completely new Citroën car the TPV (Toute Petite Voiture – Very Small Vehicle) which is eventually marketed as the 2CV.

1937 Pierre Michelin is killed in a road accident. He is succeeded as the head of the Michelin-Citroën organisation by two co-directors, Robert Puiseux (his brother-in-law) and Pierre Boulanger, who has specific responsibility for Citroën.

Michelin introduces low-profile Pilote wheels and tyres for touring cars, which greatly improve grip at high speeds.

1938 The first tyres specifically designed for trucks – the Michelin Metallic series – are launched, employing metallic filaments in their casings instead of the textile cords used previously. These give greater resistance to the overheating caused by heavy loads.

1939 England and France declare war on Germany. Petrol rationing is introduced in the UK which effectively ends private leisure-time motoring for the time being.

Morris becomes the first British manufacturer to build a million cars.

1940 Édouard Michelin dies at the age of 81. France is invaded by Germany.

In the UK, Purchase Tax at 33$^{1}/_{3}$ per cent is introduced for motor vehicles, but the manufacture of cars for civilian use ceases in October.

A night-time speed limit of 20mph is introduced to cut down traffic accidents caused by the blackout, but they rise to unprecedented levels all the same, and 8,609 people are killed during the year.

1941 Cut off from its parent company in France, Michelin's Stoke-on-Trent factory is turned over to war production, making tyres for military vehicles and assembling trucks for the Allied armies.

Vehicles from the Ministry of Supply's Wheeled Vehicle Experimental Establishment were based at Stoke during the latter stages of the war. From April 1944 to June 1945, its fleet of test vehicles covered well over a million vehicle miles.

placed by the Ministry of Supply. For Michelin at least, the task was made doubly difficult. First; until June 1940, the Stoke plant had relied on its parent company at Clermont-Ferrand for all matters related to the research and testing of new materials and processes, and for the design and supply of new manufacturing methods and machinery. Now, suddenly cut off from France, it had to rapidly create a self-sufficiency in all these areas, and with a greatly reduced staff – many key employees had already returned to France, or been called-up for military service. Four new departments were quickly established: the Development Department, responsible for all new tyre and process studies; the Installations and Moulds Departments which were concerned with the design and erection of new production machinery and facilities, and a Technical Department, which took charge of all questions regarding tyre fitments and testing, both in laboratories and on the road. During the dark days of 1940 and '41, when invasion seemed imminent and inescapable, these new departments and the factory as a whole worked with desperate urgency, designing and producing the special types and sizes of tyres required to equip the enormous range of military vehicles needed to transport the new con-

script army. This comprised 55 divisions then being assembled and trained in the UK to liberate France and the other occupied countries of Europe.

The second major difficulty related to raw materials. No sooner had the UK subsidiary accomplished the immense task of changing over to independent operations than a new blow fell, not just on the Michelin Tyre Company, but on the whole Allied tyre industry world-wide. In December 1941, the Japanese swooped on the US naval base at Pearl Harbour and followed up this initial attack by the swift conquest of all the richest rubber-producing areas of the Far East, including Michelin's own plantations in Indonesia. This came as a staggering setback – the armed forces moved on rubber tyres and it was essential to keep up supplies of raw materials and, indeed, increase them. To replace the loss of natural rubber resources, plans were introduced immediately for the production, in the United States, of synthetic rubber, derived from oil and coal, which could be mixed with ground-up natural rubber obtained from recycled tyres, to make a highly effective substitute. Even so, a completely new manufacturing technique, involving an alternative type of mould, had to be invented. Throughout this gruelling period,

Michelin's own fire tender which served at the Stoke factory during the Second World War – and for some time after that!

A Chevrolet 15cwt Canadian Military Pattern lorry of the type also assembled from CKD kits at Stoke during the war. In this case, however, the vehicles came from General Motors' independent Canadian factory and were part of the Canadian government's contribution to the war effort.

Michelin's technicians were always the first to complete their experiments and produce tyres with the correct admixture of ingredients. What is more, this change-over from natural to synthetic rubber was accompanied by another change almost as fundamental – the replacement of the cotton fabric reinforcement in the tyres by artificial rayon fibres, a development which caused enormous problems of its own. In spite of these difficulties – greater perhaps than those faced by any other of the major motor transport industries at that time – the Michelin Tyre Company not only maintained but vastly increased its output during the war years, while retaining the highest standards of quality for which it was already widely renowned.

The contribution to the war effort made by the Stoke-on-Trent factory was not confined to tyre production alone, however. It also embraced the assembly of military vehicles sent from the USA under the Lend-Lease scheme, and shipped across the Atlantic as Completely Knocked Down (CKD) kits contained in large wooden packing cases to be put together in the UK. Besides completing a total of 4,765 specialist vehicles such as Mack recovery units, Federal tank transporter tractors, Willys Jeeps and Indian motorcycles for despatch riders, the firm also specialised in the construction of tank transporter trailers. Also, various parts for tanks and other armoured vehicles were made under contracts placed by the Ministry of Supply.

Moreover, in 1943, the Engineering Department assembled 317 examples of the distinctive Canadian Military Pattern lorry, designed by a team of Canadian engineers and manufactured in CKD form by the independent Ford and Chevrolet plants in Canada, funded by the Canadian government. This work had been commenced in 1940 by the Citroën factory at Slough, which produced 23,480 CMP vehicles during the conflict, the last being built in 1945. Throughout the war years, the Stoke factory maintained its own Home Guard unit, responsible for fire prevention and aircraft spotting duties. Yet strangely, in view of its strategic importance, it was never once subjected to enemy attack, much less put out of action, even temporarily, by the Luftwaffe.

This was very different indeed to the situation in France where both the Citroën factory in Paris and Michelin's Cataroux plant at Clermont-Ferrand were deliberately targeted in carefully planned bombing raids carried out by the RAF, in September 1943 and March 1944 respectively. As the production of vehicles for the civilian market in France had been suspended following the German invasion, the parent company had no alternative but to continue making tyres and trucks for the Wehrmacht, its only substantial customer, merely to safeguard its continued commercial existence and the welfare of its work force.

Even so, its management avoided all direct personal contact with the Nazis and reduced production to the lowest output levels possible. Although the company managed to steer a stable course through these difficult times, the Michelin family itself was not without its tragic casualties, notably the death of André's son Marcel, who was deported and died in the Buchenwald Ohrdruf concentration camp in January 1945.

A 40-tonne Federal Tank Transporter unit, one of the 4,765 military vehicles assembled at the Stoke factory between April 1941 and April 1944, from Completely Knocked Down kits supplied by the USA under the Lend-Lease scheme.

The Snubnose Morris technical service vans

When, in January 1931, regulations requiring the fitting of pneumatic tyres to all wheeled motor vehicles and trailers in Great Britain came into force, manufacturers such as Michelin were presented with an unprecedented sales opportunity. Not only would all the new commercial vans, lorries and buses that were coming on to the roads in ever-greater numbers have to be so equipped but all existing vehicles running on solid tyres (which were causing severe damage to the highways) would soon have to be re-equipped with pneumatic tyres. The prohibition of solid tyres created almost overnight a great new market, over and above the rapidly expanding demand then being experienced

as a result of the huge increase in the ownership of private cars that was taking place. Between 1930 and 1935, the production of cars and commercial vehicles in the UK was virtually doubled, from 236,528 to 403,720 units.

In the light of this development, Michelin, in common with certain competitors, lost no time in embarking on a major marketing campaign to advertise and promote its pneumatic tyres. And as was typical of Michelin's methods even then, the emphasis was on increasing technical awareness and understanding among its existing and potential customers, and on preaching good practice in all things pneumatic.

Thanks to the large scale of its operations in the British Isles and Europe, the company possessed the resources to go about this educational

Like all the main buildings at the Stoke factory, the tyre warehouse (Building No. 14) was painted with camouflage during the war. The evidence remained for many years, as can be seen from this 1950s photograph.

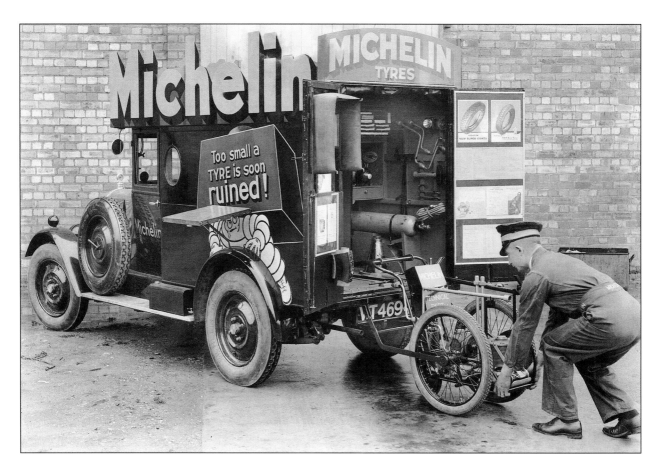

campaign in a very substantial way, as is born out by the impressive fleet of technical service vans that took to the roads in the middle of 1930. It is known that at least a dozen of these vans existed, and that they remained in use until 1932 at least, each crewed by a two-man team comprising a salesman and a specialist technical fitter-driver, both dressed in natty Michelin uniforms. Around fifty technical fitters were recruited in 1930 alone.

Based on the 11.9hp, 10cwt capacity Snub-nose light commercial vehicle (a derivative of the well-known Bullnose saloon car) produced by Morris Motors from 1923 until 1930, these vehicles were fully equipped for their work of providing instruction, assistance and general customer support. Each one was kitted-out with all the necessary hand-tools, jacks, axle-weighing devices and air pumps to demonstrate the task of fitting and inflating a pneumatic tyre to the correct pressure, or to show how to change or repair one in the event of a puncture. No stock of products was kept on board the vans, but their crews were certainly not forbidden from taking orders! Even so, their declared role was to dispense information on the choice of tyres available within the Michelin range and to advise on the right type and size to suit the particular make and model of vehicle belonging to prospective customers.

In truth, there could be no mistaking the true commercial nature of their mission, for the vans carried large Michelin signs on their roofs, while their sides were decked-out with eye-catching placards and posters featuring Monsieur Bibendum. Some may even have had a large representation of a cut-away section of a tyre fastened to their bodywork, which gave them the appearance of a mobile advertising hoarding. Touring the length and breadth of the country and following a regular itinerary, they would visit the depots of major freight transport or bus companies, or merely park in town centres or on village greens, where leaflets reading: 'The Michelin Technical Department is here today. Please stop us. We welcome your enquiries,' were handed out to attract the interest of private motorists and the ordinary public. It was all so indicative of Michelin's energetic and innovative way of doing business.

Unfortunately, none of these service vans survived beyond the 1930s, the only evidence of their existence being a series of photographs taken then, and now preserved in the archives at Stoke-on-Trent. As a fitting way to mark the Centenary of the company, therefore, it was decided to attempt a complete recreation of a Michelin service van, accurate in every detail, and following almost exactly the specifications of the original vehicles, just as they were when delivered to Stoke brand-new in the early 1930s. The first step in building this replica was to acquire a rolling chassis including an engine and transmission and this was accomplished in December 2003 with the help of the Bullnose Morris Club. The vehicle was then given a thorough overhaul including a complete engine rebuild, all undertaken by the specialist restorer, Cooke's of Leicester. The brief was to produce a robust and reliable vehicle that would require only minimal maintenance beyond that laid down in the original Morris Motors owner's hand book, and which could be driven with confidence all over Europe. Naturally, special attention was paid to the wheels and tyres, which had to be Michelin 14x45 Bibendum Comfort, as produced by the Stoke factory throughout that era, fitted on Bibendum rims. Although not standard equipment for the Morris light commercials, these were known to have been fitted on the contemporary Citroën C4 cars and would certainly have been chosen for the fleet of service vans.

The construction of the cab and exterior body-work, formed from sheet aluminium, was a relatively straightforward task. The real challenge lay in recreating the interior and locating the many different tools, jacks and other items of equipment which were carried by all the service vans, as was revealed by the archive photographs. Since little of this kit could be found among the surviving period pieces at Stoke, they had to be located elsewhere, at auto-jumbles or motoring memorabilia dealers, or remanufactured entirely by specialist engineering firms. It all involved a country-wide search. The so-called load jack was one such example. An accurate axle weighing device, a pair of which was carried by each vehicle was required, but there was only one example left in the entire Michelin organisation. Thanks to the assistance of a highly-skilled group of Michelin employees, current and retired, plus numerous engineering organisations in the Stoke area, the original now has its twin. Similarly, the wheeled trolley that carried these special jacks was missing, but a perfect replacement has now been made.

It is planned that over the coming years the replica Snubnose service van will visit automobile shows, race meetings, classic car gatherings and other motoring events all over England, France and the rest of Europe to demonstrate that the Michelin tradition of providing customer service goes back seventy-five years at the very least!

Opposite and Left: Two views of the original Michelin technical service van, specially built on the Snubnose Morris chassis. A sizeable fleet of these vehicles operated around the country during the early 1930s, but none has survived – so Michelin has built an exact replica for use during its centenary celebrations and beyond.

The Traction Avant is built at Slough

Just like the Michelin brothers, the dynamic and progressive French motor-magnate André Citroën (who had founded his Double Chevron marque in 1919) was an internationally minded entrepreneur whose interests, activities and ambitions extended well beyond the borders of France. As a pioneer of modern manufacturing, marketing and publicity methods (rather than an automobile engineer or mechanical inventor in the mould of Louis Renault), he recognised that, to expand production, bring down prices and increase sales it was essential to achieve the economies of scale that can only flow from world-wide, multinational operations.

So it was that, also seeking to escape the restrictions of the McKenna Duties recently introduced in the UK, in 1926, he opened the first of his foreign factories at Slough on the outskirts of London, to build the cars that were currently in such great demand among British motorists. In its first full year of operations, no fewer than 5,299 Citroëns

were assembled there (a very large number for that era) using a high proportion of components supplied by British-based manufacturers. As the tyres and wheels for these vehicles were sourced solely from Michelin, Citroën Cars Ltd soon became the Stoke-on-Trent factory's largest and most important customer, just as was the case with the relationship between Michelin and Citroën in France.

There, by that time, the Double Chevron firm had already outstripped its older Continental rivals, Peugeot, Renault, Panhard and Fiat to become the largest automobile manufacturer in Europe. In 1929, as many as 102,891 cars and light commercial vehicles rolled off the production lines at the Quai de Javel factory in Paris, to join the tally of almost half a million Citroëns then running on Michelin wheels and tyres along the roads of France. Yet despite this extraordinary success, achieved within the space of only ten years, André Citroën was unsatisfied. By the early 1930s, he had become bored with his reputation as the Henry Ford of France. He thus decided to abandon the entirely conventional, American style of cars that he had been producing up until then, and to manufacture instead something far more adventurous. Moreover, he planned to do so at the rate of 1,000 units a day in a modernised factory, entirely reconstructed and re-equipped with the latest and most costly machine tools.

The result was the Traction Avant, the world's first mass-produced front-wheel-drive car, now generally acknowledged to be the vehicle that set the pattern for the modern family car. Designed by André Lefèbvre, it featured such novelties as chassisless monocoque construction, independent front suspension by torsion bars, and hydraulic brakes all round. Launched in June 1934, the Traction Avant met with universal acclaim, even in the British motoring press which hailed it as 'the car we could not overturn' on account of its very low centre of gravity which gave it remarkable stability. The following year it went into production at the Slough Works, in right-hand-drive form.

When taking over Citroën's French operations, the Michelins also made the brave decision to keep open the works at Slough, the future of which was uncertain to say the least, due to the greatly diminished production experienced there during the Depression. Their anglophile faith in the long-term prospects for the sales of cars and tyres in the British Isles and the British Commonwealth was fully justified, however. In due course, the Traction Avant proved to be a major success for the British motor industry also, by playing a key role in the export-drive. No fewer than 24,970 right-hand-drive examples were 'Made in England' at Slough, firstly between 1935 and 1940 and then later, between 1946 and 1955 – 5,922 of them pre-war and 19,048 post-war. Almost 16,000 of these cars were exported throughout the British Commonwealth, mainly to Australia, New Zealand and South Africa. All of them were shod with British-made Michelin tyres, produced at Stoke, as were those for the successors to the Traction Avant made at Slough, the 2CV and the DS19.

The Michelin Pilote tyres and wheels

The Michelins were entrepreneur-industrialists who were never afraid to risk their money on a promising venture. Consequently, throughout the forty-odd year history of their tyre-making enterprise, the profits had consistently been re-invested in further research and development. Having begun in 1895 by producing the first detachable pneumatic automobile tyre and then, in 1899, the first tyre capable of withstanding speeds of over 100km/h, the brothers had gone on to launch, in 1923, the world's first low-pressure (2.5 bars) balloon tyre, the Comfort. In this, the tread-carrying

A right-hand-drive version of the Citroën six-cylinder Traction Avant, built at Slough for the British and Commonwealth market in 1949. It is equipped with Michelin's Pilote wheels and tyres.

rubber outer casing containing the pressurised inner tube, was reinforced by layers of textile material, laid in a criss-cross pattern. By reducing hysteresis, or internal friction, this technique allowed the tyre to run much faster without risk of overheating, and therefore greatly improved both its safety and its service life. The Comfort was normally capable of covering at least 15,000km, double that of ordinary contemporary tyres. In 1932, the Comfort was followed by the very low-pressure (1.5 bars) Super Comfort, capable of lasting 30,000km, and in 1934, by the world's first rain tyre, the Super Comfort Stop, which featured a tread pattern moulded, not cut, into its circumference, specifically designed to clear water

away from the central area of the tread, thereby reducing the danger of skidding in wet conditions.

The next great innovation from the Clermont-Ferrand firm was the Michelin Pilote tyre, which made its appearance at the Paris Motor Show in 1937 and the London Show in 1938. The Pilote was the world's first low-profile tyre, with an aspect ratio of 0.80; in other words, its sidewall measured only 80 per cent of the width of its tread. Designed specifically to enhance the road-holding and ride-comfort of high-performance cars, it duly became standard equipment on the Traction Avant range, in conjunction with the special lightweight steel wheels of the same name, also made by Michelin. Designed to reduce unsprung weight and weighing

Below: A new advertising van, mounted on a 1-tonne Morris chassis, was commissioned in August 1937 to publicise the Stop tyre. The large hand on the roof showing off the flexible anti-rain tread was turned by a small electric motor.

Above: Nicknamed the 'Travelling Laboratory', this 5-tonne Commer lorry of 1937 had a specially built body. Its primary purpose was to test and demonstrate the non-skid properties of the Stop tyre, with the aid of a built-in water tank and sprinkler system. The vehicle also featured a customer reception office complete with a mini-bar for dispensing hospitality!

a kilo less than their predecessors, these Pilote wheels featured a novel open-centred form of construction. Welded in between the hubs and rims was a series of slats that acted like the vanes of ventilating fans to help cool the brake drums.

Michelin golf balls

One of Michelin's lesser-known activities before the Second World War was the production of golf balls. Although the manufacture of sports equipment and play-things had been one of the parent company's sidelines from the earliest days, it is known that golf balls were only ever made at Stoke-on-Trent. Production had begun there sometime during the late 1920s, shortly after the factory had opened, for distribution throughout the United Kingdom and the British Commonwealth where the game of golf was rather more popular than in France.

To promote sales, the company employed five travelling sales representatives, whose task it was to visit all the golf courses in the country, from Land's End to John O'Groats, playing golf with the members and cultivating the professional staff. There

can have been few better opportunities to combine work and pleasure in the history of the game! The job – if it can be called a job – attracted a very high calibre of employee. One of the representatives was an ex-minister of the Church who had graduated from St Andrews University with a degree in Greek and Hebrew. He was paid a starting salary of £4 a week plus expenses.

These Bibendum golf balls were very popular indeed – business was brisk and highly profitable; records show that in late 1930 the product brought in more sales revenue than bicycle tyres and tubes. However, it appears that production stopped with the outbreak of war, never to be resumed.

The last document referring to golf balls in the company's archive is an order from New Zealand dated 8 November 1939. Hundreds of thousands – if not millions – of the golf balls must have been made throughout the previous decade, but strangely enough, only one single example is known to have survived. Mounted on a small plinth it is presented every year as a trophy to the winner of the annual golfing competition held by the Michelin Athletic Club at Stoke.

This poster advertising Michelin's golf balls was seen in the UK during the 1930s. Millions were sold but production did not resume after the war. By then the company had decided to concentrate entirely on tyre production.

1945–1954
Bibendum bounces back

The Michelin Athletic Club

Because the Michelin firm was established in a relatively remote rural location in France, lacking the normal facilities of an industrial centre, in order to attract sufficient labour during those early years of rapid growth it was compelled to build or provide a wide range of company-owned facilities. So in addition to its factory buildings it also constructed sufficient modern accommodation for its

1945 Production of cars – mainly for export only – is resumed in the UK.

The first British car to spearhead the export drive – an Austin Ten – is shipped to the USA.

1946 In June, Michelin patents the steel-braced radial tyre in France.

Production of cars is restarted at Citroën's Slough Works with 1,050 examples of the Traction Avant built there during the year, of which half are exported.

Austin builds its millionth car, with Ford having achieved this feat in the UK six years earlier.

1947 Posters advertising Michelin tyres appear on London buses for the first time.

1948 In January, a flat rate of car tax is introduced to replace the horsepower system that has been in existence since 1921. The new rate is set at £10 per annum.

The first UK Motor Show for ten years is held at Earls Court in October and attracts a record 275,493 visitors, 96,940 on one day alone.

Earlier, at the October Paris Motor Show, Citroën exhibits the 2CV, the French People's Car, but sales do not begin until the following year.

This year also, Jaguar launches the XK120 sports car and Rover brings out the Land Rover.

The first double-decker bus in the UK to be fitted with Michelin tyres goes into service.

Stoke factory celebrates the production of its first Metallic tyre in June 1948.

1949 In June, the Michelin X tyre enters regular production, available as optional equipment on the Traction Avant.

Great Britain becomes the world's leading exporter of cars, a position it holds until 1956 when overtaken by Germany.

1950 Pierre Boulanger, the co-director of Michelin and Citroën, is killed in a car crash, en route from Paris to Clermont-Ferrand. He is succeeded as the head of Citroën by his deputy, Pierre Bercot, who reports to Robert Puiseux, the new chief executive at Michelin.

In the UK, petrol rationing (which has been in force since 1939) ends in March. The basic allowance had been sufficient for only 200 miles a month. Food rationing continues until 1953.

1951 Zebra crossings appear on the streets of Great Britain and Northern Ireland.

In Europe, Lancia is first to adopt the X tyre as standard equipment, on the Aurelia sports saloon.

The Michelin group is reorganised into two companies: Manufacture Française des Pneumatiques Michelin and Compagnie Générale des Établissements Michelin, a Group holding company.

In April, trains on the Paris Metro run on Michelin pneumatic tyres for the first time.

1952 Michelin produces the first radial tyres for trucks.

The Montagu Motor Museum – later the National Motor Museum – is opened by Lord Montagu at Beaulieu.

Austin and Morris merge to form the British Motor Corporation, bringing the Austin, Morris, MG, Riley and Wolseley marques under one commercial roof.

1953 Pool petrol is withdrawn and replaced by branded premium-grade petrol.

The Michelin Motoring Map of Great Britain, a new production, goes on sale, timed to coincide with the Coronation of HM Queen Elizabeth II.

1954 Flashing direction indicators become a legal requirement in the UK.

Bosch introduces fuel injection for cars while Standard launches the first British diesel-engined passenger car, a version of the Vanguard saloon.

The Bristol 404 becomes the first British-designed car with Michelin X radial tyres as standard equipment.

The output of the British motor industry exceeds a million vehicles for the first time.

work-force plus the schools, hospitals and shops needed to support them: a policy that later led to unfair accusations that the company was excessively paternalistic in its attitude towards its employees and their dependents.

Moreover, to encourage a sense of community and comradeship among these migrant workers and their families, the company established a sports and social club, the Association Sportive Montferrandaise (ASM), which duly assumed a very important role within its corporate culture. Therefore, when Michelin opened for business in the British Isles, it was only natural that it should seek to repeat this success with the establishment of the Michelin Athletic Club (MAC), an institution that has flourished ever since, and has played an important part in the lives of all its UK employees over the past century. The activities of the club have in no way been confined to athletics, cricket, tennis, swimming or sport in general, but have also included all manner of other leisure pastimes and pursuits such as music and drama, together with the normal gamut of darts matches, dances, concerts, children's parties and other traditional social gatherings.

Only two years after its incorporation in 1905, the payroll of the Michelin Tyre Company Ltd had

risen above 100 people, more than enough to form a cricket team. So, in 1907, the first interdepartmental sports event took place with the 'Offices' playing the 'Stores'. The match took place at Battersea and the 'Offices' won, reportedly by a considerable margin. Sporting events continued until the outbreak of the First World War, when practically the whole of the staff joined the army, the navy or the air force, partly encouraged by Édouard Michelin who paid a weekly allowance to all married men enlisting. Inevitably, some men lost their lives in the conflict and an illuminated scroll exists which lists 29 such men who had served in Michelin's British operations.

During the boom years that followed the cessation of hostilities, sales increased at such a rapid rate that it was almost impossible to train staff quickly enough to deal with the orders. It was now, that what eventually became the Michelin Athletic Club, began to play an important part in both the life of the company and on the amateur sports scene in London.

The company rented a ground for the club at Boston Manor in Harrow, at which cricket, tennis and football were played. The respective teams attained good positions in the local leagues and Business Houses' competitions. Even at this early

Seen outside the Fulham Road building is the new style of van that entered service in the London area in 1952 for the sole purpose of collecting tyre casings for retreading.

Michelin vehicles at Fulham Road in late 1953.

A Michelin representative delivers the goods with his Vespa scooter combination in 1953.

Opposite: On the road with a Michelin representative, crossing Westminster Bridge in 1954. The French beret was not part of the uniform!

was time to move on. However, he thought that Michelin might still wish to retain certain facilities for providing refreshment for its employees. He therefore offered to sell his interest in the canteen, which Michelin accepted and duly took over the enterprise. This consisted of the hut, its equipment and stock, together with a bank book with an unexpected credit of £100 representing the accumulated profits from the sale of alcoholic liquors.

This windfall formed the foundation of the sports provision for employees. The Sports Club, firmly established as the MAC, has evolved in direct relationship with the evolution of the company in all its major locations over the years. The work initiated by Chairman Alexis Chadeyron and especially by Secretary Horace Cole in the late 1920s, led to a facility which has become synonymous with employment at Michelin in the UK.

Marcel Michelin, who was the chairman of Michelin Tyre Company Ltd before the war, was a keen sportsman and became the president and founder of the Association Sportive Montferrandaise, in Clermont-Ferrand. It was therefore highly appropriate that he should also become the first President of Michelin's British sports organisation, the MAC, and he was awarded this honour in 1930. In December 1936, he presented two silver cups to the MAC, one to be competed for by relay teams entered by English sports or athletic clubs; the other to be used for another purpose to be decided upon by the Club's executive committee. Ultimately, it was agreed that this latter Marcel Michelin Cup should be given to the bowls section for an inter-departmental competition.

Initially, employees paid three pennies (3d) per week for membership which enabled them to play tennis (the first facility offered), and later, cricket, football, billiards and snooker. Stoke's original clubhouse, only recently demolished, was built in 1935 at a cost of £6,000 and officially opened by Alderman Harvey in his capacity as Lord Mayor of Stoke-on-Trent. In his address he said that 'A man employed at Michelin works hard, but he also plays hard, and he has every encouragement to play well'. The clubhouse had a bar and kitchen, with a range of indoor sports facilities and even boasted a rifle range in a specially constructed basement.

Following repeated lobbying by theatrical activists, a stage was added in 1937 to enable plays to be performed; the first was a one-act play called 'The Wrong Flat'. Drama was to become a popular feature of the MAC's activities; an ambitious production staged in December 1938 was a three-act thriller called 'Murder Party'. There was even music added, played by an orchestra led by Mr Simpson of Wood Mitchell and accompanied by 'The Two Mrs Camerons'. War stopped such productions

stage in the development of the club, the football team was invited to play a match with the Clermont-Ferrand team. The team travelled to France but did not return with the cup!

In the late 1920s, when work was progressing on the construction of the factory at Stoke-on-Trent, a gentlemen named Mr Barker approached Michelin and obtained permission to erect a hut in which to provide meals for the contractors' men engaged in the building work. The hut was built and business begun, and within a short time these same men requested the pleasant accompaniment of a glass of beer with their meals! Having obtained the company's permission to allow the Michelin name to be used, the proprietor obtained a licence for the 'Michelin Club'.

Time passed, beer was drunk and the profits began to accumulate. Club law of the time meant that alcohol sales had to be kept separate from food sales. By 1928, when the bulk of the construction work had been completed, Mr Barker decided it

until January 1947 when the show 'Junior Michelin on Parade', with its complement of 40 children of Michelin employees, was presented.

The club was a popular and thriving activity from the outset and represented a major employee benefit, a rare facility in the district in its day. Membership in 1929 was 49, by 1934 it had risen to 1,100. In the first club magazine, dated November 1934, there are reports and information on the following sections forming part of the club's regular activities: angling, athletics and cycling, billiards, cricket, football, golf, hockey, rifle, tennis, table tennis, socials and lectures. The second magazine contains a report on the MAC annual dinner, a function held on 1 December 1934, and which begins:

Three hundred and twelve members and guests sat down at the Grand Hotel, Hanley to the most important and notable Annual Dinner ever held by the Michelin Athletic Club. Monsieur Marcel Michelin, our President, travelled specially from France to attend, and there was a record number present, fully representative of every section of the club and every department of the factory.

Monsieur J. A. Domenet, the Chairman, presided, and among the many guests were the Lord Mayor and Lady Mayoress of Stoke-on-Trent (Alderman and Mrs A. C. Harvey), Major Kent DSO (President of the Longton Branch of the British Legion), and Dr B. S. Bhandarkar (Medical Officer of the company).

Major Kent's presence was significant. Michelin's post-First World War stationery exhibits the 'National Scheme for Disabled Men' logo, an indication that the company gave particular assistance in finding work for ex-service men. In the November 1937 edition of the company house magazine *Bibendum*, an advertisement states that 'over 50 per cent of the men employed in this factory are ex-service men. No other industrial concern in this country can equal this'. Major Kent acknowledged this in his response to a toast for the visitors at the dinner. Following Michelin's well-established support for the British Legion, the first 'House Branch' of the association was formed in 1937. This was a branch confined exclusively to the employees of one firm, in this case Michelin. Later, in 1938, female employees had the opportunity to lend their support when a women's section was formed; a full-size flag in the company's archives is marked with the words 'British Legion, Women's Section, Michelin Branch'. This was dedicated on Sunday 18 June 1939 on the MAC sports ground.

The first of the MAC's full-scale annual sports meetings took place on 30 June 1934 and the proceeds, some £80, were donated to the North Staffordshire Cripples' Aid Society. These meetings, open to all competitors, soon developed into important athletic events in the Midlands, attracting a very high calibre of contestants.

The second meeting, held on 29 June 1935, included various races for competitors drawn from

In September 1947, Michelin's chief, Robert Puiseux, visited Stoke to play in a friendly tournament on the new MAC tennis courts. M Puiseux can be seen wearing white, seated with crossed legs in the front row, with his wife to his right. Two places to his left is J. A. Moore, the Staffordshire Champion and Wimbledon entrant who was an invited playing guest.

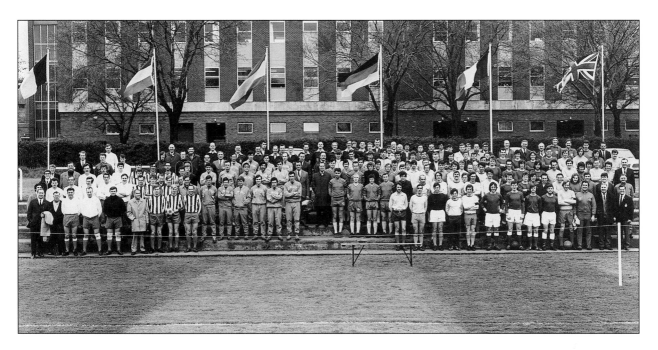

both Michelin and the surrounding country, such as the Schoolboys' Relay and the AAA Championships (Staffordshire and Midlands). The British six-mile champion, J. T. Holden took part. The third annual sports, run on 27 June 1936, also attracted national runners, such as W. E. Eaton, British Native Record holder of Salford Harriers, and A. Burns, of Elswick Harriers, captain of the English cross-country team. The Dunlop and GEC Magnet companies also fielded teams. The story was the same for the fourth annual sports, held on 3 July 1937 with more national athletes such as W. Roberts (Olympic runner, quarter-miler) and F. R. Handley (Olympic runner, half-miler) taking part. That year, the proceeds from the event, which amounted to £186 7s 6d, went to the Stoke-on-Trent Children's Convalescent and Holiday Home in Rhyl. By the time of the fifth annual sports day on 2 July 1938, the event had become a very big occasion indeed. The prospect of watching competitors of international and county standard attracted more than 11,000 spectators, who thronged to the Michelin track to see the Countess of Shrewsbury present the prizes.

Tennis and swimming were not neglected either at this time as both sports had an annual tournament or gala, held on the MAC's own tennis courts in All Saints Road, Boothen and at the baths at nearby Newcastle-under-Lyme. Similarly, cricket had a big following, with matches played regularly on the MAC ground in Campbell Road. The pitch was of sufficient quality for a county match between Staffordshire and Northumberland to be played there in July 1938.

As befitted a manufacturer of golf balls, the MAC also boasted a nine-hole golf course which had been opened in the early 1930s alongside the Campbell Road site at Stoke. The facilities comprised an 18-hole putting course and a 9-hole mashie course. Later, turf was taken from the course for the creation of a bowling green which was completed and opened by the Lord Mayor of Stoke-on-Trent (Alderman J. A. Dale) on 4 June 1937. A report in the company house magazine, *Bibendum*, published in June 1938, announced 'the entry of ladies in our competitions, for the first time in our history'.

Clearly, by then the MAC had become a large, important and very busy organisation, so much so that it demanded the services of a professional club official to organise its activities. Accordingly, in September 1935, a well-known athlete, John Flower, had been appointed to the full-time post of secretary/manager. The British ABA welterweight Boxing champion in 1920, '21 and '23, he came from the Phoenix Club in Mitcham and was a playing member of Surrey County Cricket Club and joint trainer of Crystal Palace FC. When he later resigned, he was replaced by the then retired former Club Manager, Alexis Chadeyron.

Evidently, around the middle of the decade in the 1930s, a group of less-actively sports-minded individuals had formed in the MAC, who felt that it lacked sufficient

Michelin teams from six countries participated in the 13th Marcel Michelin Football Tournament, at Stoke in 1971. Left to right: Zuen (Belgium), Bois-le-Duc (Holland), Lasarte (Spain), Bad Kreuznach (Germany), Clermont-Ferrand, Troyes (France), Burnley and Stoke.

cultural activities: 'Those members who have cultural leanings must go to outside organisations, to WEA classes, to amateur operatic societies, to discussions groups – why should this be so? In this matter, the MAC is far behind not only the clubs of such English firms as Unilever, Cadbury's, or Morris Motors, but behind its own counterparts the ASM of Clermont-Ferrand and the MSC of Turin,' they complained.

The outcome was a widening of the MAC's activities into arts and crafts and music. In October 1935, the MAC Dance Band made its debut as 'the purveyor of melody and rhythm for the Saturday evening dances', although it seems that it was not wholly composed of MAC members. Four years later there was an appeal to recruit instrumentalists for a company brass band. Twenty members were recruited by August that year, but the war delayed its development. It was to be almost twenty years later that the dream became a performing reality. Its first public appearance took place on 21 December 1956 in a Christmas carol concert held in the clubhouse. In March 1958, the band competed in the Midland area competition of the National Brass Band Championships and came seventh out of 28 entries.

The last of the pre-war annual sports meetings, the sixth, took place on 10 June 1939. That year an executive committee of leading Stoke-on-Trent personalities including the Lord Mayor, the Earl of Shrewsbury and Gresham Copeland of Spode was formed to develop six local clubs for young boys who had just left school. Representatives of the MAC had already been on a fact-finding mission to Cadbury's at Bournville where a similar club was in existence, to learn how Michelin's support for such an organisation might be beneficial. In due course, these local Stoke boys' clubs became part of the National Association of Boys' Clubs, the NABC. Its president was the Duke of Gloucester who attended a civic luncheon at Stoke-on-Trent on 29 June 1939 when the local appeal for funds was launched. Jacques Domenet, a member of the local executive committee, represented Michelin.

In October 1967, the entertainer Frankie Vaughan, a big supporter of the Boys' Clubs movement, visited Stoke-on-Trent to present fitness awards to apprentices.

Opposite: The 14th annual sports day organised by the Michelin Athletic Club took place on 9 July 1955. Thousands attended to watch local and national athletes compete in what had already been established as a major Midlands sports meeting.

Michelin's autumn dance at Trentham Gardens, Stoke, on 21 November 1970 was attended by 2,400 people. Entertainment was provided by the Humphrey Lyttelton Band (seen here) and the Reg Bassett Band. Proceeds from these dances, which were a regular event at this time, went to various local charities.

In the grim years immediately after the war, economic and social conditions in the UK were as difficult as they had been throughout the conflict, if not more so, with shortages rife in almost every area of work and play. Thus the athletic activities of the MAC were not resumed until 5 July 1947 when the seventh annual sports day took place. The pre-war format was restored and a well-supported event was held. Athletics, cycling and tug-of-war predominated. The following year, the event got back into its stride and the eighth annual sports day, held in July 1948, which included the Staffordshire 100 and 220 yards championships, was in the finest MAC tradition. That year, Jack Riseley was appointed sports organiser to the MAC. He had been wing-half for Charlton Athletic Football Club and fast medium bowler for Essex County Cricket Club. The year was also distinguished by two important social occasions, the visit of the Dagenham Girl Pipers who gave a display in the clubhouse and the first MAC annual dance, held on 16 November in the Kings Hall of Stoke-on-Trent Town Hall. Entertainment was provided by Reg Bassett and his band, with tickets costing 3 shillings (15p).

Earlier, the summer of 1946 had been notable for the first seaside outing organised for MAC members' children. In August, 260 children in seven coaches, went to New Brighton for the day. In subsequent years, other outings to places such as Rhyl and Dudley Zoo were arranged, as well as

Christmas parties in the clubhouse. This latter tradition remains to this day in the form of special cinema showings for employees' children at various locations. Although the very first events were financed by MAC fundraising activities, the company provided the funding for many years after the war and until such time as the club became self-financing.

In May 1947, the first arts and crafts exhibition was held in the clubhouse. Some 200 visitors passed through the exhibition which included paintings, drawings, photographs, needlework, woodwork and model railways, all of it the work of MAC members and their families. Two months later an exhibition darts match was played in the clubhouse when Mr J. Hitchcock, the current No. 1 British darts player, gave an exhibition in aid of St Dunstan's Hospital for the Blind.

Undoubtedly, the big event of the year, however, occurred in September when the then Head of the Michelin Company, Robert Puiseux, visited Stoke with his wife and played tennis on the MAC's new courts sited alongside the clubhouse. He played Mr W. Hook of the staff department and won 6-2, 6-4. This was really the first time since the Liberation of France that it had been possible to resume normal social relationships with the Clermont-Ferrand headquarters. When inaugurating the tennis courts, M Puiseux made a speech praising the work carried on at Stoke. 'During the war, the factory at Stoke-on-Trent was our banner factory', he said, 'It had the largest production of all the Michelin factories and gave the best service in the Allied cause.' Two years later, in September 1949, a full-scale tennis team from Clermont visited the MAC. Stoke lost by 18 games to three. Despite there being some good local players in the home team, Clermont had fielded some crack sportsmen in their team, such as Robert Puiseux and François Michelin.

Monsieur Puiseux's visit marked the start of a long series of sporting exchanges between the English and French works which continued for many years. At the ninth annual sports day held in June 1949, an ASM team from Clermont participated. Jean Michelin (André's eldest son) was present with his wife. The Lord Mayor of the City of Stoke-on-Trent, Dr A. P. Spark, gave an address in English and French, in which he thanked the Michelin Tyre Company for their interest in sport, which had been of great value to the city. That November, the MAC sent over a football team to play the ASM at Clermont, when speeches of welcome were delivered by Robert Puiseux and Jean Michelin. France won 1-0. On 18 March 1950, however, a return football match, the MAC vs

ASM, was played on the former's home ground and for the first time, a British team had defeated the French, the result being 1-0. A dinner was given in the evening at the North Stafford Hotel in the presence of the Lord Mayor and Lady Mayoress of Stoke-on-Trent.

At the tenth annual sports day, on 1 July 1950, Monsieur and Madame Puiseux were present at Stoke and the event that year was held in aid of the Stoke-on-Trent Children's Convalescent Home at Rhyl. A party of eight athletes from the Gold Coast AAA participated, as did some national cycling champions. The BBC broadcast the event, which was publicised in Radio Times. The annual general meeting report for 1950 indicated that membership of the MAC at the end of 1949 was 1,652.

There then began a long-running series of international, inter-factory football matches known as the Marcel Michelin Tournament. In the first of the series, played at Clermont on 11 and 12 November 1950 a team from Stoke competed against others from the company's factories at Clermont, Brussels and Turin. Stoke played Brussels in the final and lost 2-1. In May 1951, the tournament was played in Turin, Stoke losing to the Italians in the final,

Michelin's Leeds distribution branch opened in January 1947. Note the Bibendum mascots on the delivery vans, seen in 1957.

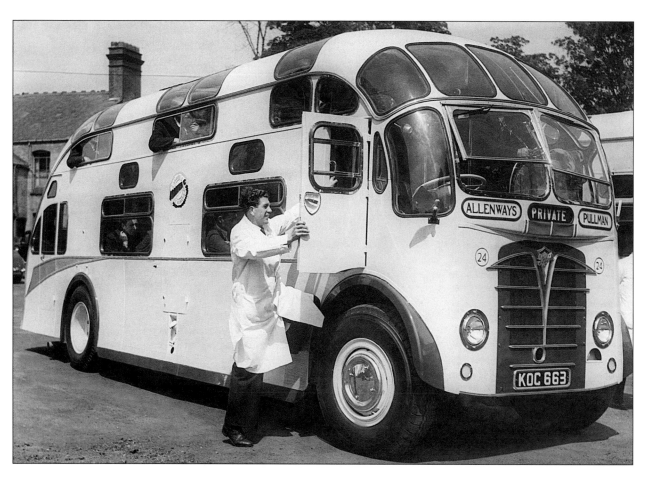

Clearly inspired by Dan Dare's spacecraft in the contemporary comic, The Eagle, *this double-decker long-distance coach of the 1950s ran on Michelin tyres.*

3-1. M Daubrée, the managing director at Turin, presented the winners' prizes at the dinner held on the evening of the event. In 1952, when Brussels was the venue for the tournament, it was won by Stoke in the final against Belgium, with a score of 5-1. On 18 and 19 September 1953, it was the turn of Stoke-on-Trent to host the competition. The final, between Stoke and the Belgians, resulted in a one-goal draw, but the visitors were awarded the cup on an extra corner. Mme Guy de Bourgues (wife of Michelin Tyre Company's managing director, and the daughter of Marcel Michelin) presented the cup in the presence of the Lord Mayor of the City of Stoke-on-Trent. The fifth tournament was held in Clermont on 29 and 30 May 1955. Spain joined the event this time, adding to the UK, Belgium and France (Italy was unable to send a team that year). In the final, the Stoke team beat France 1-0. The following year, Spain won the competition which was played in Turin with teams from Stoke, France, Italy, Belgium and Spain all competing. In June 1957, the seventh tournament was played at Lasarte in Spain where the home side won. At Easter 1960, the eighth tournament was held at Orleans in France with

teams from England, France, Italy, Belgium and Spain competing.

With the expansion of Michelin's international factory network, the tournament grew bigger year by year. For example, in the tenth tournament in 1962, a team from the new Nigerian plant joined those from France, Belgium, Spain and Britain. Stoke beat Clermont in the final. The 11th tournament was held at Clermont when Belgium, Spain, France and the UK competed for the major cup while a subsidiary cup was played for by French-only teams raised by the company's domestic factories. In May 1971, for the 13th tournament, the competition returned to Stoke. Teams from Belgium, Holland, Spain, Germany, France and the UK were present – Spain (Lasarte) won. For the 14th tournament, played between 30 April and 1 May 1973, it was the turn of Clermont-Ferrand to play host. A team from the Burnley factory represented the UK, having earlier won the UK knock-out competition at Dundee on 1 April. The Lancashire side beat the French for the cup, 2-0, making them Michelin European Champions of 1973.

To return to athletics, however, on 7 July 1951,

the 11th annual sports day was held as part of the City of Stoke-on-Trent Festival of Britain celebrations. A 15-mile road race was included for the first time. As usual, the tug-of-war competition was especially popular and this year it was won by a team new to the event, entered by the Metropolitan Police. In common with previous years, some Staffordshire Championship races were run. Probably the most famous athlete present was the distance runner J. T. Holden of Tipton Harriers, running his last race. He came third in an exciting race which saw C. Cerou, from the Clermont ASM team, win. In Mr Guy de Bourgues's absence, Mr Hubert Michelin addressed the crowd and invited Mme Guy de Bourgues to present the prizes.

In February 1952, a Midland Counties hockey match was played at the MAC – a typical example of how the company's sports facilities, among the best in the Midlands, were offered for use for special events. Later in the year, a cycling section was formed within the MAC, together with a rugby section. On the Whitsun weekend of 1953, a cricket match between the Australian touring side and the Minor Counties was played on the MAC ground. The visitors won handsomely. A new ground was officially opened by Mr Calonier on 3 October that year.

For the 14th annual sports, held in July 1955, teams of French athletes from the University of Paris and the ASM at Clermont attended, as well as Michelin employees from London and throughout the country. Big crowds of spectators turned out as, by then, the membership of the MAC had turned the 2,000 mark. The 16th annual sports, on 29 June 1957, were again devoted to raising funds for the Stoke-on-Trent Children's Convalescent and Holiday Home at Rhyl. The world's current fastest miler – Derek Ibbotson – attended and ran his two-mile race in 9min 6sec. Olympic runner Peter Driver also took part. Robert Puiseux and his wife attended, as part of a visit to Stoke-on-Trent as guests of the city. Two years later, the 18th annual sports saw the participation of international runners Peter Radford and Fred Norris. All the usual events were held and Jean Michelin and Mme Guy Michelin attended to present the prizes.

Finally, on 2 July 1960, the 19th annual sports event was held, again in aid of the Rhyl charity and organised in conjunction with the City of Stoke-on-Trent's Jubilee celebrations. Peter Radford, Britain's champion sprinter, participated again. A 15-mile road race through the city was held, attracting approximately 60 runners; local athlete Don Shelley was the winner. This was to be the last sports day held in its traditional form although in future years there would be an employee-only sporting element to the event that replaced it, the Michelin Carnival Day.

Nevertheless, the MAC continued to be deeply involved in athletics events at a national level.

In April 1962, the club played host to the NABC National Cross-Country Championships, held at Trentham Park in Stoke-on-Trent, the first of several such events. For example, on Sunday, 1 June 1975 the MAC organised the Michelin AAA Marathon for which 10,000 people lined the streets of Stoke-on-Trent to see national and international runners in action: 179 started the course which took them through various streets of the Potteries and 149 finished. Neil Allen of The Times newspaper commented that 'Yesterday's race, so magnificently organised by Michelin Athletic Club was warmly supported by the people of Stoke …' Jeff Norman of the Altrincham & District AC won in 2hr 15min 50.2sec.

A typical Michelin cycle tyre stockist of the period – Mrs Lightbown's of Ellesmere Port, Cheshire.

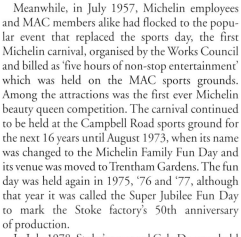

Meanwhile, in July 1957, Michelin employees and MAC members alike had flocked to the popular event that replaced the sports day, the first Michelin carnival, organised by the Works Council and billed as 'five hours of non-stop entertainment' which was held on the MAC sports grounds. Among the attractions was the first ever Michelin beauty queen competition. The carnival continued to be held at the Campbell Road sports ground for the next 16 years until August 1973, when its name was changed to the Michelin Family Fun Day and its venue was moved to Trentham Gardens. The fun day was held again in 1975, '76 and '77, although that year it was called the Super Jubilee Fun Day to mark the Stoke factory's 50th anniversary of production.

In July 1978, Stoke's renamed Gala Day was held at the new MAC sports ground at Trent Vale. These facilities were created as a result of the loss of the Campbell Road grounds when the A500 (Queensway or Potteries' 'D' Road) was built and much of Michelin's recreational property was compulsorily purchased for the road. As a result, the MAC emerged as a two-site organisation: the original 1935 clubhouse in Sideway Road remained in use for many of the social functions, and still with its snooker room and the rifle range in the basement, and the Trent Vale sports centre which had extensive grounds for football, rugby, hockey and athletics, together with squash courts, tennis courts and, ultimately, a fishing pond for the angling section.

Not surprisingly, Stoke's MAC history is considerably richer than that of the other factory sites. It was started earlier and it was very much a pioneering initiative in its day, most especially in North Staffordshire. This fact does not diminish the achievements of the other clubs, all of which have played an important part in the life of their respective factories. They, like Stoke's MAC, have provided support beyond that for employees alone and have entered into the life of the local community through hosting events and celebrations.

By the early 1980s, the MAC had reached the height of its growth throughout Michelin's British organisation. For the majority of employees, it had become a natural part of life within the company, providing sports and recreational facilities in impressive surroundings. Inter-departmental games and inter-factory sports events and competitions regularly took place. In response to changing leisure and sporting fashions, new or improved facilities such as squash courts, sports halls and fitness suites were regularly added. Over time, individual sections came and went – activities

such as beer & wine making and drama are long gone, having been replaced by aviation, aerobics and spinning! However, these days many individuals are attracted by the competing facilities provided in commercially-run health and fitness clubs or leisure centres. The MAC has weathered these changes and still provides Michelin employees at its three major UK sites with a local, personal service at an affordable price. Certainly, the cricket match played in London way back in 1907 began a very proud tradition of Michelin sports and leisure activity that endures to this day, having been enjoyed by many thousands of employees over almost a century.

The 2CV in the United Kingdom

As soon as the Traction-Avant had been refined and re-engineered into a reliable and profitable product, Citroën's new Michelin management, led by Pierre Michelin and Pierre-Jules Boulanger, turned their attention towards a completely new type of machine. This was to be a small and inexpensive passenger vehicle that would act as a French People's Car, especially suited for rural and agricultural use. The Michelins had been studying such a concept for many years, long before their acquisition of the Citroën firm, and had already carried out numerous engineering and market-research studies.

As defined in a design brief laid down in 1936, this new *Toute Petite Voiture* (TPV) was to be, in effect, a motorised pony-cart, ideal for farmers, small-holders and wine-growers, with no previous experience of owning motor cars or machinery of any kind. Since France was still predominantly an agrarian nation, the TPV was intended to be an ultra-simple, light-weight, go-anywhere means of transport that would cost the very minimum to purchase, operate and maintain. No more than ' four wheels under an umbrella' it was to be capable of carrying two people plus 50kg of potatoes or a small cask of wine in the greatest comfort over the poorest roads, so that even when carrying a basket of eggs over a ploughed field, not one single egg would be broken. Economy, reliability, versatility and practicality were what counted most – the appearance of the finished vehicle would be quite unimportant.

Unfortunately, when Pierre Michelin was killed in a car crash in December 1937, this left his deputy, Pierre-Jules Boulanger in sole charge of activities at Citroën, including the development of prototypes and the supervision of its Bureau d'Etudes (design office), led by André Citroën's

protégée, André Lefèbvre. Consequently, although Boulanger was not an automobile engineer (he was actually an architect who had joined the Michelin organisation in 1920 to supervise its building programme at Clermont-Ferrand), stage-by-stage the spartan TPV, constructed largely of aluminium and canvas, came more and more to represent his austere and frugal personality.

By 1939, the TPV was judged ready to be launched at the Paris Motor Show in October, but the outbreak of war the previous September put paid to this plan. The show was cancelled and the 250 completed examples of the TPV that had been made ready for the exhibition were hidden away. So it was that during the Occupation of France the TPV was completely redesigned in secret, as the Nazi authorities had forbidden all design and development work on new or prototype projects within the French motor industry.

It was not until the Paris Motor Show of 1948, therefore, that the TPV finally emerged on to the market, in a drastically revised form and renamed the 2CV. This reflected the French road-tax rating of its ingenious 375cc capacity, air-cooled, flat-twin-cylinder engine, capable of achieving 63mpg and a top speed of 40mph. Sales did not commence until the end of the following year and it was to be five years before its annual rate of production exceeded six figures.

As conceived and funded by Michelin, and designed by André Lefèbvre, the 2CV represented an idiomatically French answer to a specifically French transportation problem. Displaying many radically inventive and original ideas which were at the same time entirely logical, it approached the problems of automobile design from an entirely different perspective, which made the quality of suspension and ride-comfort the top priority. Its simple construction was also intended to overcome the difficulties of manufacture using minimal tooling and materials as the Germans had made off with most of Citroën's body presses during the Occupation, and supplies of steel and other materials were still in short supply.

As is well known, despite its lack of conventional automobile gloss and glamour, the 2CV turned out to be a huge success, lasting for five decades and serving three generations of motorists. Indeed, following the Energy Crisis of the 1970s its outstanding fuel-economy and reliability allowed it to enjoy a completely new lease of life for a further twenty years, until eventually it fell victim to increasingly

In 1953, the Citroën 2CV entered production at the Slough factory in right-hand-drive form. The Citroën company was under Michelin ownership for 40 years, from 1935 to 1975.

In 1948, Michelin was chosen as the tyre supplier for a fleet of 50 Leyland PD1 buses with 'White Lady' bodies built by Burlingham. The vehicles were destined for use on long-distance express services in Lancashire run by the Ribble bus company.

severe exhaust emissions and accident-safety legislation and it was withdrawn from the market in 1990.

In its issue of November 1949, the British company's house magazine *Bibendum* carried a report on the arrival of the long-awaited new Citroën. 'If ever a car was likely to popularise motoring among the masses, it is the 2CV', it avowed. 'Whereas all other cars launched on the market under the name Popular - even the German VW - are more or less a scaled-down standard car, the new Citroën constitutes something absolutely different from all those on the road today. Will this machine be a success?' it asked. 'At first sight one may doubt it. The first reaction is that… the average motorist will turn away from the austere lines and cheap appearance of the coachwork. One must recognise, however, that this is the first car likely to take motoring a step further ahead by offering the possibility for tens of thousands of people to obtain a vehicle, from which they were barred hitherto.'

In 1953, the 2CV entered production at Slough in right-hand-drive form with three versions made available: a saloon, a van and a pick-up truck, the latter unique to the United Kingdom with no French equivalent. The British Government purchased 65 of these pick-ups between 1959 and

1961 for use by the Royal Marine Commandos. Based on the helicopter carriers HMS Bulwark and HMS Albion, they saw service during the anti-terrorist operations in Malaysia and Borneo during the mid-1960s, being carried into action by the aircraft of the Fleet Air Arm.

Assembly of the 2CV at Slough ended in 1961 and for a number of years it was unavailable in this country. In 1975, however, imports from France were begun, continuing until 1990 when the model was withdrawn from all markets including France. Ultimately, 108,415 examples of all types and origins were sold in the UK, including the 735 vehicles built at Slough, but this number pales into insignificance in comparison with the huge total of 5,114,969 2CV saloons and vans that were constructed in the car's homeland during its 41-year life-span.

The launch of the Michelin X radial tyre

At exactly 11am on 4 June 1946, a messenger from the Michelin headquarters at Clermont-Ferrand walked into the French Patent Office in the rue de Leningrad, Paris, bearing a fat file of paperwork.

The bulky dossier contained a patent application covering the technical principles and manufacturing technology of the steel-belted radial tyre, the invention which Michelin's engineers had been perfecting over the previous four years, and which was set to revolutionise not just the tyre industry but the entire automobile world at large.

The application was made in the name of Michelin's technical chief, Pierre-Marcel Bourdon, who had taken over the post following Marcel Michelin's death in 1945. Although he was not related to the Michelin family by birth, Bourdon had joined it by marrying Édouard Michelin's daughter Simone, thus becoming Robert Puiseux's brother-in-law and François Michelin's uncle.

Michelin's research into the steel-belted radial tyre could be traced back as far as 1929, when attempts were made to improve the service life of the rubber-shod wheels of the Micheline railcars, by introducing various forms of metal reinforcement. But serious work on the concept had really begun in 1944 when a major investment in a programme of fundamental research was approved by Robert Puiseux, who had taken charge of the company on Édouard Michelin's death in 1940.

The true begetter of the radial tyre concept, however, was a certain Marius Mignol, who held no qualifications as a scientist or engineer whatsoever. He had originally joined the company as an accounts clerk in its sales department where his skill in calculating foreign currency conversions with a slide rule had been quickly spotted by Édouard Michelin, who transferred him to the experimental department, so that his abilities as a mathematician could be put to better use.

Before the war, there were two main technical problems facing tyre manufacturers. First, how to overcome the heat generated through hysteresis by tyres running under heavy loads, which is not easily dissipated due to the poor conductivity of rubber, so resulting in fatigue and failure. Secondly, how to prevent the distortions transmitted from the casing to the tread in fast or intensively run tyres, and which leads to a loss of adhesion with the road surface. The tyre is not only the most crucial part of a car from the safety point of view, but it is also perhaps its hardest working load-carrying component, supporting more than 50 times its own weight. All the useful traction power produced by the car's engine and transmission passes through the small area of tread that forms the contact patch between the vehicle and the road, thus subjecting the tyre to permanent stress.

Consequently, in the early 1930s Michelin engineers had begun to study vehicle dynamics in a systematic, scientific manner, to measure the role of tyres in steering, roadholding, braking, suspension and ride comfort. Part of this research programme had centred on exploring the questions of rolling resistance and directional stability, which entailed a study of how a tyre absorbs energy and dissipates the resultant heat. It was already well understood that these heat build-ups and losses occurred separately in both the tread area and the side-wall region, but identifying and quantifying the exact source-points of the heat, and then tracing the flow-paths by which it escaped, proved to be a difficult task. In other words, it was impossible to measure exactly how and where, either in the side-walls or the tread, the heat was being generated. Not having had the benefit of any formal technical education, Mignol was able to come up with the answer, which a professionally trained tyre engineer would doubtless have dismissed as frivolous, facile and naive. 'Make a special test tyre without side-walls', he suggested.

In the early 1930s also, Michelin had begun a series of experiments to investigate the possibility of substituting the cotton textile cords used in the reinforcing plies of truck tyres with thin and highly flexible steel wires. As trucks got bigger and heavier, their tyres required as many as 22 cord plies to achieve the required strength. Disliking the idea of simply adding more and more fabric, Édouard Michelin had begun to think of using stronger materials such as finely drawn steel wire and had eventually solved the extremely difficult problem of making these steel plies adhere to the rubber compound of the tyre body, through the use of a powder coating. As a result, the first heavy-duty metal-cord tyres were tested in 1934 and marketed in 1938, for use on trucks and buses. By this time the company had also acquired the metallurgical

Robert Puiseux (1892-1991) head of the Michelin company from 1938 to 1959, at the wheel of a Citroën DS19. He gave the go-ahead for the manufacture of the radial tyre and the Citroën 'Déesse'.

The 1963 UK fuel-saving demonstrations with X tyres used two coaches, each equipped with a special fuel tank and a trailing fifth-wheel by which speed, mileage and fuel consumption could be accurately measured.

know-how to produce the wire itself and to weave it into plies and cords, there being no other source of supply. Experience with these metallic tyres, as they were called, showed that two or four steel plies not only did the job of 16 to 20 fabric plies but that the wear resistance of the tread was quadrupled, extending the life-expectancy of the tyre from 10,000 to 40,000 miles.

To construct Mignol's sidewall-less test tyre (nicknamed the cage à mouches – fly trap – on account of its appearance) the tread area was anchored to the hub by a carcass formed from loops of wire spaced widely apart, running from bead to bead and located radially like the spokes of a wheel. Set at right angles to the crown, corresponding to a cord angle of 90°, the loops were embedded in the thinnest possible sheet of rubber so as to offer minimal internal friction. High-speed running tests established right away that Mignol's tyre ran with very low energy consumption and at very cool temperatures, showing that the heat problem lay in the sidewall area rather than in the tread region. Clearly, the explanation was that the heat build-up in a conventional crossply tyre was produced not by the tread surface as it rolls along the road, but by the friction that occurs when the criss-crossing reinforcing plies in the sidewalls rub together as they flex under load. Lacking the normal cross-wise reinforcing layers of textile plies found in conventional tyres, the thin walls and wire hoops of Mignol's experimental tyre flexed without friction and exhibited very low rolling-resistance. Unfortunately, without the bracing effect normally provided by the sidewalls, and with the position of

the wire hoops corresponding to a 90° cord angle (ie at right angles to the crown line) – the test tyre was completely devoid of directional stability and would not steer satisfactorily.

Again, Mignol came up with the solution. 'If the tyre lacks stability because there's nothing under the tread, so that it lacks support, maybe we could put something in there, more or less in the direction of the crown line – nothing extra in the sidewalls, just under the tread, like some sort of a belt', he suggested. So, to correct this defect, a second-stage test tyre was made, incorporating a steel-cord belt plus two steel wire plies laid at the angle that had been found to give the highest directional stability in conventional bias-ply tyres – at 20° from the crown line with one layer to the right and the other to the left. This arrangement proved to be the perfect triangulation required to stabilise the carcass and the tread.

When the experiments were resumed, even greater advantages were revealed. Not only did the new version of Mignol's test tyre possess the required directional stability but it also offered extraordinary cornering power. It ran even cooler than the earlier unbelted version and the rolling resistance was greatly reduced, and as the test mileage mounted up, it was found that tread wear was minimal. Unwittingly, Mignol had stumbled on a novel and superior principle of tyre construction – a major advance in automobile engineering. Not only did the light and flexible sidewalls mean that the maximum foot-print area was kept in contact with the road in all circumstances – even when the tyre was tilted under lateral thrust, so giving better grip and hence improved traction, braking and road-holding performance, but the steel belt construction actually extended the life expectancy of the tyre into the bargain.

Next, further research studies were conducted to determine the exact configuration of the new product. The construction method finally adopted involved a girdle laid radially under the tread made up of three plies of woven steel wire, with the layer closest to the tread being wider than the other two, but the steel wire cage supporting the side walls of Mignol's test tyre was replaced by a single layer of cotton cord laid at a 90° angle to the crown. An 0:80 aspect ratio was chosen and the tyre ran at inflation pressures as low as 25psi. The familiar double zigzag tread pattern adopted was not new, however. Created by Marcel Michelin specifically to improve braking ability in wet conditions, it had made its first appearance on the Stop tyre of 1934.

Limited production of the steel-belted radial began early in 1948, for large-scale field testing by selected customers all over France. At this stage, the product was referred to as the Pilote 165-400 SP or

185-400 SP, according to the size. In June 1949, however, it was renamed the Michelin X and put into volume production. Again, only two sizes were offered, 165-400 and 185-400, tubed of course, for use only on Pilote and certain other wide-rimmed wheels. Naturally, the first examples went to Citroën for fitting on the Traction Avant, but as optional equipment only. There was no question of the Quai de Javel factory switching over to radials completely at this stage, as Michelin's manufacturing capacity was quite unable to keep up with the widespread demand, despite the premium price being charged. As the X tyre could not be made on existing equipment new machinery had to be introduced, and of course, Michelin still had an enormous investment devoted to the production of the traditional cross-ply tyre. It was not until the end of 1954 that supplies were sufficient for Citroën to be able to fit the Michelin X as standard on the Traction Avant.

In fact, the first car to feature the X tyre as standard equipment was the Lancia Aurelia, introduced in May 1950, but by 1952, Alfa Romeo had also standardised on the X tyre for its 1900 series. Ferrari began to recommend it to its dealers and clients, while continuing to fit Pirelli products as original equipment. Indeed, it can be claimed that it was the Italian motor industry rather than the French or British which was the first to recognise the advantages of the X tyre. Before long, the

Michelin men realised that they had a major success on their hands. Consequently, in 1956 Robert Puiseux took the decision to commit the company to the exclusive production of the steel-belted radial tyre and to abandon bias-ply tyres entirely. The design of the X tyre was simplified, with the steel belts in the crown being reduced from three to two and the aspect ratio changed to 0:78. Similarly, the cotton fabric employed in the casing was replaced by rayon, polyester or nylon. In 1964, the first tubeless version of the X tyre made its appearance, on the Citroën 2CV and 3CV models, of course.

Between 1956 and 1970, no fewer than 15 new factories dedicated entirely to the Michelin X tyre and its successors such as the XAS, XVS and ZX were built in France and abroad, an expansion that eventually transformed the Clermont-Ferrand firm into a substantial multinational business trading in 140 countries world-wide, owning more than 75 centres of production and employing over 130,000 people. By 1969, the company was making 30 million X tyres a year. Today, the radial tyre has completely eclipsed the cross-ply and Michelin products are used in virtually every transportation application involving the wheel, be it for cars, motor cycles, lorries, buses, tractors, earthmoving machinery and aircraft – even the Space Shuttle. By any standard, this achievement is a monumental feat of industrial creativity and enterprise.

This photograph published in The Autocar *in December 1953, shows its reporter Michael Brown testing a set of X radial tyres on his 1½-litre Riley. Mr Brown described the X as a 'revolution in tyre technology'.*

1955–1964

Bibendum sweeps all before him

Expansion during the 1960s and '70s

The success of the steel-reinforced metallic tyre and the revolution created by the advent of the Michelin X steel-braced radial presented the company with the challenge to meet a vast potential for international growth. The first major phase took place in the 1960s, when 14 new factories were built and then the pace accelerated to such an extent that 17 more were opened during 1970 and 1971, part of the total of 24 constructed during the 1970s. In this first phase, three new plants were opened in the British Isles, located at Burnley (1960), Belfast (1965) and Ballymena (1969). British personnel also formed a major part of the team that built Michelin's Port Harcourt factory in Nigeria, which opened in 1962.

Burnley

Burnley was Michelin's second new European factory to be built outside France after the Second World War. The following internal announcement was made on 21 May 1957:

Negotiations have been proceeding for some time between the Michelin Tyre Co. Ltd and the Board of Trade and it has been decided to establish a large new factory in the North-East Lancashire Development Area. This will help to meet the growing demand for the company's steel-cord tyres, especially from overseas markets, and will

1955 François Michelin (Édouard Michelin's grandson) joins Robert Puiseux and Emile Durin as a co-managing partner.

Citroën introduces the DS19 at the Paris and London motor shows in October.

A purpose-built apprentice school is opened at the Stoke factory.

1956 Petrol rationing is introduced in December as a result of the Suez Crisis. It remains in force until May 1957.

1957 Double white lines appear for the first time on the roads of the UK.

Felix Wankel builds the first rotary engine. It is later commercialised by NSU, Mazda and Citroën.

The first Michelin television advertising campaign to be screened in the UK is transmitted on Saturday, 2 February 1957 on Midlands ITV.

1958 In July, parking meters appear in London. The first stretch of motorway in the UK, the Preston bypass, now part of the M6, is opened in December.

A Lancia Aurelia fitted with Michelin X radial tyres wins the Monte Carlo Rally. X tyres are also fitted to the cars in third and fourth places.

1959 François Michelin becomes head of the company.

In the UK, the first speeding conviction resulting from a radar speed trap is recorded. The fine imposed is £3.

The first Mini rolls off the BMC production line and features front-wheel drive, a transverse engine and all-round independent suspension. Its price is £469.

1960 The first 67-mile section of the M1 motorway between London and Birmingham is opened, Michelin-tyred earthmoving machinery has played a major part in its construction.

A Citroën DS19 equipped with Michelin X tyres wins the Monte Carlo Rally.

MoT tests are introduced for all private vehicles over ten years old. The period is reduced to three years in 1967.

Michelin's new factory at Burnley is opened.

1961 The Ford Motor Company appoints Michelin as the standard supplier of tyres for all commercial vehicles built in the UK.

Jaguar launches its E-type roadster in 3.8-litre form. It costs £2,098.

The Morris Minor becomes the first individual British model to sell more than a million units (between 1948 and 1961).

The fitting of front seat belts on all new cars becomes compulsory, although there is no obligation for drivers and passengers to wear them at this stage.

1962 On 22 August OAS terrorists attempt to assassinate President de Gaulle in Paris. His life is saved by the hydro-pneumatic suspension system of the Citroën DS19 in which he is travelling.

Ford introduces the Cortina, billed as the big car at a small car price.

British personnel play an important part in the creation of Michelin's new Nigerian plant at Port Harcourt, which opens in September.

1963 General de Gaulle vetoes British entry into the European Common Market.

Michelin introduces a new version of the X radial tyre, developed especially for use on London taxis.

The annual output of the British motor industry exceeds two million units – 1,607,939 cars and 403,781 commercial vehicles.

During the decade, the number of UK car owners increases from 5.6 to 11.8 million. As a result of this huge increase in vehicle registrations, the first suffix letter 'A' appears on numberplates.

1964 The Citroën 2CV becomes the first series production car to be fitted with tubeless radial tyres, introduced by Michelin.

The first performance of the Michelin Works Brass Band, under the baton of Doug Oakman, was on 21 December 1956. The band soon grew to 38 musicians and well-and-truly hit the road in 1958! It rehearsed four evenings a week, and on Sundays too.

contribute to the greater diversity of industry of which that area stands in need.

It is foreseen that the new factory will be built on the Heasandford Industrial Estate, on a site to be acquired from Burnley Corporation.

Present plans are to have the new factory in operation during 1959. It is expected that employment will be provided in due course for several hundred workers (nearly all men) who will be drawn mainly from Burnley, Nelson and Colne.

This expansion will involve additional activity at the company's Stoke-on-Trent factory, where extensions are already under way for a greater production of the steel cord which will be required by the new factory.

Although the text confirmed a substantial expansion at Stoke-on-Trent, notably in the production of steel cord, the question of why it was necessary to create an entirely new site elsewhere was certainly raised by many of the 4,700 employees already at Stoke. The answer was that the job-creation and industrial development rules and incentives of the day encouraged new industries to be sited in areas of high unemployment. Grants were normally made available in such areas, while development

was hindered at others by a lack of governmental support. In short, in the late 1950s, Burnley qualified for new development status, but Stoke did not.

A special department was created at Stoke in January 1958 to oversee and support the complete project of establishing the factory at Burnley. Notes of the time refer to Burnley being a satellite factory, because of its dependency on Stoke. The factory would comprise buildings for tyre assembly and storage plus the essential associated service buildings such as the boiler house, central engineering and the canteen. There would be no facilities for the production of steel cord or, initially, for the mixing of rubber compounds; these supplies would come from Stoke.

Local employees had to be recruited and much effort was made to encourage applications from suitable candidates. The *Blackburn Evening Telegraph* ran a feature on the training schemes that were being run at Stoke for the new people. The newspaper wanted to show its Lancashire readers the employment opportunities that were becoming available and an interviewer from the paper toured the Stoke training centre.

The factory's design was based on a daily output

of 1,000 truck tyres in five sizes ranging from 6.50 x 20 to 9.00 x 20, in two types, X and XY. The first phase of construction, which followed site clearance work late in the summer of 1958, envisaged some 16,000sq m of building at a cost of £3 million.

Traditionally, Michelin's tyre factories had included a water tower to ensure an adequate supply for production purposes. However, a tower was not necessary for the 50-acre Burnley site because there was adequate quantity available from the town's water supply and from the three boreholes that were sunk, two of them on site. In the early days of construction, the idea of sinking boreholes to get even more water during a period of excessive rain must have seemed crazy – the site was a sea of mud for weeks!

In the original projections for Burnley, a complement of 500 employees was envisaged. The first tyre was produced there on 21 July 1960 and within two years the output figure was regularly exceeding the initial expectations. In fact, the Burnley factory remained in production for 42 years – the last tyre being made there on 27 March 2002. Its closure resulted from the fact that, although still efficient and productive, the site had become too small by modern capacity standards. Industrial logic dictated that less investment in other much larger factories would produce a significantly greater increase in output.

Inevitably, throughout its long presence as a major employer in Burnley, Michelin developed a strong connection with the borough and the towns and villages that surround it. The traditions established during the development of the Stoke factory were duplicated in Lancashire: a strong training culture was fostered through the creation of an apprentice school on the site, a Michelin Athletic Club with its own premises was opened, and all manner of social functions and events were held such as retirement parties, carnival days and the presentation of long service awards. The factory had an impressive safety record, regularly winning a British Safety Council annual award. One of its greatest national achievements was gaining *The Times* newspaper award in 1992, following-on from winning a National Training award. *The Times* award was given for 'training to meet the challenges of international competition' and was presented at a gala event in London.

The history of the Burnley site is not complete without reference to its wheel-making activity. The tyre factory had expanded with the addition of a rubber compound mixing department and a purpose-built warehouse, while a completely new manufacturing process was introduced for the production of drop-centre (or well-based) steel truck wheels. The first wheel came off the production line on 23 March 1972 and many thousands were to roll out of what became a factory in its own right. Michelin has produced steel wheels since the early part of the 20th century and a wheel works was

Michelin's stand at the 1958 Cycle Show at Earls Court. The Bibendum figures were worked by air. They were inflated and pedalled furiously as a result, then gradually came to a halt, whence the cycle resumed!

established in London, long before the first Michelin tyres were made in the British Isles,.

The Burnley operation became part of the quartet of European wheel-producing factories and largely supplied the market for ready-fitted units (the tyre and the wheel combined) for the original equipment market. Following the major re-organisation of Michelin's British operations, announced in January 1985, wheel manufacturing at Burnley ceased in April that year. Thereafter, the factory concentrated on tyre production alone, although receiving supplies of tyre-making components, or semi-finished materials from other UK sites, until its final closure in 2002.

Port Harcourt, Nigeria

Michelin tyres have been used in Nigeria since the early 1930s, gaining a good reputation for reliability, durability and value for money. Most of these tyres came from Britain, and in particular from the Stoke-on-Trent factory which made a range of car, truck and cycle tyres over the years. With the coming of independence in 1960, the eastern region of Nigeria turned to the outside world for the means of developing the country as an industrial nation. What was more natural than to look to Britain, and Michelin, for the means to establish a new industry – one that could directly keep Nigeria on the move by providing that essential requirement of modern road transport, tyres for trucks and cars.

A Nigerian delegation therefore requested the

opportunity to visit a Michelin factory, preferably in England. This was arranged early in 1961 with the result that by July, work had started on clearing a 50-acre site on the new Trans-Amadi Industrial Estate at Port Harcourt. In November, the historic act of the laying of the foundation stone was performed by the Premier of Eastern Nigeria, Dr the Honourable Michael Okpara. Less than a year later, on 29 September 1962, the first tyre came out of the production workshops.

The Nigerian factory was very much a British project and since its establishment many Michelin employees from throughout the British Isles have spent time there. Right from the start, Nigerians were brought to Stoke for training and there was a steady flow of personnel from both sides back and forth as the site got under way. This link has never been broken and, indeed, UK employees have served as members of the Nigerian company's Board, or as senior managers, and training and technical staff throughout the factory's life.

Belfast

Early in 1962, the company considered its existing productive capacity in relation to the expected future expansion of the tyre industry and decided that greater capacity must be provided to supply the Michelin share of this enlarged market.

After long negotiations, the company obtained firm assurances from the, then, Board of Trade that expansion could take place in the future at the Stoke and Burnley locations. As a result of this,

In 1964, cycle tyre representative Vernon Edwards travelled to Nigeria where he spent three months promoting Michelin products in towns and villages throughout the country. His specially built Morris 30cwt van was kitted out with equipment for demonstrating the tyres and showing films. Naturally, a large inflatable Michelin Man went with him on the trip.

Michelin agreed to build a third factory, in an area which was currently experiencing high unemployment.

The site finally chosen was at Mallusk, on the northern outskirts of Belfast in Northern Ireland. Building work was scheduled to begin early in 1963 with production commencing in 1965. André Bouet, as Head of Michelin's British factories, together with the Northern Ireland Minister of Commerce, John Andrews, announced this news jointly at a press conference held in Belfast on 16 November 1962. Initial investment was foreseen to be £14 million in a factory planned to solely produce radial car tyres, with a workforce of 700 at the end of the first production phase and then rising to 1,900. The construction contract was awarded to the Belfast firm of McLaughlin & Harvey and work at Hyde Park Industrial Estate at Mallusk started on 1 May 1963. Some 3,000 tons of steel were supplied by Harland & Wolff of Belfast for the buildings, which covered almost 100,000sq m on the 100-acre site. A special ceremony took place on 21 June when The Rt Hon Frederick Erroll MP, in his capacity as President of the Board of Trade, laid the foundation stone.

Twenty months later, on 6 March, Belfast's first Michelin tyre, a 5.20 x 10 X suitable for the Mini, was made. By this time, 350 people were employed at the site and a further 170 new employees were undergoing training at Stoke-on-Trent for the various phases of the production build-up.

Unlike Burnley, Belfast was planned largely as a self-contained unit with its own workshops for rubber compounding and steel cord production and hence required a much larger workforce.

Ultimately, this was a key factor in the decision to close the site in the troubled economic climate of the early 1980s. In fact, a wide combination of adverse factors led to this situation. Over a period of time, falling tyre demand both at home and abroad resulted in a large excess of manufacturing capacity; abnormally high stock levels built up in Europe and in North America, a major export market at the time. The decline of the British motor manufacturing industry greatly reduced outlets for original-equipment tyres. Despite

A new building designed specifically for the maintenance of the company's growing fleet of vehicles was opened at Stoke at the end of 1958. Every possible aspect of maintenance could be undertaken there.

What the new Michelin factory at Ballymena will look like when completed.

various measures to reduce costs, by changing work patterns, stopping recruitment and encouraging early retirement, Michelin's British financial performance became progressively worse at this time. The trend towards declining profits experienced throughout the late 1970s led to £100 million losses over the three years 1982-84. Fundamental restructuring was essential.

In an announcement made on 17 December 1982, the UK company revealed that jobs would be lost in both its commercial and manufacturing operations in the months ahead, the major action being the total closure of the Belfast factory. The independence of Belfast, in that it neither received from nor supplied large quantities of tyre-making components to other factories, was a crucial factor for the decision. The last of the 40 million tyres made at Mallusk since 1965, came out of the presses on 25 October 1984. McLaughlin & Harvey, the original contractors who built the factory, bought the site and redeveloped it for other industrial uses, although Michelin retained a small presence on site in the form of a commercial office and a distribution centre for the home trade market in Northern Ireland.

In much the same way that Michelin's Burnley factory had developed an impressive range of employee benefits so, in its turn, did Belfast. Training, a major part of Michelin's culture in all countries, was an important element and facilities were created to provide Northern Ireland employees (for in later years, Ballymena was to be part of the scheme) with all the professional services needed. Just as with other sites, apprentices were recruited and trained in the skills needed to maintain a regular flow of young people through the organisation. An MAC was created and all the sports and social functions which were to be found in the equivalent clubs in England, were established at Belfast.

For almost twelve months from the middle of 1981, low sales demand enforced a four-day week at all three of Michelin's UK car tyre factories. Despite the difficulties, Belfast's daily production climbed slowly, such that by February 1982, it produced a record 14,303 car tyres in one day. The production size breakdown included 1,500 145 x 10 Mini tyres, 1,000 205 x 16 XM+S Range Rover tyres and 220 175 x 16 XC TL 6PR Taxi tyres; three sizes unique to this factory for a long time.

Ballymena

From the end of January 1967 right up to the company's official announcement in September, speculation was rife in the Northern Ireland press, that Michelin was about to create a truck tyre factory in Londonderry, with the most likely site being the former BSR factory at Drumahoe. At a press conference on 22 September, Brian Faulkner, Northern Ireland Minister of Commerce, announced that Michelin had decided on a site on the Broughshane Road in Ballymena, County Antrim. The Minister's statement indicated that the new plant was intended to be complementary to the Mallusk (Belfast) factory which had been opened as the first stage in a programme of long-term development within the province, provided that labour relations were satisfactory and economic production was found to be possible in the region. His text hinted that Michelin had experienced difficulties in certain aspects of labour relations, but he understood that improvements were being made.

On 30 November that year, the local Ballymena press reported the outcome of a meeting in London between the Minister, M François Michelin and senior representatives of the Michelin Tyre Company. 'Work on the new tyre plant in Ballymena is to start early in the New Year and production is expected to get under way before the end of 1969.'

Anticipating that a workforce of 700 would be required within three years, Michelin began to search for employees in earnest. A recruitment weekend in November at Ballymena's Town Hall saw more than 600 people attending to view an exhibition and to talk to company representatives. Within three months a local Michelin office was opened in former bank premises in the town; the development was underway and new staff were recruited and sent to Stoke-on-Trent for initial training. However, the following April clouds appeared on the horizon in the form of an industrial dispute at the company's Mallusk site, and Michelin was forced to call a temporary halt to the project. To the relief of all concerned, the green light to recommence activities was given on 29 April 1968. The formal statement read: 'In its reappraisal of the project, the company has been most impressed by the goodwill extended towards Michelin at the Ballymena site.' That goodwill extends to the present day and Michelin is proud to have become a substantial part of Ballymena's, and hence Northern Ireland's, economy. Mrs Terence O'Neill, wife of the Ulster Prime Minister, inaugurated the new factory by planting a copper beech tree on the site on 1 October 1968. In traditional fashion, building of the engineering department's workshops had already started and subsoil surveys of the 127-acre site were imminent in order to establish if the large quantities of water required could be drawn from the gravels known to be there.

Michelin Tyre Company's fourth 'first UK tyre' was produced at Ballymena on 3 December 1969. It was a D.20/10.00-20 X, a typical popular radial truck tyre of the time. On 30 January 1970, M François Michelin visited the site to see it for himself and also went to the Mallusk factory.

Now, more than 35 years since that first tyre was produced there, Ballymena has made millions of tyres which have been sold in many parts of the world. During the first few years of production, the output was typically the tubed-type tyres of the time and only in two or three sizes, such as the D.20 or the E.20/11.00-20, and all of the XZZ pattern. Drop-centre tubeless tyres were then

Seen on the steps of a BEA aircraft at Belfast's Aldergrove Airport are three employees from Northern Ireland who are about to take part in the Parade of Floats in the 1966 Belfast Lord Mayor's Show.

In 1959, the prototype Saunders Roe SRN1 hovercraft was transported by road from Lee-on-Solent to the Farnborough Air Show. Bakers Transport of Southampton chose G.20 Metallic Y (1400-20) tyres to do the job safely. The craft made a 5-tonne load and was 21ft wide.

gradually introduced as the market developed, in sizes such as 11-22.5in and 12-22.5in. By 1975, the new XZA pattern was introduced into the planning and in May 1979 all the old tubed-type tyres used with flat-base rims, such as the D20X, were stopped. Ballymena emerged as a major all-tubeless radial truck tyre plant, the situation which remains to this day. Production has increased enormously as a result of expansion over the years, improved productivity and, not least in importance, by the introduction of continuous working, 24 hours a day, seven days a week. Michelin factories throughout the United Kingdom have often led the way in making substantial gains in output through flexible working arrangements.

Michelin's major structural reorganisation in 1996 led to a fundamental change in the way that the Ballymena factory operates. It had progressively produced a substantial percentage of its output for the North American market at the time, making

tyres which were unique for that market, typically of 24.5in rim diameter. It therefore became logical that it would become part of Michelin's North American truck tyre operation, the situation which still exists today.

Although the Mallusk factory had a training facility on site when it opened, a purpose-built establishment was foreseen for the vast number of young trainees and management and work study trainees needed to keep pace with the company's developments at both factories. Michelin's Northern Ireland Training Centre (NITC) was formally opened in a new 24,000ft^2 building close to Ballymena factory, on 22 January 1970. Almost 100 apprentices were in training by this time and an 'Apprentice of the Year' scheme instituted in 1971.

Michelin's culture of sports and social activities was also established at Ballymena and an MAC was formed in the hostel buildings originally used for workers at the time of the factory's construction. It has evolved over the years and still provides a range of facilities for the 1,300 employees currently on site.

Dundee

In the same way that Stoke-on-Trent was only one of a wide range of potential factory locations appraised by Michelin in the mid-1920s, so too was Northern Ireland in the mid to late 1960s. However, areas of Scotland were also always under serious consideration during the site selection process. Its North East, particularly Tayside and Grampian, was a favoured potential region and, like Ulster, it had the added attraction of various economic development grants available. In 1970, the Tay Study Report foresaw the development of Tayside as 'an area of great attraction which could hold a greatly increased population'. Industrially, Dundee had been losing jobs due to the contraction of its docks and the jute industry, its neighbour Perth too was about to be affected by the run-down of jobs resulting from the closure of the Almondbank naval stores depot.

Against this background of the need to secure new industry and jobs, behind-the-scenes discussions had been under way between Michelin and the various Scottish authorities since 1969. In January 1970, *The Glasgow Herald* picked up a rumour that something was in the air and ran a story headlined 'Michelin may open a Scottish factory'. The report made reference to a previous project, in 1966, to open a factory in Livingston, a plan which had fallen through.

By June 1970, speculation about possible sites was more widespread. The Tayside area had been selected by the Labour government as one of three major special growth areas in Britain; its prospects for a large new factory looked highly promising. Informed 'leaks' from the company suggested that a car tyre factory was distinctly likely but that it 'might be expanded to manufacture commercial vehicle tyres as well if the market demands it and labour is available'. All rumours ceased on 2 July when an official press conference was held. Michelin announced the creation of two factories; one, a car tyre plant, on a 28-hectare (70-acre) site at Baldovie in Dundee, the other, a steel-cord production unit, at Redmoss in Aberdeen. The new Secretary of State for Scotland, Gordon Campbell, welcomed 'the good news'. Investment was understood to be more than £10 million providing jobs for more than 1,000 men (women were not mentioned as conditions of recruitment were not subjected to the strictures of political correctness in those far-off days!).

It is worth noting that Dundee and Aberdeen were not the only major sites to figure in Michelin's Scottish plans at this time. Early in 1970, the local paper covering Perth, *The Courier*, reported: 'Perth in line for third plant'. After 18-months' of discussions with the local authorities, Michelin applied for planning permission on a 13.5-hectare (33-acre) site at Huntingtower just west of Perth in April 1971. This application was eventually the subject of a public enquiry the following year, which ruled against permission. Moreover, there was yet another potential development in Scotland when, in 1970, Michelin took an option on a 28-hectare site on the new Chapel Industrial Estate at Kirkcaldy, but again the development did not take place.

The Dundee factory site originally comprised 31 hectares (77 acres) of largely open, flat farmland. A stream, the Fithie Burn, ran through part of the site and was re-aligned as part of the initial earthworks. Some buildings were part of the original purchase, notably Baldovie House (now part of the company's MAC) and Baldovie Farm. Michelin paid a flat purchase price of £2,000 per acre and the total cost of the land and buildings came to £157,400, a sum that would only buy an acre or two today. The major factors influencing the choice of Baldovie were: government financial incentives, availability of labour and, as usual, ample water supplies. The initial agreement with the water authority was to ensure that there was a 3,400,000-litre (750,000-gallon) daily supply available by 1 April

During the 1950s and '60s, scooters were highly popular among young people in Great Britain and the country was one among many European nations to have its own Vespa Club. Here, a Michelin representative talks to club members at an event in Sandown Park in the summer of 1958.

1971. This is about equal to nine complete fillings of an Olympic-sized swimming pool every day.

Barely two months passed before the main contractor for the factory's construction, Sir Robert McAlpine & Sons Ltd, began work on site by building various access roads. Dundee's planning committee gave outline approval of the project on 18 August, including a change of use for 100 Nethergate in the city centre as Michelin's temporary office and recruitment centre. Serious industrial disputes among the building contractors delayed the start-up of Dundee by almost a year and so the first tyre, a 165-13 ZX tubeless radial, was not produced until 6 November 1972. Since then, tens of millions of radial car tyres have been produced at the site for use on vehicles throughout the world. Initially, there was a very small number of popular dimensions destined primarily for UK original equipment sales, mostly 12in and 13in, the typical rim sizes used on high volume cars such as the BMC 1100, Ford Cortina, Hillman Avenger and Vauxhall Victor. Production climbed steadily using highly-automated equipment that was being used for the first time in Britain. In 1975, after almost three years' production, Dundee celebrated its 5 millionth tyre, two years later it had made 10

million, and it only took three more years to reach the 20 millionth.

The Dundee factory has now been producing radial tyres for 33 years. Much has changed during that time: the nature of the tyres, their composition, and their markets. The 900 employees at Baldovie today operate in an industrial environment which could never have been contemplated way back in the early 1970s.

Aberdeen

The 44-acre site at Altens, Redmoss, on the south side of the city, was bought for £45,000 and preparatory work began in August 1970. Unlike the company's other British factories, Aberdeen was intended to produce one specific component only, for use in the tyre manufacturing process: steel cord.

Following Michelin's pioneering work in the development and exploitation of steel cord as a reinforcing agent in tyres, the company sought to develop the capacity to make this fine, brass-plated metallic cable itself. The impetus towards self-sufficiency began in the late 1940s when it was realised that vast amounts would be needed if international

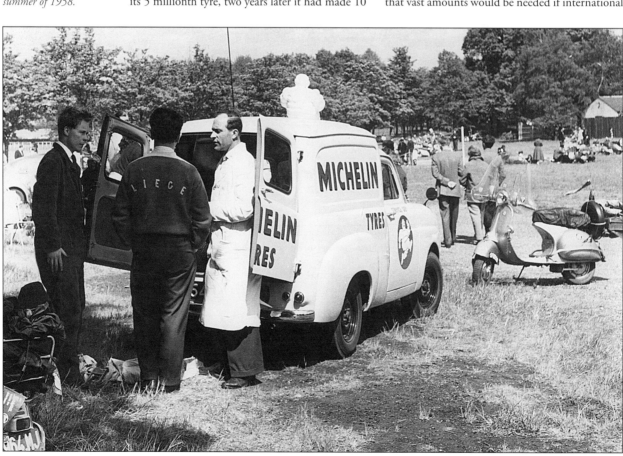

expansion was to progress: 1,200ft of cord goes into the simplest small car tyre, but five times more can be used in the average truck tyre.

Steel cable workshops were constructed at Stoke progressively from 1948 onwards and by the time that the plants required to make the new all-steel Michelin X radial tyres were being planned for the 1970s (a period when, on average, two new factories a year were being opened world-wide) a specific need for greater steel cord capacity had arisen. In this context, Aberdeen was destined to be the supplier for the planned Scottish group of factories. The first cord from Redmoss' workshops was produced on 24 August 1973. Aberdeen Lord Provost John Smith joined the 200 employees on site to mark the occasion and to receive a special plaque for the city. In 1979, the Redmoss site became the

location for one of Michelin's latest 'super-depots' for the storage and distribution of tyres, which was built along side the factory.

With the restructuring of Michelin's organisation that took place in the mid-1980s, in order to improve the UK Group's efficiency and long-term profitability, it was found that Aberdeen's output could be absorbed by the Stoke-on-Trent factory. The overhead costs of running another complete site could thus be saved and the operational costs ameliorated by an increased load on just one site. Thus, Aberdeen made its last cable on 7 July 1986, 13 years after opening. Much had been done beyond producing cable in that time. Young people had been recruited and trained, sports and social events had taken place, including children's outings, and employees had received their families on

In 1961, vehicles belonging to the sugar refiners Tate & Lyle, a well-established user of X tyres, were used in the company's press and TV campaign. Responsible for refining half the sugar used in the United Kingdom, Tate & Lyle transported some 12,000 tons to the grocery trade every week.

site at open days. Michelin's family culture touched a part of the Grampian region of Scotland for quite some time.

Michelin and the Citroën DS19

On Édouard Michelin's death in 1940, following the old tradition of keeping control within the family, the new supremo of the Michelin organisation was named as his son-in-law, Robert Puiseux. Born in Paris in 1892, Puiseux had joined the firm in 1921 after a distinguished military career in the Great War, during which he had served in the artillery and then latterly as an aviator in the Army Air Corps. Although he had not enjoyed the benefit of higher education and was entirely without formal engineering training and

The revolutionary hydro-pneumatically sprung Citroën DS19 was launched at the Paris Motor Show in October 1955.

qualifications, just like Édouard he proved to be a leader of considerable commercial acumen and vision, and a worthy successor as patriarch of the Michelin dynasty.

Then, in November 1950, Pierre-Jules Boulanger also met an untimely death, killed outright at the wheel of an experimental Traction Avant, while travelling between Paris and Clermont-Ferrand, just as had happened to Pierre Michelin thirteen years earlier. His role as President-Directeur-General (Chairman) of Citroën passed to Robert Puiseux, who with effect from January 1951, became ruler of both realms of the Michelin empire. Based at Clermont-Ferrand, Puiseux left the day-to-day management of the automobile subsidiary under the control of a new managing director, Pierre Bercot, who was located in Paris.

Unusually among the higher echelons of the Michelin empire, Bercot was not a member of the family either by birth or marriage. Born in 1903 he had studied languages (he spoke both ancient and modern Greek) before gaining a doctorate in law. However, he had joined the Michelin firm in 1937 not as a lawyer but as an economist, and in this capacity he had later been transferred from Clermont-Ferrand to Paris by P-J. Boulanger, shortly after Michelin had acquired the Javel company. Over the years, he gradually became the de facto managing director at the Quai de Javel, with ever greater responsibilities being delegated to him. Thus, when Robert Puiseux eventually retired in 1959, this situation was formally recognised and Bercot took on full responsibility for Citroën affairs with the title of President-Directeur-General, but reporting to the new supremo at Clermont-Ferrand, François Michelin (Édouard Michelin's grandson) who assumed control of the holding company, the Compagnie Générale des Établissements Michelin, in May 1955. Four years previously, Michelin's tyre manufacturing and marketing activities had been re-organised in a subsidiary company, La Manufacture Française des Pneumatiques Michelin.

By this point in time, early in 1951, work was well underway at Citroën's Bureau d'Etudes on the prototype intended as the replacement for the Traction Avant. Codenamed the VGD (Voiture de Grand Diffusion – mass-market car) this design

PRESENTING THE NEW **CITROEN** 2 LITRE SIX SEATER

FEATURES

had evolved under Boulanger's direction to resemble a strange-looking, round-snouted, humpbacked beast, disrespectfully christened the Hippopotamus by those who thought that its somewhat out-dated specification and appearance could be improved upon, now that P-J. B. was no longer on the scene. In forming this opinion they had the full approval of their new patron, Pierre Bercot. Taking stock of the situation, he recognised that by adopting a long-term view and delaying the production of a replacement for the Traction Avant for the time being, an opportunity existed for Citroën to create yet another truly advanced and radical vehicle that would, once again, give it a lasting lead over its competitors, just as the Traction had done some twenty years earlier. Moreover, he was quick to see that here lay the chance to create a car that would enhance the prestige of France as an automobile producer and industrial power, and so he readily agreed to a complete revision and up-dating of the project. No expense was to be spared in making the Traction Avant's replacement the finest, fastest, most comfortable vehicle that had ever been produced in France, using the very latest materials and methods. And not least among

the innovations to be incorporated, of course, would be Michelin's own recent invention, the X-series steel-braced radial tyre.

André Lefèbvre, the designer of the Traction Avant and the 2CV, was instructed to carry out a total rethink of the VGD, employing the revolutionary hydro-pneumatic suspension technology that had been invented by a young Citroën engineer, Paul Mages, during the war. It was also to incorporate an extremely unusual and highly sophisticated front suspension layout, designed to exploit the advantages of the new Michelin X steel-braced radial tyre, which had been launched at the October 1949 Paris Motor Show. Clearly, the grand idea – although never explicitly stated – was that the new car should act as a demonstration vehicle to show-off the virtues of the Michelin X tyre. By this point in time the Michelin firm had already committed itself to developing the capacity to manufacture the X tyre in very high volumes, with the intention that it should eventually replace the conventional cross-ply tyre completely throughout its product range.

Naturally, Bercot's decision to proceed with the commercialisation of Mages's hydro-pneumatic

The right-hand-drive version of the DS19 (built at Slough between 1956 and 1965) was launched at the London Motor Show in October 1955.

self-levelling suspension technology was fully endorsed by his boss at Clermont-Ferrand, the current gerent Robert Puiseux. In 1951 he gave the go-ahead for the huge investment required to enable Citroën to begin the manufacture of hydro-pneumatic systems and components. It had been Puiseux who, in 1944, approved the research and development programme that led to the patenting of the radial tyre concept by Michelin, in June 1946.

It is hardly surprising then, that when revealed at the October 1955 Paris Motor Show, the DS19 created a world-wide sensation – a staggering 12,000 orders were taken on the first day alone. When it was exhibited at the London Motor Show a few days later, the reception accorded by the press and public alike was almost as rapturous. The technical editor of *The Motor*, Laurence Pomeroy, called it; 'One of the biggest advances in the whole history of motoring'. Today, it has become a cult object, placed third in the 1999 International Car of the Century competition, as well as being voted Industrial Product of the Century by a panel of British automobile design and engineering experts.

The list of fresh ideas and innovations included in its specification was surely unparalleled for its boldness and ambition. Besides its revolutionary fully independent hydro-pneumatic self-levelling suspension and front-wheel-drive transmission, the DS19 also featured high-pressure hydraulic servo operation of its braking, steering and gear-selection systems, as in an aircraft. Its highly aerodynamic body work, styled by Flaminio Bertoni, also broke new ground in that the detachable panels forming its superstructure were mounted on an exceptionally rigid

caisson or punt-like infrastructure, a method of construction that, with the exception of the 2CV, was quite unlike that used on any other motor car before or since.

In 1957, the DS19 was joined in the Citroën catalogue by the ID19, a simplified version having manual transmission, braking and steering, but also powered by a 1911cc engine. Unlike the DS19, however, this was also available in estate car form. Later D series versions included the 1,985cc DS20, the 2,175cc DS21 and the 2,347cc DS23 saloons plus the 1,985cc ID20, D Special or D Super saloons, and the 2,175cc or 2,347cc ID estates. Production of the range continued for 20 years until 1975, by which time a total of 1,456,115 D-series vehicles had been sold, surely a testament to the uncompromisingly advanced conception of the original design.

Throughout the course of the Fifties, Sixties and early Seventies, Michelin's car-making subsidiary Automobiles Citroën gradually recovered from its earlier financial difficulties and the production problems of the immediate post-war years, to re-establish its reputation as the largest and most technically advanced automobile manufacturer in Europe. In 1965 it took 30.5 per cent of the French market, going on to capture 9.3 per cent of total European sales the following year. By 1973 its output was topping 750,000 vehicles.

The following year, however, production plummeted by almost 100,000 units to approximately 689,000 cars, lorries and vans. The cause, of course, was the first world-wide Energy Crisis, brought on by the Yom Kippur Arab-Israeli War of October 1973. The price of petrol quadrupled almost overnight,

The only vehicle of its type in the country, this 35ft long ambulance owned by West Hendon hospital during the 1960s was actually a mobile clinic. Completely self-contained it could be halted by the roadside while a minor operation was carried out. On trial runs on the M1 in 1962 it reached speeds of over 75mph with perfect stability, thanks to its Michelin X tyres.

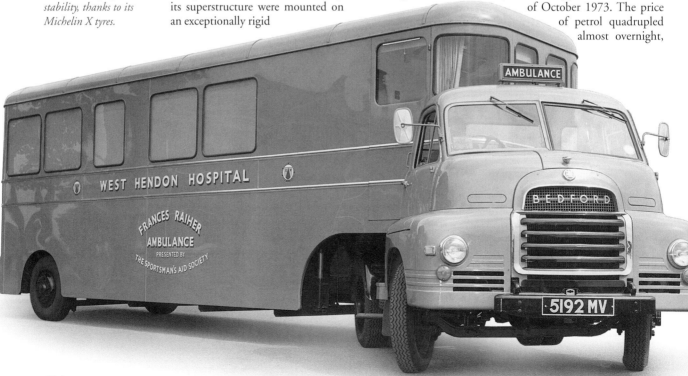

drastically reducing demand for all but the smallest, most economical vehicles, such as the 2CV.

Having recently invested heavily in the development of two brand-new models, the SM and the GS launched three years earlier, in 1970, (plus another car, the CX, intended as the replacement for the D-series models, but not launched until 1974) Citroën was more exposed than most other automobile firms to the effect of this recession. Moreover, it was also faced with the task of recouping the costs of constructing brand-new production facilities at Aulnay-sous-Bois on the outskirts of Paris, to replace the outdated Quai de Javel factory which was closed in 1974.

In the circumstances, at a time when demand for tyres was also greatly depressed, the parent company had little alternative but to cut its losses by selling, albeit reluctantly, its 89 per cent stake in the Citroën group to Automobiles Peugeot in order to concentrate its resources on the expansion of its tyre-making activities, which demanded the construction of numerous additional factories around the world. With French government backing, therefore, in July 1974 Citroën was released from Michelin ownership and control to join a new industrial conglomerate, the PSA Peugeot-Citroën group. It is worth noting that Michelin's stewardship of the Double Chevron marque had spanned 40 years, well over twice the duration of André Citroën's ownership.

The DS19 – also 'Made in England', 1956-1966

In 1956, a right-hand-drive version of the 1,911cc engined DS19 saloon replaced the Traction Avant on the assembly line at Slough, to be joined two years later by the ID19, in both saloon and estate car form, always known in the UK as the Safari. Production of this trio continued until 1966 when all three models were briefly superseded by the improved DS21 and ID21 versions, equipped with a new, 2,175cc engine.

But by this time the Slough works, which had always been reliant on the Australian and South African export markets to be fully viable, was experiencing a severe decline in demand due to the establishment of rival Citroën assembly plants in those countries, supplied directly from France. Accordingly, it was decided to close down the facility and to import all right-hand-drive models for the British market from Paris. Production ceased in February 1966, exactly 40 years to the day since it was opened by André Citroën, and thereafter the Slough establishment operated solely as a sales, distribution and replacement parts base. In total, 8,668 right-hand-drive D-series models had been produced there, of which 22 per cent were exported. All these cars ran on Michelin X radial tyres supplied by the Stoke-on-Trent factory, although their wheels (a unique type with a single central fixing, specially designed for the DS19 by Michelin) came from France.

At the 1961 Earls Court Motor Show the 5.20 x 10 X tyre for the Mini was exhibited on the Michelin stand for the first time, promoting the theme of fuel economy. Eight telephones provided potential customers with a 'Dial-for-the-Answer' service.

1965–1974
Swinging through the Sixties

The London to Sydney Marathon of 1968

When the DS19 first appeared in 1955, few commentators predicted that the model would enjoy a long and successful career as a competition car extending across three decades, from 1959 to 1975. Its design was far too complex – delicate even – to survive the rough and tumble of the rally circuit, was the experts' verdict. In fact, the very reverse was true; the construction of the D-series models was immensely strong, robust and durable, while the special characteristics of their hydro-pneumatic suspension systems enabled them to survive conditions that wrecked the springing of conventional designs. Time after time, experience in long-distance endurance events showed that their astonishing ride-comfort over poor road surfaces cushioned both car and crews alike from shocks and fatigue. The Citroën's drivers were never as tired as their competitors, even after very long runs over arduous terrain.

The first notable victory occurred in 1959 when a standard ID19, privately entered by a team

1965 Michelin opens its new research and testing centre at Ladoux, north of Clermont-Ferrand.

The world's first asymmetric tyre, the Michelin XAS radial, is introduced for high-performance cars.

The Michelin organisation now employs 81,000 people world-wide, including 9,500 in the British Isles. A new factory is opened in Belfast (it closes in 1984).

By this time, no fewer than 60 million X tyres have been produced by Michelin and sold throughout the world since the first examples were introduced in 1948.

Due to the vast increase in traffic on British roads, AA patrol men cease saluting members.

1966 The Citroën factory at Slough is closed after 40 years of activity. Henceforth, all right-hand-drive Citroën cars will be built in France.

A Citroën DS21 is awarded first prize in the Monte Carlo Rally after the BMC Mini Cooper team is disqualified for alleged lighting infringements.

François Rollier is appointed a co-managing partner.

The new Michelin XAS tyre is promoted at the London Motor Show.

1967 A blanket 70mph speed limit is introduced in the UK. Breathalyser tests are also introduced for British motorists.

The Michelin ZX radial replaces the X tyre for enhanced comfort and driving pleasure. It is advertised as being safer in all kinds of weather.

1968 The *Daily Express* stages the first London-Sydney Marathon.

British Motor Holdings (formed in 1966 by the merger of BMC and Jaguar) joins forces with the Leyland Motor Company (owner of Rover and Triumph) to form the vast, but ill-fated British Leyland Motor Corporation conglomerate. BLMC becomes the first British manufacturer to build more than a million vehicles in a year.

1969 The new Michelin factory at Ballymena, Northern Ireland, opens.

The American astronauts of the Apollo mission walk on the moon wearing their bulbous space suits and a TV commentator likens them to Monsieur Bibendum.

1971 Decimal currency is introduced into the British Isles.

Michelin's first International Test Day takes place at Silverstone, where members of the press are invited to try out various makes of foreign cars. Hundreds of journalists and celebrities tested hundreds of cars at this annual event which Michelin sponsored up to 1976.

1972 The Wembley-Mexico Rally is run.

The Range Rover appears at the London Motor Show for the first time.

A total of 2.3 million cars and commercial vehicles leave Britain's factories, an all-time record for the industry.

Michelin opens its first Scottish factory, at Dundee, for the production of radial car tyres.

1973 Britain joins the European Economic Community and purchase tax is replaced by VAT.

Michelin opens its second Scottish factory, at Aberdeen, for the production of steel cord (it closes in 1986).

The Energy Crisis caused by the Arab-Israeli war brings recession to the motor industry world-wide.

1974 The Wembley-Sahara-Munich World Cup Rally is won by a Citroën DS23.

In January, British industry experiences the Three-day Week.

The Driver and Vehicle Licensing Centre at Swansea is opened.

Michelin re-introduces the Red Guide to Great Britain and Ireland.

Michelin sells its shares in Automobiles Citroën to the Peugeot Group.

One of Citroën Cars Ltd's works-entered DS21 team leaves a reception at the Royal Gardens Hotel in Kensington, heading for the start of the London-Sydney Marathon at the Crystal Palace, in November 1968.

The first notable victory for the Citroën Déese – and the Michelin X tyre – occured in 1959 when a standard ID19 privately entered by Paul Coltelloni won the Monte Carlo Rally, gaining for Citroën the Coupé des Constructeurs.

Rallye Monte Carlo 1959

1er CLASSEMENT GÉNÉRAL
COLTELLONI · ALEXANDRE · DESROSIERS
SUR
ID 19 CITROËN
GRAISSÉE PAR

YACCO

L'HUILE DES RECORDS DU MONDE   300.000 Kms. A MONTLHÉRY

comprising Paul Coltelloni, Pierre Alexandre and Claude Desrosiers won the Monte Carlo Rally, gaining for Citroën the Coupe des Constructors (manufacturers' prize). This success caused the Double Chevron company to open a competitions department for the very first time, with Citroën preparing the cars and funding the entry costs and expenses. Naturally, the tyres were provided by Michelin.

Several years of strong achievement followed, with both ID19 and DS19 entrants participating in numerous international events, the latter usually being equipped with the manual transmission introduced early in 1963 on the DS19M and which was preferred by drivers such as Neyret, Terramorsi, Toivonen and Bianchi. But from 1965 onwards, the team competed formally under the Citroën banner, initially entering a batch of DS19Ms in the April 1965 East African Safari, then regarded as one of the toughest challenges in the competition world. Five out of the 17 finishers were Citroëns. Because the course lay in the former British territories of Kenya and Uganda (which being part of the right-hand-drive zone remained within the sales territory controlled by Citroën Cars Ltd) the team was actually entered and supported by the Slough subsidiary, although left-hand-drive cars were used.

In 1966, Citroën won the Monte Carlo Rally once again, but under controversial circumstances. The team of Mini Coopers entered by BMC, which had finished first, second and third was disqualified for alleged lighting infringements, leaving the DS21 of Pauli Toivonen to claim the laurels. This decision generated a reaction of outrage in the British press and soured Anglo-French relations for many years, at least within the motor industry. Thereafter, Citroën's competitions department began to concentrate on off-road endurance events such as the Moroccan and Portuguese rallies and the long-distance marathons of the Sixties and Seventies, which better demonstrated the unique advantages of the D-series range. These included the 1968 *Daily Express* London-Sydney Marathon, the 1970 Wembley-Mexico Rally, the 1974 UDT Wembley-Sahara-Munich World Cup Rally and the second London-Sydney Marathon sponsored by UDT in 1977. All four events were organised and sponsored by British interests, all had their starts in England, all had predominantly British cars and drivers among their entrants, and all generated enormous coverage and publicity in the British press. Citroën teams put up outstanding performances in all four events. A DS23 driven by

the Australians Welinski, Tubman and Reddiex actually won the 1974 race, while in the 1977 Marathon Citroën gained the manufacturer's trophy, with a CX2400 driven by Paddy Hopkirk being placed third.

But none of these later rallies ever equalled the drama and excitement of the first of the trio, the 1968 London-Sydney Marathon. In this event, organised and sponsored by the *Daily Express*, the Citroën team was actually entered by Citroën Cars Ltd, the cars being prepared in the workshops at Slough. Two official works-entered DS21 cars took part; the first, No. 87, was driven by Bianchi and Ogier, and the second, No. 74, by Neyret and Terramorsi, although a third DS21, driven by Vanson and Turcat, was entered privately by the Automobile Club de France.

The longest and toughest rally so far devised at that time, its course covered 10,000 miles through Europe, Asia and Australia, crossing 12 countries in over 250 hours of non-stop driving time, a unique test of both men and machines. Representing 20 makes and 15 nations, 98 cars set out from the Crystal Palace, London, on 24 November, but on arrival at Bombay eight days later, after covering 6,800 miles through France, Italy, Yugoslavia, Bulgaria, Turkey, Iran, Afghanistan, Pakistan and India, only 72 were left in the race. At the end of this stage the Bianchi-Ogier car was placed third, an excellent result for Citroën as not one DS21 had required the slightest repair since leaving London. Many other entrants needed a complete rebuild in Bombay, however.

After a nine-day sea crossing to Freemantle,

The Citroën DS23 shod with Michelin's XM+S mud and snow tyres that won the UDT World Cup Rally in 1974. Michelin was also responsible for the unusual wheels that were made in France solely for the 'Déesse' range.

In January 1967, demolition started on the all-concrete Stoke factory water tower which had provided the reserve supply for the site for over 40 years. The concrete reservoir at the top of the tower carried the word 'Michelin' flanked by depictions of Michelin Men, and was illuminated at night.

a head-on collision at high speed. The DS21 was wrecked, although both driver and navigator escaped with only minor injuries. After running a magnificent race, involving no fewer than 11 days of flat-out driving, sometimes in appalling weather conditions and almost always over abysmal road surfaces, the high expectations of the Citroën team were crumpled in just a fraction of a second.

At the time of the impact, Bianchi was lying 11 minutes and 21 penalty points ahead of his nearest opponent, a Hillman Hunter driven by Andrew Cowan. Arriving in Sydney nearly a quarter-of-an-hour behind the time at which Bianchi and Ogier would have reached their destination, Cowan was declared the winner and awarded the *Daily Express* Trophy plus the £10,000 first prize.

The return of the Michelin Red Guides

It has to be admitted that for many people the name Michelin stands as much for restaurants as it does for rubber. If so, then that is certainly due to the remarkable success of the famous series of Michelin Red Guides which first appeared in France in 1900. Listing a choice of congenial hotels, pubs and restaurants offering good food and drink, as well as much other information of value to motorists and tourists, these renowned guides have long been regarded as the ultimate tourist reference.

In March 1974, the Red Guide to Great Britain and Ireland, was reintroduced after a long absence, publication having been suspended in 1931 for reasons that are still obscure. The first edition had been published in 1911, yet although the English language versions of Michelin's Continental guides covering German, Italy, Spain and Portugal and Belgium and the Benelux countries had all been available since the early 1920s, except for the interruption caused by the Second World War, it took over 40 years for the service to be resumed. Since 1974, however, the British Guide has been brought out on a regular annual basis, not merely in English but also with texts in French, German and Italian, for the benefit of tourists and other visitors to this country. Compiled and produced by Michelin Travel Publications, a subsidiary of Michelin in France, the Red Guide to Great Britain is now in its 32nd post-war edition.

Because of this long interval, the task of research and inspection had virtually to start from scratch, so that the new, 1974 edition took no less than four years to compile with over 15,000 establishments being examined and evaluated. The result was a comprehensive list of 2,330 hotels, 331 motels and

Australia, on the P&O liner *Chusan*, the Marathon recommenced at Perth, heading for Sydney on the final three-day, 3,500-mile leg, run mostly on dirt roads. Mid-way across the Outback, some 8,700 miles from London, Bianchi took first place, consolidating his position with every following hour until it seemed that he had built up an unassailable lead. No other competing car could cover the rough ground as fast as the DS21, due to the advantage conferred by its hydro-pneumatic suspension. To the reporters on the spot and the millions following the event around the world on television, radio and in the newspapers, it appeared that a stunning Citroën victory was inevitable.

But suddenly, at 9am on the morning of 17 December, just an hour or so short of the finishing line, disaster struck the Citroën. At Nowra, a mere 100 miles from Sydney, it collided with a Mini driven by two local youngsters who had strayed into its path, on a road that was supposedly closed and entirely clear of on-coming traffic. For all his skill, driver Ogier (who was at the wheel while Bianchi snatched a little sleep) was unable to avoid

981 restaurants located in over 1,400 towns and villages throughout England, Scotland, Wales, Northern Ireland and the Irish Republic, all graded and recommended according to Michelin's unique system of classification. In addition, its 478 pages were packed with route maps and town plans, a table of distances, information about places of interest, an explanation of British licensing and motoring laws, a lexicon of useful words and expressions and of course, hints on tyre care and maintenance! There was also an 86-page companion booklet to the Red Guide, covering Greater London and listing restaurants by type and nationality. The set cost just £2.50!

The work of investigation and information-gathering had been carried out by a team of 12 inspectors, all of them British citizens, although trained in France. Their task, then as nowadays, was to visit, incognito and unannounced, literally thousands of hotels and eating-places to decide which establishments were worthy of selection. In those days, however, unlike some other guides, the Red Guide did not include verbal descriptions or comments. Instead, to save space, the accommodation and facilities on offer were indicated by a system of over 90 visual symbols. Restaurants were graded by crossed knives and forks while hotels were ranked in comfort, from the grandest and most luxurious down to the more modest and homely, by a similar method. Again, unlike other publications, the quality of the cuisine available was judged separately, independently of other considerations, and indicated by the award of the

famous Michelin rosettes or stars, three being the ultimate accolade.

Only 25 of the restaurants listed in the 1974 guide were considered worthy of a star, all but one of them in London, which indicated the very high standard required to achieve this distinction. Doubtless, it is a sure sign of the general improvement in cuisine that has taken place in the United Kingdom over the past 40 years that the 2005 Red Guide lists no fewer than 120 Michelin-starred establishments.

A vital principle behind the success of the Michelin Red Guides was – and remains today – the objectivity, independence, integrity and anonymity of the inspectors. This caused some problems when the UK guide was re-introduced in 1974, for although the team of inspectors was available for interview by the many journalists and broadcasters invited to the press reception held at Michelin House, photography was forbidden. To preserve their anonymity and prevent all possibility of recognition while going about their duties, their faces could not be shown in the ensuing television, newspaper, and newsreel reports.

The Maps and Green Guides are also revived

As mentioned earlier, the first edition of the Michelin Guide to the British Isles appeared in 1911. Packed with information for the motorist, it was intended first and foremost as a reference tool,

The Green Guide to London was launched in August 1977.

Three out of the four class winners in the 1967 Mobil Economy Run used Michelin tyres. This Daimler 2¹/₂-litre saloon running on X tyres won the over 2,000cc automatic transmission class.

and even had a symbol to show where an aeroplane could be serviced! The third in the series, published in 1913, announced the planned introduction of a series of road maps of the British Isles, to the scale of 1:200,000. The format would be exactly the same as for the maps of France, which was covered by 47 sheets: Great Britain would have 22 and Ireland nine.

It seems that these British maps were delayed for some reason; they actually started to appear in 1914. Of a novel 'concertina' format, the series developed with the decades. The first series of maps, from 1914 to 1921, were produced by the British publisher William Clowes & Sons. The second series, 1921/22, were produced initially by William Clowes, Waterlow & Sons and Delamotte of Paris, but the Paris company produced them all in 1922. The third series, introduced in 1923, and the fourth series (1931) were produced by companies such as Buttner-Thierry, Levallois and Gaston Maillet in France. The covers of these latter two series state 'Michelin Map of Great Britain'; Ireland was not included. A special map of Great Britain was published in 1921, the first road map of the country to bear road numbers, pipping Bartholomews to the post and well in advance of the Ordnance Survey's series.

Certainly, it is recorded in the minutes of a Ministry of Transport meeting dated 18 November

1920 that M André Michelin had provided 'some helpful suggestions' towards devising a British system of road numbering. An issue of the company's house magazine *Bibendum* dated September 1948 carried a report on a letter to the editor of *The Motor Cycle*, published in its August edition. The letter stated that 'By far the best map and guide system in my opinion was the now-unobtainable Michelin's. Incidentally, in the Michelin Guide is an excellent description of the method of road numbering used by the Ministry of Transport'.

Following the completion of the main administration building (General Offices, Building No. 10) on the Stoke-on-Trent factory site in 1930, the Fulham Road premises were demoted to the status of a depot and virtually all of the UK company's administration activities, including sales, were transferred to Stoke. It seems likely that a decision was taken around that time to substantially reduce the maps and guides activity, indeed, a sticker dated 13 February 1928 was attached to maps stating that 'Michelin itineraries for Great Britain are no longer available'. As the free provision of itineraries had begun when Fulham Road opened in 1911, its closure marked the end of an era. The last Great Britain Guide, was the 11th edition and was issued in 1930. The next was not to appear for another 44 years.

Similarly, there was a reduction in the availability

of Michelin's maps and no new UK maps were published until Coronation year, 1953, when a new map of the United Kingdom appeared. Although there was no specific British Isles map on offer by Michelin in the 1940s, however, it is known that the company's continental mapping systems of France were then being used by the British military and their allies, in preparation for the invasion of France. The Directorate of Military Survey's Volume 5 'Mediterranean France' of 1944, for example, gives 181 through-way town plans based on the 1939 Michelin Guide.

The June 1953 edition of *Bibendum* commented on the return of the road maps. 'A new map is now on the market, called The Michelin Motoring Map of Great Britain. This map, which includes Great Britain and Northern Ireland on the one sheet, will be a boon to all road users… It is early yet to see the

sort of reception this map will receive but its publication is timed for the Coronation and it has a Coronation wrapper. Employees of the company can obtain the map at retail price 3s 6d less 20 per cent', it declared. Between 1953 and 1969, this was the only Michelin map on offer for the entire British Isles. Covering only Great Britain and again excluding Ireland, and printed on a scale of 1:1,000,000 (14 miles = 1 inch) it was re-issued spasmodically until 1970 when it was revised and relaunched. Its popularity was such that it has been produced annually ever since, together with five 1:400,000 series maps covering parts of the British Isles.

Earlier, in June 1954, a special metal motoring map was introduced, printed on an enamelled plaque that could be attached to the walls of a garage forecourt, alongside a similar plaque that

A Michelin articulated truck prepares to set off from Stoke's tyre store on the nightly run to Liverpool Docks at some point in 1970, loaded with a consignment bound for export.

Distributors Roger Hook Tyres of Teignmouth gained first prize in the Commercial Section of the Shaldon Water Carnival in 1970, with this unusual float featuring Monsieur Bibendum surrounded by a bevy of bathing belles.

Michelin had produced giving the correct inflation pressures for its various tyres when fitted to different vehicles. This was available in two versions: England and Wales, and north of England and Scotland.

The late 1980s saw another surge in Michelin's map-making activities in the British Isles. In May 1985, a new road map covering Ireland was launched, while in 1989 came its first comprehensive Road Atlas of Europe produced for British motorists, a handsome hard-backed volume containing 224 pages covering the entire Continent. Later that year, the atlas was made available as a special presentation pack contained within a wallet made of black simulated leather with stitched edges and gold corners, and packed together with the four regional motoring maps of Great Britain, all in a gold-coloured box. Next, in 1990, the Motoring Atlas of Great Britain and Ireland was launched, in the same format as the Road Atlas of Europe. That

same year a special Golf Map of Ireland was produced, to cater for golfing enthusiasts on touring holidays in the Emerald Isle by motor car. Currently, the 2005 series of Michelin's small-scale maps for the British Isles is printed on a scale of 1:400,000: four maps cover Great Britain and one covers Ireland. In 1984 these Michelin UK maps were chosen as the official reference for the Lombard RAC Rally.

Another publications milestone took place on 12 August 1977. The British Isles were to be covered in Michelin's famous tourist guides to towns, cities and regions. Now sporting a green cover, these English-language publications were also to be made available in French, German and Italian versions for the benefit of tourists from abroad. They were designed to complement the established series covering holiday destinations on the Continent and which had long been the favourite guides of British tourists heading across the Channel. The first to appear was the Green Guide to London – 'Be a Londoner for £2.50' proclaimed the posters and advertisements that heralded its arrival. In December 1984, the Green Guide to the West Country was launched, the first in a planned series of regional tourist guides to the British Isles. Consequently, this was soon followed in January 1986 by the Green Guide to Scotland, in 1991 by the Green Guide to Great Britain and in 1992 by the Green Guide to Ireland. A completely new English-language Green Guide to France, designed specifically for the British tourist, had also been published in 1991.

Since then, there have been a host of other interesting issues from Michelin Travel Publications, prepared especially for English-speaking travellers and tourists. Notably, the first, which appeared in 1996, was the In Your Pocket series of guides covering various towns and regions such as Amsterdam, Madrid, New York City, California, the Greek Islands and four French areas including the Auvergne and the Rhône Valley, all containing a wealth of easy-to-use, practical information in a pocket-sized format. Next, in 2000, in response to the demand from hitchhikers and backpackers came the NEOS Guides to off-the-beaten-track destinations such as Cuba, Morocco and Vietnam. More recently, 2004 saw the publication of Eating Out in Pubs, a brand-new guide which contains the annual award of Michelin Pub of the Year. Pub food has changed a great deal during the last decade, as more and more establishments have put greater emphasis on achieving excellence in their cuisine. This guide opened the door to a large selection of some of the very finest hostelries – in fact, 500 of the very best pubs to drink and dine in throughout Britain and Ireland.

Another, little-known string to the Travel Publications company's bow was its adoption, in February 1991, of the I-Spy series of children's books, which had first been devised in 1948 as a means to keep children amused when on a holiday outing or a long car journey. At the outset the relaunched series comprised 12 titles including Sports, Birds, Cars and At the Zoo. Priced at 99p (softback) or £1.99 (hardback), the principle was the same as when the booklets had first come out, ie children were invited to look for things in the books, tick them off, and then to claim an I-Spy badge when 1,000 points had been collected and verified by parents. The series also appeared every Saturday in the *Young Telegraph* at the time of the re-launch. Subsequently, there have been several variations using the I-Spy theme, such as the Big I-Spy Book in 1991, two guides to cars and British birds in 1996, and a range of mini-atlases for various European countries. Ultimately, over 50 I-Spy titles have been produced in the Michelin format.

Electronic media has developed in many aspects of modern life, not least in navigation systems. Michelin has been there from the start and has developed a web-based information system, incorporating information from its vast cartography and Red and Green Guide database, which has been extended to in-car navigation route planning under a separate subsidiary, ViaMichelin. Many of the established European navigation system hardware providers have opted for partnerships with Michelin, both for vehicles and for portable, hand-held mapping devices.

The Duchess of Sutherland LMS locomotive being transported using a Scammell tractor shod with 14.00-24 XS tyres, on its journey to Bressingham Steam Museum, Norfolk in 1971.

Bibendum joins in the celebrations with a crowd of enthusiastic motorists during the MG marque's Golden Jubilee Year, 1975.

BBC TV 'Top of the Pops' star and rally driver extraordinaire Noel Edmonds meets Bibendum and Wellington (from the Wombles) at Michelin's International Test Car Day at Silverstone, 21 May 1975.

A special Michelin tyre for London taxis

In 1963, Michelin introduced a special version of the X tubeless steel-braced radial tyre produced exclusively for use on London taxis, and designed to offer as much as 100 percent greater mileage than the conventional crossply tyres with which the large fleet of taxis currently circulating in the capital was equipped, as well as better fuel economy, extra reliability and greater passenger comfort into the bargain. Sixteen years later, a new tubeless version of this tyre became the standard original equipment fitted to all examples of the familiar model of black London taxi, the FX4, then being produced in large numbers by Carbodies of Coventry, in association with the British Leyland Motor Company. Over 75,000 examples of these black cabs were eventually produced, of which a fleet of about 19,000 would have been in service throughout the Greater London area each and every year throughout the 1980s. Like the original first-ever radial tyre for taxis, the new version was available in one size only, and was developed after an extensive

programme of additional research into the requirements and idiosyncrasies of the London vehicle and its drivers, as regulated by the Metropolitan Police.

In common with all Michelin radials, the new taxi tyre incurred low rolling resistance so that it absorbed less power. Fuel consumption tests in central London traffic showed results in line with RAC tests on other Michelin radials where the saving was as high as 8 percent. Not only that, but the radial tyre's steel-cord bracing and flexible side-walls (which controlled the contact patch) ensured that the maximum area of tread was kept in contact with the road under all circumstances, so that squirm and distortion (the main cause of tyre wear) were reduced. At the same time, the grip imparted by the tread was improved, leading to easier steering and braking and thus maximum manoeuvrability. Moreover, since a taxi tyre has more than its fair share of brushes with the kerb, the Michelin Taxi radial was designed with this problem specifically in mind and incorporated special features to minimise the damage. The Michelin London taxi tyre was produced exclusively at the Mallusk factory in Northern Ireland.

Above: In November 1978, Michelin's 175-16 XC tubeless radial tyre was adopted as the standard fitment for all British Leyland London Taxis. The tyre had been developed for the vehicle in 1962, as the 5.75-16 X, an optional item for owner-drivers.

'Trying to connect you now, sir!' Before the advent of digital technology, telephone switchboard systems were operated manually by plugging wires into sockets, as this picture of Michelin's main exchange in 1972 shows.

1975–1984

Bibendum beats inflation

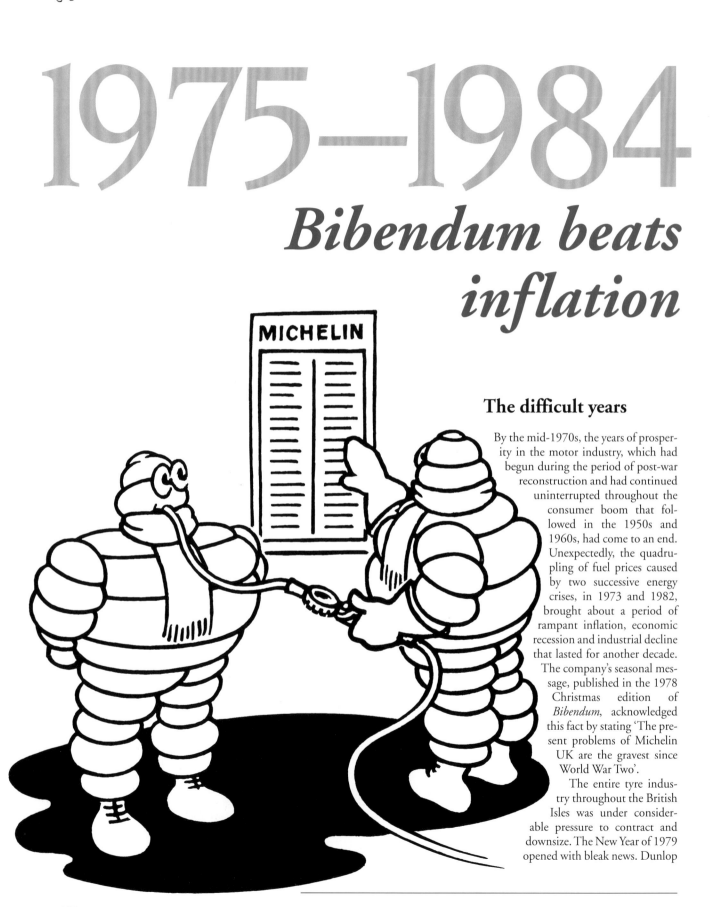

The difficult years

By the mid-1970s, the years of prosperity in the motor industry, which had begun during the period of post-war reconstruction and had continued uninterrupted throughout the consumer boom that followed in the 1950s and 1960s, had come to an end. Unexpectedly, the quadrupling of fuel prices caused by two successive energy crises, in 1973 and 1982, brought about a period of rampant inflation, economic recession and industrial decline that lasted for another decade.

The company's seasonal message, published in the 1978 Christmas edition of *Bibendum*, acknowledged this fact by stating 'The present problems of Michelin UK are the gravest since World War Two'.

The entire tyre industry throughout the British Isles was under considerable pressure to contract and downsize. The New Year of 1979 opened with bleak news. Dunlop was reducing its workforce by 3,000 jobs through closure of its factory at Speke on Merseyside and redundancies at Birmingham and the crossply tyre factory near Glasgow; Goodyear announced a reduction of 1,000 employees, while Firestone was negotiating the future of its Brentford plant with the government.

At the outset of the 1970s, the UK tyre industry had boasted 17 factories, employing some 47,000 people, but by 1981, five of these factories had closed and employment had halved. It halved again within another ten years, and by the turn of the 20th century, the industry had just seven principal sites employing around 6,000 people. Whereas in 1970, ignoring competition from overseas, there had been no fewer than 14 different makes or brands of home-produced tyre, all competing for sales in original equipment and replacement markets, ten years later there were just six.

The problems had really begun at the start of 1974, due to the emergency three-day working week, a measure which lasted for three months. From January until the end of March, Michelin employees were urged to conserve energy in order to reduce costs at a time of severe shortages in fuel and materials. Even so, by 1976, 'Michelin was still in full production and progressing with confidence', according to a contemporary company statement.

By 1977, approximately 72 per cent of all tyres supplied as original equipment to car manufacturers were steel-braced radials, although unlike ten years earlier, when Michelin was the dominant supplier, there now existed a wide range of suppliers of this type of tyre, and comparisons could be more easily made across the range. The days of a clear and easy choice between Michelin's products and competitors' textile radials or even crossply tyres, were over. Competition was hotting-up, in a market that was being greatly influenced by issues such as rising oil prices. *The Economist* reported: 'During the past six months, competition in the tyre replacement business has become cut-throat. Dealers, never previously noted for their price competitiveness, are having to offer the public the big discounts formerly reserved for garages, in an effort to keep their market share. Many small distributors have already gone bust. There are several other reasons, besides the radials, why Europe's tyre market has gone flat. The high price of petrol is at last having an effect on motoring. Europeans are buying more cars again, but using them less. In Britain, although total car and van mileage since the early 1970s has gone up from about 120 billion to over 140 billion miles a year, growth has lately slowed to a stroll'.

Against this background, Michelin's financial performance in the UK was subject to an adverse

1975 The Michelin TRX car tyre is launched and the XZX replaces the ZX.

The British Leyland Motor Corporation ceases to exist and is nationalised as British Leyland, with the government owning a 99 per cent stake.

1976 Michelin sponsors the sixth stage of the Milk Race, a cycling Tour of Britain which finishes at Stoke-on-Trent, in June.

The Chrysler name replaces the old Rootes marques, Sunbeam, Humber and Singer. Two years later, Hillman also vanishes.

1977 Michelin's Stoke-on-Trent factory celebrates its 50th birthday.

The first Green Guide to London is published.

The SMMT's London Motor Show moves from Earls Court to the National Exhibition Centre in Birmingham.

1978 Peugeot buys Chrysler Europe's car and commercial vehicle operations and acquires the Ryton factory at Coventry. Henceforth, until 1987, its products are branded as Talbots.

EEC Type Approval regulations are introduced in the UK.

The first radial agricultural tyre, the BibX, is launched.

1979 Michelin tyres help Ferrari to victory in the Formula One World Championship.

1980 Car production in the UK falls below a million units for the first time in 30 years.

1981 The Michelin Air X is announced, the first radial tyre for aircraft.

Michelin becomes the majority shareholder in the French tyre firm Kléber-Colombes.

1982 Michelin develops an association with Dunlop in producing a new tyre/wheel design which reduces the effects of a puncture at speed. The tyre, designated Michelin TDX, is produced in volume at the Dundee factory the following year.

1983 At a Buckingham Palace ceremony, HRH Prince Philip, the Duke of Edinburgh, presents François Michelin with the Prince's Award of the Plastics and Rubber Institute.

The use of front seat belts becomes compulsory in the UK.

Heavyweight Boxing Champion Henry Cooper being shown the correct way to regroove a truck tyre, on the occasion of the opening of a new Avis truck depot in Norwich in 1979.

Sean Kelly (Ireland), winner of the Michelin-sponsored sixth stage of the Milk Race, which finished in Stoke on-Trent on 5 June 1976.

trend which would cause a progressive erosion of profit over the next five years. This resulted in drastic restructuring measures which, regrettably, were implemented in the 1980s with the closure of the Belfast and Aberdeen plants. Such action was inevitable given the decline of the British automotive industry, the pressure on manufacturing costs, the emergence of good-quality products from non-European sources, and the loss of traditional export markets around the world.

Even so, Michelin UK still represented more than half of the UK's total tyre manufacturing workforce, a position that reflected the efforts made by all its employees to serve its customers, maintain efficiency, uphold quality and remain innovative and competitive. In fact, during the second half of 1980, the home market collapsed to such an extent that the only opportunity to keep sales up was to export. However, exporting was becoming increasingly difficult due to the strength of the pound. Nevertheless, Michelin UK managed to do so – over 60 per cent of UK production was destined for export. In this way, the factories were kept going and jobs protected.

Coincidently, on 1 January 1982, Michelin Tyre Co. Ltd became Michelin Tyre Public Limited Company, a change that resulted from the requirements of the Companies Act 1980 which made it obligatory for all publicly quoted companies to end their titles with the letters plc.

The prospects for 1982 were not rosy either. Tyre markets had shrunk, at home and abroad, exporting had become more difficult, and stock inventories rose. In 1981, UK truck production had dropped to 50 per cent of 1980 levels while car production, although better, was still down on the previous year.

Yet against all the odds, more Michelin tyres were sold in 1981 than in 1980 in the car, truck, tractor, earthmover and cycle tyre sectors of the UK replacement market, an achievement that took place against the background of a sharp fall in total market demand and savage price discounting by competitors. However, the original equipment market had shrunk – over the two years 1980 and '81 UK car production dropped by around 35 per cent, truck production by more than 50 per cent. Meanwhile, the world recession was reducing the opportunities for export sales.

However, recognising the need to reduce costs and output at this time, Michelin had implemented a five-day production week towards the end of 1980, largely eliminating week-end working and overtime. This dropped to four days in the middle of 1981 and did not return permanently to full, five-day working until 1983. Various schemes were introduced to encourage older employees to

retire early and for employees in general to consider voluntary redundancy. This was to set the trend for the years to come and Michelin began to develop systems that would provide help and support to employees, at whatever level, for new employment or retirement.

Employee Advice Centres were created at Stoke and Mallusk in 1983. Manned full-time by Michelin personnel, these centres provided advice on such matters as state benefits, employment opportunities, retraining and education, and investment. Government and local enterprise agencies were invited to assist by providing lectures and one-to-one discussions by specialists in areas such as becoming self-employed, obtaining enterprise allowances and understanding tax issues. This system of employee support has been used throughout the periods of major change in Michelin's UK organisation, such as during factory closures and the transfer of activities from one location to another. Michelin has received tremendous support from local and government agencies during times of great difficulty for its employees, and has been sincerely grateful to them all for the work that they have done.

The 1982 financial results, published in June 1983, showed the first loss in living memory for Michelin's UK operation. This was to be the first of three such losses, from 1982 to 1984 inclusive, resulting in a total deficit of £38 million over the period, excluding £66 million allocated to restructuring costs, largely redundancy payments. The launch of the new MX car tyre range in 1983 was a step towards gaining more sales, but the signs overall were not bright.

The archives tell us that the mid-1980s was not the brightest period in the life of the company. Industrial disputes were commonplace and some-

Monsieur Bibendum was a regular participant in the Belfast Lord Mayor's Show. This picture is from 1981.

Bibendum in action at BikEx 77, an event organised by the South Yorkshire Police.

world's tyre manufacturing industry.

The 1980s also saw significant changes in the commercial side of operations. The local sales structure was reorganised, involving a rationalisation of the number and size of premises throughout the British Isles. In 1977 the network comprised 38 branches/depots, by 1985 this had been transformed into 24 commercial distribution centres, and within seven years this number had been halved.

The painful restructuring of the early 1980s bore fruit in 1985 – the company recorded a profit of £18 million, the first for three years. This was a relief to all concerned and gave comfort and recognition to all the employees in the UK. The positive trend continued for several years, but the industry was still facing ever-growing pressure on its margins, largely as a result of the flow of cheaper products from overseas. Things were definitely better, but there would be much more sustained effort necessary in the years ahead to remain competitive, both within Michelin and externally.

Michelin UK's financial performance remained relatively stable until 1993 when market conditions deteriorated once again: European vehicle registrations dropped dramatically, cars by 15 per cent and trucks by 20 per cent. Price competition was keener than ever, especially in the UK where Michelin's turnover fell 12 per cent. Although employees had made major efforts to keep the rise of expenses down as low as 2 per cent, the reduced turnover resulted in a trading loss, the first since 1984. New ways of working and organising the business were needed to keep costs down. Contracting out non-core activities became commonplace: catering, site security, cleaning and aspects of maintenance, logistics and distribution. Two particular initiatives were to see a revolutionary change in the way that the company went about its business.

Long before the 1990s, Michelin had established links with local business and enterprise agencies, often providing help and expertise to other organisations that needed specific skills. In matters such as occupational health and training, areas where Michelin had considerable experience and knowledge, the company was regularly solicited for advice or support. It was decided to formalise this somewhat ad-hoc response through the formation of a separate group, initially managed by the Personnel Department. The group was called Michelin Pioneering Consultancy Group (MPCG) and was set-up at the beginning of 1993. MPCG could now offer professional services on a consultancy basis using in-house personnel. The idea was extended to Michelin's other UK sites and a network established which has since seen the group bought-out from the company and now trades

times lengthy. The announcement made late in 1982 that the Mallusk factory would close was a tremendous shock to the UK organisation, although it continued in production without difficulty, right up to the actual closure in October 1984.

Despite the work that had been planned and done to stem the UK Group's losses and return the company to profit, it was still insufficient. The UK's tyre manufacturing capacity was still too great and so further measures were needed. An announcement was made in January 1985 that major changes would have to take place. Burnley factory would stop producing wheels, van-type tyres and rubber compounds, while Stoke would concentrate on car tyres and the production of tyre components for use at other sites. Stoke's truck tyre production and the cycle and inner tube manufacturing workshops would close. All remaining activities would see changes in work patterns, notably in terms of moving to continuous (24hr, seven-day) working, a trend which had started at Burnley in 1983. Twenty years on and continuous operation is a feature which is commonplace throughout the

successfully as an independent concern in its own right, regularly providing Michelin with specific consultancy services. In the case of the Dundee factory, a separate wholly owned Michelin subsidiary, Xm Services Ltd, was created in 1995. This company provides a vast range of support services to the factory site and also sells its services to external clients in the Tayside region, and further afield.

These two examples demonstrate the flexibility of approach that is to be found in Michelin. Nothing is written in stone or fixed for ever and changes take place as often as business needs demand. The setting-up of a British office in 1904, rather than using agents, was found to be necessary to ensure the optimum business growth at that time. The creation of a factory in 1927 and the subsequent manufacturing growth in the 1960s and '70s was essential to respond to the explosion in demand for Michelin's radial technology. The reduction in Michelin-owned depots, branches and warehouses since the start of the 1980s has been a reflection of the trend towards third-party logistics specialists and, more recently, the efficiency of electronic communications systems.

One major change which affected the company's operation world-wide was the decision, in 1996, to change from a largely nationally or country-based organisation to one which is international and largely product-based. Today, there are product line groupings such as car and van tyres, two-wheel vehicle products, aircraft tyres and travel publications. By way of example, this structure enables the entire organisation of truck tyre activity, be it manufacturing, marketing or sales, to be managed as one entity across the European continent. Research and development continues to innovate and respond to customers' needs while support services, such as information technology and finance, provide their expertise across the range of product lines. Michelin's organisation in the British Isles reflects this new international structure, with new European groupings having been formed in recent times. These include a financial shared service centre responsible for many of Michelin's core accounting activities in Europe. Originally developed at Stoke-on-Trent in September 1999, the centre was expanded and relocated to Manchester in October 2002.

Another initiative, created in the UK and run from Stoke-on-Trent, was Michelin Lifestyle Limited (MLL). Michelin and its world-renowned mascot Bibendum are among the strongest brand names on Earth and not surprisingly, many individuals and organisations long for the chance to own such brand equity. It has immeasurable value as a result of over 100 years of use, generating instant awareness and a feeling of quality and reliability. Although in the past, Michelin has developed some products outside its core-business of tyres, tyre-related products and travel publications, these have tended to be associated with vehicles, such as pressure gauges, tyre levers and compressors, or directly related to Bibendum in a publicity sense. The company has not entered the market for 'associated' products in the way that other companies have.

This policy changed with the creation of MLL. This company was created in 2000 and works with The Licensing Company (TLC), a London-based specialist, to promote the Michelin brand by entering new, non-tyre related, consumer markets world-wide. Michelin does not make the products but allows others to do so, under approved licences. This venture is now well established and is introducing the Michelin brand in many diverse ways to consumers around the world. It may be a set of snow chains or a powerful trolley jack, a first aid kit, or a chef's apron sporting a starry Bibendum, a pair of tennis shoes incorporating Michelin's rubber technology, or a set of workwear. The product range is growing by the week and Bibendum is now to be seen popping up in even more places!

A culture of training for all ages

Michelin has always upheld a strong tradition of training, which represents a fundamental part of the company's culture throughout the world. It exists to develop skills and knowledge among its employees, of all ages, so that they can undertake specific jobs and, wherever possible, develop a career in the company, although this may often mean one or more changes of direction as the years pass. A teenager, for example, taking an engineering apprenticeship may find him or herself in charge of personnel later in life; a customer service assistant may become the head of the purchasing operation, or a fork-lift truck driver could become a technical service manager, and so forth. These fundamental career changes are not uncommon

within the Michelin organisation and represent a concept of flexibility which has existed in the company for many years.

Following the initial training of factory personnel that took place in the mid to late 1920s, with the establishment of the Stoke facilities, the first extensive training scheme run by Michelin in the UK evolved out of the national needs that became apparent during the war. A government scheme was set up whereby unskilled workers were trained at engineering factories to work as fitters and mechanics. After training, successful applicants were absorbed into industry as 'dilutees' and a good many of them ultimately made a long career with the company. Post-war, the government, recognising the need for improving industrial efficiency, encouraged best practice and ran a course called 'Training within Industry' for factory supervisors. Michelin participated, ultimately running the course internally. This led to the review of hourly-paid charge-hands' rates of pay by individual assessment, ultimately leading to merit-pay and monthly salaries for such employees.

Around this time, a training programme for young persons began to be formalised. Previously there had always been a craft apprentices school in Clermont-Ferrand which turned out carpenters, bricklayers, fitters and electricians annually. These youngsters, who were also trained in physical education and singing, did not necessarily become

employed by Michelin after training however. By 1948, Michelin at Stoke had established a similar form of apprenticeship training. Reg Sweetmore was one of the first entrants and, in recognition of gaining a First Class City & Guilds examination success in electrical installation work, he received a slide-rule from the company. Reg was one of 21 apprentices in that first group of young trainees, a group that was to set the scene for many hundreds of engineering, rubber-technology and administration apprentices over the next 57 years.

A *Bibendum* house journal article of 1949 reporting on the new apprentice scheme stated that 'Young lads desirous of learning a trade are interviewed in the first place by an apprentices committee consisting of Mr Barraclough (Head of the Engineering Department), Mr McCombie (Head of the Labour Office), Mr W. Parton of the Engineering Department and Mr R. Dennis, Apprentices' Supervisor. The lads selected are tried on various jobs in the Engineering Department and if they show particular aptitude for one of the many different branches they are placed on that job. For one full day each week they attend the Stoke Technical College and their wages are paid by the company. If they progress satisfactorily they may eventually be selected to take the Diploma Course which means a complete six months at school. Such selections are not made by the company – the lad's own efforts at college earn him the right. A teacher from the college suggests that a suitable person be allowed to take the six months' course and the company has always agreed, in both the interests of the person concerned and the future of good engineering'.

The scheme progressed to such an extent that within three years a dedicated Apprentice School was opened at Stoke, in September 1951. This replaced the previous system whereby craft apprentices were trained by attachment to the appropriate departments, to learn a particular trade. The training was given in a traditional way, 'Nellie fashion', little different from that employed in the British engineering industry since the 1920s. George Swift was the workshop instructor and Jack Riseley was the physical training instructor (PE was equally important in the scheme) for the first group of eleven boys who entered the new school.

As the years passed, the success of the scheme in producing quality, skilled craftsmen was judged to be such that a purpose-built 8,000ft² building was erected on the factory site in 1955, to serve as the Engineering Apprentices Training School. Seventeen boys joined that year, several of whom were ultimately to complete 40 years' service with the company.

As Michelin's UK group of factories expanded, starting with Burnley in 1960, so did the need for skilled engineers and technicians. Apprentice schemes were extended progressively to all sites, encouraging applications from young men and young women alike. To establish an ethos of excellence, encourage a spirit of competition and promote the recognition of achievement, merit awards were presented to individuals within each group of annual intakes. This practice developed into the holding of special presentation events, attended by apprentices, parents and local dignitaries, and usually featuring a special guest speaker. Representatives of major customers such as motor manufacturers, senior personnel from national training organisations and chiefs of industry, have all been welcomed as VIPs at Michelin training awards functions throughout the UK over the years.

The apprentice training scheme, established in France and taken up in the British Isles, was originally based on the methods proposed by the Swiss industrial psychologist Alfred Carrard who wrote several books on training-related topics, notably Le Chef, sa formation et sa tâche ('The manager, his training and his job'), published in 1956. The

A pair of 50-tonne Caterpillar 773 dump trucks at a demonstration held at Bagshot, Surrey in October 1981, to show the fuel-saving benefits of radial tyres on heavy earthmoving machinery.

principle was to train through a technique of personal observation and self-criticism, but the training programme has never been confined to the classroom and the workshop. Developing the individual's overall competences has always been paramount; apprentices have been given physical training on the sports field, in the gym or in the swimming pool. Moreover, from an early date, Michelin apprentices were encouraged to participate in the activities of both the National Association of Boys' Clubs and the Duke of Edinburgh's Award Scheme. Community projects have also been encouraged and many young people over the years have given support to local factory initiatives with projects associated with schools, elderly persons and those with disabilities.

Other training routes have also been available to potential young Michelin recruits. The Youth Opportunities Programme, the Youth Training Scheme and Modern Apprenticeships are just some of the initiatives with which the company has been involved since their inception. Although the systems may be different, the company's philosophy of supporting young persons' training has not changed since the first schemes of the late 1940s.

On the adult education front, Michelin's success with winning six National Training Awards is an indication of the quality and status of training in the organisation. The first award, gained in 1987, was for a novel computer-based training system. The Awards' patron, Sir John Harvey-Jones, commented that 'training is essential'. He added

that 'the National Training Awards give public recognition to exceptional training programmes, such as Michelin's'. Ballymena factory has won three Awards over the years, a unique achievement in the tyre industry.

As with youth training, adult training has taken many forms over the years as systems and procedures, and the types of training evolve. Pure 'chalk-and-talk' disappeared many years ago, to be replaced by systems which are more sympathetic towards allowing individuals to learn at their own pace. Electronic methods are now much more commonplace and computing courses ever-popular. Today, the company trains its employees in a wide variety of courses such as health and safety, IT, finance and language. As ever, the company's maxim remains 'not to be trained, but to stay trained'.

One adult course which today may seem somewhat quaint and old-fashioned was far from that when it was introduced in the mid-1950s. At that time, Michelin started a training scheme for potential supervisors, be they existing or prospective employees, and which had several unusual features, including visits to external organisations to learn about such matters as local government. It also included instruction on how to use a slide-rule. Probably its most interesting feature, however was that it set trainees the task of building a bridge from prefabricated parts. The bridge exercise duly became legendary among Michelin personnel and management, from its inception until it was phased

This GM Transmode, developed in the UK in the late 1970s, was a special test vehicle used by Michelin for many years throughout the 1980s. It was based on a conversion of a 26ft American GMC Motor Home, completely stripped of its internal living accommodation, and powered by a GMC 455 V8 engine.

out in the late 1970s. Groups of trainees were required to erect and dismantle a bridge across the River Churnet in the depths of the Staffordshire countryside. The task – somewhat similar to that used by the Army for leadership training today – was designed to reveal personal characteristics which could otherwise be discovered only by seeing candidates in action as supervisors. Over a three-day spell at the bridge site, with Youth Hostel Association accommodation thrown in, groups of eight to ten trainees would be monitored and assessed as they set about the bridge-building task, as previously outlined at a factory briefing. Many candidates passed, despite their considerable apprehension brought on by the horror stories related by those who had undergone the test before them – but there were others who had great difficulties and soon realised that the supervisor's life was not for them!

Most of what is described above is training as it relates, either directly or indirectly, to tyre production. However, when tyres are made they still have to be sold, and sold in a highly competitive market. The training of those people directly involved in

sales is therefore just as important and serious a business as the education of manufacturing personnel. Undoubtedly, the enviable reputation for thorough product knowledge enjoyed by Michelin's sales force throughout the trade has been established and supported by the vast range of Michelin publications produced over the years. One of the earliest of these was the 1911 Instruction Plates book. Back in the 1950s, Michelin representatives (as they were then called) were trained in the London office in Fulham Road. The tough, three months' long course included practical experience in the field when trainees would visit Michelin users in the London area or at one of several depots or marshalling areas, where vehicles were always available for inspection. There, for several weeks, the trainees carried out physical examinations of vehicles, checked tyres and pressures, measured alignments, off-sets, clearances and calculated axle loads, all in order to determine the right tyre for the job.

Much of this philosophy, which stresses the paramount importance of providing correct advice and service information, was fundamental to a new

Knowing the track surface temperature is critical when deciding which compound tyre to use in F1 racing. Here, the surface is being checked at Brands Hatch in 1983, when Michelin secured first, second, fourth and seventh out of the first eight home.

training initiative which came about in 1980. It was in April that year that the Michelin Training & Information Centre (MTIC) opened in Battersea, London when 250 members of Michelin's UK commercial organisation, the country's largest sales force of any tyre company, assembled there for a sales conference. Having found a suitable building towards the end of 1978, work started on converting the 2,500ft² premises into a facility which would cater for both internal and external needs. The prime objective was to develop a closer relationship with customers, enabling the company to understand better their problems and, at the same time, to encourage a mutual exchange of information. MTIC was designed to cater for six basic training functions: technical matters such as tyre fitting, balancing and repairs, commerce, sales techniques, administration, understanding stock control systems, point-of-sale advertising, computer technology, accountancy, construction – providing a free advice service on extending premises, and lastly, personnel affairs including a consultancy service advising on recruitment and issues of employment law.

In 1985, Michelin's London-based commercial operations moved to Harrow and ultimately, in

1993, on to Watford, where full training facilities were provided for both internal and external needs, as before. With the transfer of these functions to Stoke-on-Trent in 2001, however, MTIC has now found a new and purpose-designed home at the south end of the factory site. Incorporating all the latest tyre inspection and maintenance equipment, this location provides modern lecture and teaching facilities, available for employees and customers alike.

Michelin's approach to training in the British Isles therefore continues the traditions and principles laid down by the organisation over a hundred years ago. Whether it be in the commercial or the manufacturing sectors of the company, there is a regular approach to reviewing business needs, such that employees can be kept abreast of new developments and be trained and prepared to meet the challenges of the future.

A century of Michelin advertising

Michelin has never shied away from advertising in the British Isles. The early advertisements, which

An irreverent sense of humour has always been a feature of Michelin's propaganda, right from the start. The cartoons seen here, published in the UK company's house magazine, Bibendum, *during the 1970s continued this tradition of poking fun at the authorities.*

The New MICHELIN Tyre

by combining

★ Michelin's 3 great tread inventions: the Zigzag design — the slits — the variable pitch (*i.e.*, every step of the tread pattern varies in length from the next).

★ an unrivalled technique in casing construction.

★ the use of the finest materials.

It costs you no more!

gives

100% tyre silence — The variable-pitch Zigzag pattern prevents sound generation and corner squeal, **throughout the tyre's life** and at all speeds, even when the wheels are enclosed by coachwork.

longest life . . . . — The tread has a deep, thick-set pattern and is made of a special rubber compound highly resistant to abrasion. It gives 20% more mileage and is immune to the scooped wear usually caused by independent wheel suspension.

greatest safety . . — Slits, especially shaped and slanted to oppose skids from every direction, add further to the multiplicity of gripping edges provided by the short pitch Zigzag pattern.

perfect comfort — The unique suppleness of Michelin tyres protects both passengers and car by absorbing road shocks at the source.

Typical Michelin publicity material of the 1960s, featuring Monsieur Bibendum, as ever.

MICHELIN
MOTOR-CYCLE
TYRE PRESSURES

	PRESSURE IN LB. PER SQUARE INCH									
	12	16	18	20	22	24	26	28	30	32
SIZE			Load per tyre in lb.							
2.50/2.75-19			140	160	180	196	210	230	250	266	280
3.00-19			160	180	200	220	240	270	300	330	350
3.00-20			160	180	200	220	240	270	300	330	350
3.25-19			200	240	280	315	350	375	400	420	440
3.50-19			280	320	350	370	400	425	450	475	500
4.00-18			360	400	430	465	500				
4.00-19			360	400	430	465	500				
3.50-8	195	230	246	260	274	290	306	320	336	350
4.00-8	260	300	320	340	356	370	386	400	416	430

Find the laden weight of your motor-cycle — front and rear — then from the table above read the **PROPER PRESSURES**

led readers of *The Advertising World* to select Michelin's adverts for the Baltimore Exhibition, the exuberance of the Fulham Road building, the technical demonstrations given around the country, and the company's signage on almost every tyre outlet up and down the land, were all proof of the company's faith in publicity as an essential means to win customer loyalty and create a popular household brand name.

O'Galop's extraordinary graphic interpretation of Monsieur Bibendum as the jousting medieval knight, complete with lance and shield, 'whose strength is as the strength of ten because my rubber's pure' appeared in Britain very soon after Michelin took up offices in Sussex Place in 1904. The poster bears the name and current address of The Michelin Tyre Co. Ltd, suggesting that it was produced in 1905. In subsequent years, right up to the 1920s, Michelin's British advertising followed the lines of that produced in France, and perhaps some other European countries as well, yet was also specific to Britain.

The First World War provided a particularly potent theme, promoting Bibendum's support of the Allies by supplying tyres and beautifully printed maps of the highest quality and reliability. 'Endurance will gain the Victory' he says. Economy is also a theme, as is long life and resilience. Bibendum even proposed a 'link with France' through a Channel Tunnel made of tyres!

Generally speaking, the bulk of this early publicity material was advertising in motoring magazines. For example, a series of adverts with political themes ran in *The Autocar* at the start of 1913. In these, Bibendum is seen speaking in debates in the Houses of Parliament, but he later becomes something of a politician himself by campaigning on certain issues, such as public concern about the proliferation of publicity hoardings around the countryside. An advert for *The Autocar* in April 1913 shows our rotund tyre man stating: 'Bibendum is removing his road signs – but what he takes away with one hand, he gives back with the other. The names and addresses of Michelin stockists are given, together with a great deal more information, in the 1913 edition of the Michelin Guide'. A company campaign which had great public sympathy therefore gave an opportunity for product promotion.

Despite ever-increasing demand, things did not always run smoothly for the tyre makers in these pioneering days of motoring. Business could be cut-throat. Claim and counter-claim were regularly made by one particular company regarding the efficacy of its products when compared with its rivals. Dunlop and Michelin had serious disagreements at this time, no doubt harking back to the ill-feelings created during the patents war at the turn of the century. Issues such as who was making what tyre where and at what selling price became an issue of libel between these two strong adversaries. The affair resulted in a court case in 1917, from which neither side could claim much credit. In March 1917, *Bicycling News* reported that the case, after a seven-day trial, left the parties pretty much where they were before!

During the 1920s and '30s, technical developments of tyre design and construction such as the advent of the Comfort, Super Comfort, RLP and STOP tyres, led to 'technical' advertisements. Readers were encouraged to check pressures and vehicle loadings. This resulted in a style of publicity which became, to some extent, standard across Michelin's main European markets. Even the rear covers of Michelin's maps sported identical adverts, printed in the appropriate language of the country in question.

One point that intrigues students and collectors of Michelin's advertising and publicity, is the question of its house colours, or, in modern parlance, its corporate identity. Although blue and yellow were always used throughout the second half of the 20th century – as now in the 21st – it is clear that during

What's small, fat and travels on the Metro?

Michelin's new low-profile XZX 70's are original equipment on the Mini Metro HLS and 1·3S.

MICHELIN
The Great British Radial.

The acceptance of the new low-profile XZX 70s as original equipment on the Metro mini-car was proclaimed by this advertising campaign, which ran in 1980.

the first half of the last century a more flexible approach was allowed; while yellow was consistently used, blue was not. There are many examples of brochures, price lists and advertising material produced in this period, which have green, orange, brown or red as the predominant colour, either by themselves or in conjunction with yellow. Hence, we can be sure that the advertising designers and creators at that time were by no means constrained by the rigid rules of a Corporate Standards Handbook of the kind that is prevalent in many large international organisations in more recent times.

Soon after the Second World War, Bibendum made a welcome return to the scene, appearing in British advertisements extolling the virtues of a wide variety of products including tyres for cycles, electric vehicles, three-wheelers, scooters, cars and trucks. In the days before the advent of the tubeless

tyre, inner tubes, especially those made from the 'finest red rubber' were also given a high profile. Maps and guides too were widely publicised, as travel and holiday motoring became more commonplace, following the abolition of petrol rationing. The variety of the content and consumer appeal displayed in this press and poster advertising was wide indeed, as is illustrated by the following examples: 'For Town and Touring you are on safe ground with Michelin tyres' (cycle, 1956); 'Michelin. Strong, Silent, Supple and Safe! – the tyre for the Bond Minicar' (1958); 'Every Renault produced in Britain is fitted with Michelin Tyres' (1959); 'Michelin supply 120 countries from their factory at Stoke-on-Trent' (1960); 'Vauxhall are fitting Michelin Tubeless Tyres on the new Victor' (1961); 'Michelin 'X' tyres are fitted as standard equipment on the new Leyland 12c Comet range'

In 1969 Michelin entered the music business again, by releasing a disc entitled 'The Michelin Theme', written and recorded by Manfred Mann.

Drive the long runner.

Switch to **MICHELIN**

Get a grip in the wet.

Switch to **MICHELIN**

Sweet cornering.

Switch to **MICHELIN**

Feel at home on the road.

Switch to **MICHELIN**

I'm clinging in the rain.

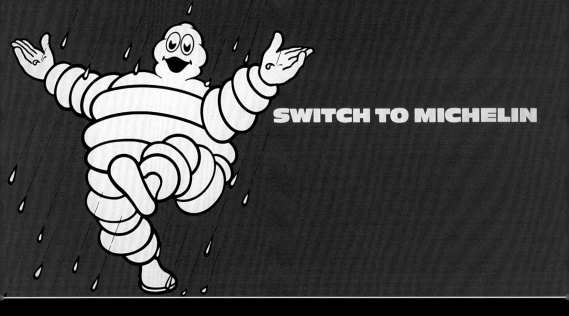

SWITCH TO MICHELIN

Rain-drops keep falling off my tread

SWITCH TO
MICHELIN

(1962); 'Twice the Motorist on Michelin 'X' tyres' (car, 1963); 'For absolute mastery of his scooter, the good rider chooses Michelin ACS Scooter tyres' (1964), and so forth.

On Saturday, 2 February 1957 Monsieur Bibendum made his debut on British television when Michelin's first-ever TV advertising campaign in the UK commenced on Midlands ITV (Channel 8). The 60-second commercial featured a soundtrack spoken by the famous radio actor, Stephen Jack, who gave Bibendum his voice in the film. In January 1959, a new commercial promoting the benefits of the 'X' tyre with the copy theme 'Twice the mileage, Twice the grip' followed, this time screened across the nation-wide ITV network in all areas where a total of more than three million motorists were resident. Three more films were created for the 1960 campaign, bringing 'X' tyres to the notice of 66 per cent of all motorists in Great Britain. Naturally, these TV campaigns were supported by extensive press advertising in national Sunday and daily newspapers.

March 1960 saw Michelin release the first of what was to become a series of three audio recordings, all of 7in single size playing at 33⅓rpm and encased in smart sleeves. The first, simply called 'A Michelin Gramophone Record' depicted Bibendum on the front, playing a guitar: one side of the enclosed record told the listener all about Michelin 'X' tyres while the other side – by way of a change – said it with music. No fewer than 20,000 copies of the disc were produced, with two different sleeves, half for the British Isles, half for North America. The second of these flexi-format records appeared in August that year and was entitled, simply 'Michelin X'. This was another double-sided recording with a sleeve depicting a Spanish or Caribbean band of six Michelin Men, of which 70,000 copies were produced in various languages. Record three was made as part of the ZX car tyre campaign in 1969. This was a one-sided recording, on a solid disc to be played at 45rpm. Entitled 'The Michelin Theme', it was composed by Manfred Mann and Mike Hugg of the then popular rhythm-and-blues group Manfred Mann, whose records Do Wah Diddy Diddy and Mighty Quinn had previously topped the pop charts. Their disc was actually the full length version of the soundtrack of the 1969 Michelin TV commercial.

The somewhat bland monochrome press advertisements of the 1950s and '60s were soon eclipsed in the public consciousness, however, when Michelin's first major launch of the radial tyre took place in the autumn of 1965. 'Learn the supple secrets of 'X' became the slogan seen in a salvo of publicity that was the biggest barrage yet fired off by the company in the UK. Twin campaigns were

mounted: widespread press, TV and other advertising media being aimed at the motoring public in general, with a comprehensive technical briefing for the garage trade. Full-page advertisements were taken in such papers as the *Sunday Mirror, The Observer, The People, Sunday Express, Weekend Telegraph* and *Sunday Times*. Each of the adverts offered a copy of a special publication on request, of which half a million copies were printed. In the spring of 1967, the 'X' campaign was reprised with the inclusion of the recently launched asymmetric XAS high-speed tyre. Television commercials and extensive press advertising continued as did a range of brochures, including novel additions such as a flick book.

The theme continued into the 1970s when a new advertising campaign started on 4 April 1971, promoting ZX and XAS tyres. The message signalled to both employees and customers alike was that the company had decided to concentrate solely on the manufacture of radial-ply tyres from then on. The crossply tyre was consigned to the history books, and in the years to come; 'radialisation' would be adopted by all sectors of the pneumatic tyre market, from two-wheeled machines to

Michelin introduced the MXT 80 high-speed tyre in 1992 to complement the MXT 70 and MXT 65, for cars with top speeds of 110mph and above. This advertisement appeared in the British motoring press in March that year.

Opposite and Previous Page: The switch to Michelin Campaign, introduced in 1982, was surely Michelins biggest advertising effort to date in the UK.

aircraft. Michelin's faith in its patent of 1946 was well-founded.

As the inexorable public acceptance and use of the radial progressed throughout the decade, Michelin took full opportunity to publicise the concept from the point of view of both its technical benefits and fuel-saving advantages. Typical was the campaign mounted in 1973 showing Bibendum sitting astride a ZX tyre with the headline 'Drive a Michelin – It makes a good (car/truck/coach …) better'. Next, at the 1974 London Motor Show where Michelin tyres took the greatest share of original equipment fitments among the vehicles on display, the company took a virtual monopoly of the advertising space along the subway approach to Earls Court from the London Underground station. Twenty Maps and Guides posters were displayed with 80 'Drive a Michelin' posters, many of which were overprinted with a car manufacturer's name, such as 'See us on Ford', Rover, or Ferrari etc.

Advertising also played a major part in the sales drive mounted in 1975. Motorists were invited to start a Michelin Economy Drive to convince them that Michelin's were the most economic tyres to run in the long-term and that the company's experience and technical superiority were second to none. This message was driven home on TV, in the national press, the motoring press, in a poster campaign and, in a rapidly growing media at the time, commercial radio. The 1976 campaign saw the ZX

symbol replaced by a new visual device showing Bibendum sitting 'astride' a tyre, sideways-on, as a solid black circle. The idea was intended to take the customers' eyes away from a specific type of tyre, the ZX, and to gain a more general awareness of the Michelin radial.

The advertising bombardment continued in 1978 with a massive poster campaign using sites all around the country. The first message was 'Switch to Michelin – for longer life' and this theme was developed over the months that followed. Posters were also fixed to the sides of Michelin's delivery fleet – some 200 vehicles at the time. TV advertising followed, beginning on 1 March. Two years later the slogan 'The Great British Radial' was introduced, in recognition of the fact that by then the Dundee factory, in particular, was supplying large quantities of radials to the British market.

Of all Michelin's advertising campaigns in the UK that have run in more recent years, the 1982 effort was probably one of the most widely appreciated by the public. This brilliantly conceived nation-wide press and poster campaign devised by the company's current London advertising agency, Connell, May & Stevenson used humorous visuals, once again bearing the message 'Switch to Michelin and insist on no other', but now displaying Bibendum riding not on a tyre or even a car, but on a wide range of domestic articles including fish, fruit, vegetables and tubes of glue. 'Stick your load to the road'; 'Get a grip in the wet'; 'Drive the long runner'; 'Sweet cornering' and so forth were among the witty copy-lines.

In 1988, there was a return to TV when two contrasting commercials produced by the company's new agency, Ogilvy & Mather, were screened. In one the action took place in the heat and sand of the desert, while in the other it was located in the freezing cold of the Arctic North. Despite appearing to be authentic on the screen, they were both filmed in Pinewood Studios.

In more recent years, Bibendum has continued to blow his own trumpet with gusto. Even so, progressively over the past 20 years, UK publicity campaigns have tended to follow more closely those that were devised for products commercialised throughout Europe as a whole. The MX car tyre was a case in point. Made extensively in the UK for home and export markets, and launched in 1983, this tyre represented Michelin's next generation of radials for the popular family cars of the day. An 80-series tyre (the cross-

sectional aspect ratio of height/width), the MX range was developed in subsequent years into the MXL and MXV derivatives having lower profile and higher speed ratings.

As the MX range evolved, just as all tyre ranges do over the years, then European markets were supplied with the MXT in 1990 and then the MXT80 in 1992. Thus, the publicity material for these tyres began to display a European approach, reflecting the convergence of motoring styles and habits that was taking place across the Continent, and more particularly, the emergence of vast numbers of European and Japanese vehicles that followed a common design approach and used common components. And so, in the light of this ever-increasing standardisation in automobile design and construction, which greatly reduced the diversity and individuality of the motor vehicle population to be seen on the roads of Europe, it was natural for Michelin to adopt a pan-European style of advertising.

Major European campaigns took place to launch the Pilot car tyres in 1993, the Classic tyre in 1994 (these were made extensively in Dundee) and the Energy tyre in 1997, for which a major European TV campaign was developed. These car tyre launches have always tended to eclipse Michelin's other product launches, but there has been considerable advertising activity in these other areas as well. This included the 1991 cycle tyre press advertisement depicting a runner with 'the wrong boots', a 1992 press advert with Bibendum dressed in fatigues

promoting XML truck tyres for off-road mobility, a brand campaign in 1993 showing Michelin tyres in action in the most challenging conditions such as on the Space Shuttle, the promotion of Michelin winning the RASE silver medal in 1994 for its agricultural tyres, a 1995 press advertisement using the 1994 World Superbike Champion and Michelin rider Carl Fogarty, an advert in *Le Shuttle* magazine in 1996 promoting Michelin maps and guides and the 'Hard Case' press advert used to promote Michelin's earthmover tyres at the time of the bi-annual Buxton Hillhead Quarry Show. These are just a few of the many examples of advertising material created by Michelin in the British and Irish media up to 1998.

That year was something of a milestone for the company, not just in Britain, but throughout the world. In recognition of the creation of Bibendum, the Michelin Man, a hundred years previously, the year was designated the 'Year of Bibendum'. Many activities took place organised by the British company including carnival days for employees at all sites, the mounting of a major interactive exhibition during the Motor Show at the NEC, the raising of £100,000 by employees for Children in Need, and the celebration of Bibendum's actual birthday. This special year achieved a very high level of press coverage and many company advertisements promoted Bibendum's achievements, culminating in a special advertisement showing Bibendum blowing out the 100 candles on his cake.

Following the extensive corporate activity of 1998, the next year saw a return to more normal levels of advertising and publicity, promoting the now well-established individual product lines. A special poster campaign for car tyres was launched, designed to make drivers understand the importance of tyres

In more recent years, Bibendum has continued to blow his own trumpet with gusto – though UK publicity campaigns have tended to follow a pan-European approach.

As well as its famous maps and guides, Michelin Travel Publications has been publishing the well-known series of I-Spy children's books since 1991. These were first seen in the 1940s.

Opposite: In 1985, Monsieur Bibendum shared the limelight with Roger Moore, star of the James Bond film A View to a Kill, *on posters advertising the movie around the world.*

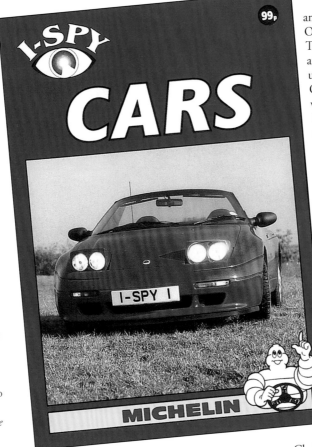

and explode the myth that all tyres are the same. One poster featured World Rally Champion Tommi Mäkinen, while the second poster drew attention to the fact that Michelin was the unique supplier of tyres for the Space Shuttle. On the corporate front, advertising hoardings were used at Premier League football grounds. In 2000, the corporate theme was developed in a special series of TV advertisements for the British Isles. Called the 'Show Me the Logo' campaign, it was backed up with point-of-sale material and brochures. The TV commercials presented individuals who wanted assurance that the Michelin logo was on the tyres of the vehicle they were buying, or having serviced. The philosophy behind the campaign was to make customers aware that when they see the Michelin logo on their vehicle's tyres, they can rest assured they are the highest performing and most reliable available.

Over the last five years, Michelin's advertising in the British Isles has exploited certain specific themes such as the company's involvement in motorsport (F1, rallying, World Superbikes etc) and the environment, promoting fuel-efficient tyres, tyres that minimise soil damage, and the company's international support for sustainability in the widest sense of mobility through its annual international Challenge Bibendum initiative. The adverts may no longer be developed purely for the British and Irish markets, but their themes are those which relate to the European consumer of today.

More awards and accolades

Michelin is proud to have received many awards and accolades during its presence in the British Isles, not merely those presented for innovation in product design and performance, but also those for excellence in other areas such as advertising and publicity, employee training, and product and system quality.

Most notably, Michelin's success in the development of the radial tyre was given particular recognition when, at a ceremony held at Buckingham Palace in 1983, His Royal Highness, Prince Philip presented François Michelin with The Prince Philip Award of the Plastics and Rubber Institute, for the company's 'courageous and determined development and popularisation of the radial tyre'. The

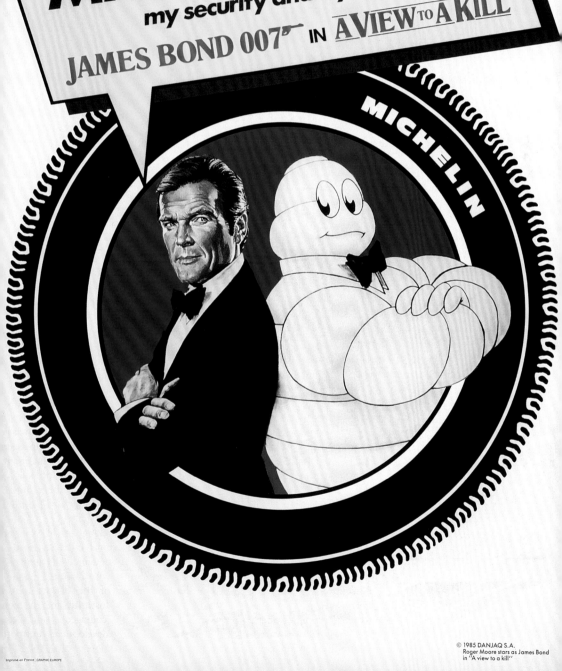

The Michelin Training and Information Centre, which opened at Battersea in 1980.

Award had first been made in 1973, but so far had only been awarded to plastics manufacturers and organisations; Michelin was the first recipient within the rubber industry. Earlier, in 1977 and again in 1982, the company won two Queen's Awards for Export Performance.

These were not the first occasions when Michelin had received an honour connected with the British Royal Family, however. On 26 February 1908, Marc Wolff (André and Édouard Michelin's brother-in-law), who was appointed the first managing director of the Michelin Tyre Co. Ltd, received permission to use the Royal warrant. At first, the style was: 'By appointment to His Majesty the King', but then, after the monarch's death on 14 October 1910 it became 'By appointment to the late King Edward VII'. Clearly, Michelin's products were as much approved by royalty and the nobility as they were by other motoring pioneers of the Edwardian era!

In 1987, the government, through its agency the Manpower Services Commission, instituted a major new initiative to reward training excellence.

Called the National Training Award Scheme, this was to be an annual competition designed to raise the awareness of the importance of training and encourage more companies to start taking it seriously. In the first year, 1,143 organisations entered and Michelin was one of 60 chosen as winners. The company's submission was for a computer-based training technique used in the truck tyre retreading department. In the years to follow, Michelin was to win no fewer than six more National awards and several Regional awards. Of the National awards, three went to the Ballymena factory, one to Burnley and two more to Stoke.

Another Manpower Services Commission honour, the Fit for Work Award, was presented to Michelin in 1984 in recognition of outstanding achievements in the employment of disabled people.

Today, Investor in People recognition is expected of any modern, caring and progressive organisation, but back in 1993 it was something unusual and special. Michelin gained this recognition then and has achieved re-accreditation, as demanded by the standard, every three years since for all its sites.

Left: François Michelin (third from left) went to Buckingham Palace on 1 November 1983 to receive The Prince Philip Award of the Plastics and Rubber Institute from His Royal Highness.

Below: His Royal Highness, Prince Philip, the Duke of Edinburgh, tours the Training Centre at Stoke-on-Trent in March 1978. Here, he is seen signing the visitors' book after being presented with a specially produced pen-set by the Chairman of the Apprentice Council.

The company has also received numerous quality awards from motor vehicle manufacturers, from vehicle fleet operators and from dealer organisations throughout the British Isles. Some are directly product related, others are service related and some represent complete system audits such as at factory level. In more recent years, environmental issues have become more important and the awards received often reflect this aspect as well.

Michelin does not forget its community responsibilities either and has received numerous awards as a result of welfare and social initiatives conducted within its factories and operational bases. When Michelin employees celebrated the centenary of the creation of Bibendum, the Michelin Man, in 1998, as part of these celebrations, its UK employees made a substantial contribution towards the cheque for £100,000 presented by the company to the BBC Children in Need Appeal that year. Michelin continues to support various local charitable and enterprise events and has taken pride in having received recognition for this work.

1985–1994

The X revolution rolls on and on

Bibendum meets James Bond

In 1985, Monsieur Bibendum found himself sharing the limelight with Her Majesty's Secret Agent 007, James Bond, on posters advertising the film *'A View to a Kill'*. In this adventure Bond is trapped underwater in a Rolls-Royce that has been pushed into a lake, but he manages to survive the prolonged immersion and escapes to safety by breathing the air from the car's Michelin tyres.

This was actually the second James Bond film in which Michelin products played a starring role. Four years earlier, in the 1981 movie *'For Your Eyes Only'* Bond had avoided capture by driving a Citroën 2CV (shod with Michelin tyres of course) at high speed in a death-defying leap across a mountain canyon to evade capture. The car was specially modified for the film with a strengthened floor pan and suspension plus a roll-over cage, and was powered by a 1,015cc GS engine. To capitalise on this publicity, Citroën produced a limited edition of 300 cars for the French market. Called the 2CV 007, these were painted bright yellow and bore stick-on bullet-hole decals as a decoration.

Bibendum Mascots & Memorabilia

In 2000, after more than 100 years of continuous presence on the transport scene, Michelin's famous mascot and trademark, Monsieur Bibendum, was chosen as the world's best-loved and most widely recognised brand symbol by a panel of design and advertising professionals. This ranked the Michelin Man well ahead of other internationally renowned logos and symbols, such as the Mercedes-Benz three-pointed star or the McDonald's arches.

Over the years, the Michelin Tyre Company's activities in the British Isles have made their own important contribution to the popularity of this avuncular roly-poly character, so that in Great Britain today (as market research studies reveal) he is recognised by no less than 98 per cent of the population. For example, late in 1956, the company announced the availability of 'a striking advertising figure for your delivery van'. This was the imposing plastic model of Bibendum that had recently been launched in the British Isles and which has since become a highly prized collector's item, to be found at auto-jumbles and on Internet auction sites commanding prices only dreamed of in the 1960s.

Made in Brownlow Mews, off Grays Inn Road in Central London by a company called Models (London) Ltd, at the specific request of the UK company, the figures were about half a metre tall. The man responsible for sculpting the original was Joseph Nardini who produced the model from which a plaster cast was taken. An acrylic cast was then made from the two parts of the plaster cast (front and back) and this was then plated with silver and nickel and copper backed, to produce the master mould, into which 6lb of PVC was poured. After hardening at 500°F in an oven for 23 minutes, the model, with its strengthening internal metal matrix, was ready to be removed and then fettled to eliminate all the flashing around the edges. It was then sprayed to a more perfect whiteness and the painting of a yellow and blue sash completed the operation. When attached to a vehicle by his metal skeleton, Bib was ready for the road!

These models of Bibendum were produced in large numbers for many years to be distributed to customers and drivers. Used in this way, in due course they became a familiar sight throughout the 1960s, perched on top of vans and trucks all over Britain, not just those owned by Michelin but also on vehicles belonging to many other transport fleets. Proud owners often fitted a light inside so the mascot could be seen at night. Carrying an illuminated Michelin Man on the roof of a long-distance lorry cab was regarded as a good luck charm by many drivers, especially when travelling in the Middle East or Africa, where tribesmen would often attack European trucks to steal their cargoes. Drivers protected by a Michelin Man would find their lorries were untouched – the natives

1985 Michelin House is sold to the Conran Octopus publishing firm.

In May, truck tyre, cycle tyre and inner tube production ends at the Stoke-on-Trent factory.

Monsieur Bibendum appears in posters announcing the James Bond film, *A View to a Kill*.

Imported cars in the UK now account for 55 per cent of sales.

1986 René Zingraff is appointed as a co-managing partner of the Michelin Group. Earlier in his career, he had spent six years at the Stoke-on-Trent plant, between 1970 and 1976, as head of the laboratory.

The 120-mile long M25 London orbital motorway is completed.

1989 Michelin is first to develop a computerised route-finding service. It is made available free of charge on the French Minitel information service, a forerunner of the Internet.

New vehicle registrations in the UK peak at 2,373,391 private cars. The British motor industry achieves a record all-time high production of 1,299,082 cars.

1990 Michelin acquires the Uniroyal Goodrich Tire Company in the USA.

1991 On the retirement of François Rollier, François Michelin appoints his son Édouard as a co-managing partner.

1992 Michelin creates an entirely new tyre manufacturing process, known as C3M. It can produce a tyre in an eighth of the time previously taken while using 60 per cent less energy than conventional processes.

In the UK, road deaths fall to 4,229 people or 187 per million vehicles. This is the lowest since statistics began in 1926 when 4,886 people were killed, thus giving the country the claim to have the safest record in the European Community.

1993 Michelin's energy-efficient Green X tyre range is launched, to promote better fuel economy. The first environmentally-conscious tyre, it cuts rolling resistance by 20 per cent, thus reducing fuel consumption.

After almost eight years at Lyon Road in Harrow, the company's Commercial headquarters moves to Watford.

1994 The Channel Tunnel is opened. The Michelin brothers had foreseen this link with France 80 years earlier.

considered Monsieur Bibendum to be a god and would leave any lorry carrying one well alone, for fear of divine retribution.

Unfortunately, the very great popularity of these Bibendum figures created certain problems and safety concerns, which eventually led to their removal from the company's vehicles. First, children were known to climb on cab roofs to get closer to the model and it was felt that this would inevitably result in accidents. But secondly, an illegal trade in counterfeit versions developed. These were not as well made as the genuine article, as was revealed one day by an incident on a motorway, when one of these crude forgeries broke free and fell off a heavy goods vehicle, shattering the windscreen of an overtaking car. Luckily its driver, a journalist, was unharmed, but after recovering the bogus Monsieur Bibendum, he began an investigation, with Michelin's assistance. A private detective was hired to track down the source of these fakes and it was soon discovered that a plastics factory in the Netherlands had been making large quantities of the counterfeit Michelin Men and distributing

them to garages all over Europe. The maker – who had been sending supplies to England by the trailer load for many months – was taken to court and convicted. Another forger of false Bibendums was tracked down to Turkey and raided by the police some time later.

Naturally, Bibendum's three-dimensional presence was never confined to the roof of a van or lorry! Then, as now, he was regularly seen at events throughout the land, either as a large inflatable figure or in human form, in a suit being worn by a company employee. He might be in a car, riding a bike, presenting an award, or just wandering about in the crowd at public gatherings, simply because people like to have him around, bringing jollity and good humour to all occasions.

Recognising Monsieur Bibendum's timeless appeal to young and old alike, Michelin, through its subsidiary Michelin Lifestyle Limited, has been progressively launching a new range of highly collectible toys, models, clothing and other items featuring the convivial figure. Visitors to the company's boutiques in Paris and Clermont-

A highlight of 1988 was the Michelin City Centre Cycling Championship. During the summer, races were held in Glasgow, Northampton, Ipswich, Lincoln and Sheffield.

Michelin won the Silver Medal award of the Royal Agricultural Society of England in 1988, the first time that any tyre-making company had received this prestigious engineering prize. The judges observed that no other tyre company in the world would allow the single-figure inflation pressures permitted with Michelin's agricultural tyres, a vital factor in reducing ground pressure and avoiding soil compaction. This was the sixth year in which the company had exhibited at the Royal Agricultural Show, fielding an impressive stand.

Ferrand can choose between a wide selection of items including genuine, legitimate and thoroughly lifelike figures of Bibendum himself!

Michelin and the London Rubber Market

Although natural rubber is believed to have been used in Central America for more than 2,000 years by the Aztec and Maya peoples, the earliest documented knowledge of its unique properties did not reach Europe until the beginning of the 16th century. This was through the writings of the first Spanish conquerors of South America, around the year 1500. The Conquistadors reported on the remarkable quality of the footwear and domestic utensils used by the native tribes of the Amazon region in Brazil, which were made from the latex or resin obtained from a local species of tree, eventually named Hevea Brasiliensis. However, it was not until two centuries later that the first proper scientifically conducted botanical and chemical investigations were made into this remarkable substance, which is elastic, malleable, impermeable and a non-conductor of electricity. In fact, it was the English 18th century scientist Dr Joseph Priestley who gave the substance its name. He found that a lump of solidified latex would erase lead pencil marks written on paper, so it became his 'rubber'. Later, it was with seeds imported from Brazil to Kew Gardens in 1876, and thence exported onwards to Ceylon, Malaya and Indo-China (Vietnam), that the

extensive rubber plantations, some originally owned by Michelin in the Far East, were established. The hevea tree can only be grown in equatorial or subtropical climates.

But before natural raw latex rubber could be transformed into the durable yet flexible material that constitutes the major, most visible component of the modern automobile tyre, three important discoveries had to be made. The first, the process of vulcanisation, generally credited to the American Charles Goodyear, can be dated to 1839. Vulcanisation or hardening involves the addition of sulphur and various other substances before heat is applied, usually in the form of steam. This solidifies the rubber while leaving it elastic, at the same time improving its resilience and resistance to changes in ambient temperature. The term vulcanisation itself was not Goodyear's, and neither did he initially register his discovery. Instead, it was probably coined by the Scottish pharmacist Charles MacIntosh (the inventor of the eponymous rainproof clothing) who obtained a sample of Goodyear's substance in or around 1841. His scientific consultant, Thomas Hancock, analysed it and filed for a British patent in November 1843.

The second really significant step forward in the evolution of the automobile tyre was the discovery, originally in 1904 but adopted in 1912, that the addition of carbon black greatly extended the life of a tyre by improving its resistance to abrasion. Before carbon black was incorporated in the mixture of ingredients – initially only as a colouring agent – 4,000 miles was the maximum life

Michelin has developed a long-standing relationship with the Staffordshire manufacturer of construction and agricultural machinery, JCB, which has employed Michelin tyres across its product range for many years. The JCB 712 articulated dump truck, launched early in 1988, was fitted with Michelin XGL TL tyres as standard.

expectancy of a motor tyre. Michelin began using carbon black in 1917 and found that it doubled or tripled tread life, to an average of 9,000 miles. Until the 1920s, the bulk of supply came from the USA, but then 'furnace' carbon black processing plants came progressively on stream in other parts of the world, such as at Stanlow on Deeside in the UK. Today, carbon black additives represent some 20-25 per cent of the weight of the modern tyre.

The third phase of development occurred as a consequence of the Japanese invasion of Indo-China in 1941, when most of the countries producing natural rubber were over-run and occupied for the remainder of the Second World War. Fortunately for the war effort, a great deal of research had already been conducted into so-called synthetic rubber materials which, having similar though not identical properties, could be used as substitutes for the natural article in the making of tyres for military vehicles. After investing huge sums of money and constructing 51 factories, the United States and Canadian governments succeeded in producing prodigious quantities of these materials, namely GRS (Government Rubber Styrene), Neoprene, Butyl and Buna, sufficient to overcome the shortage of natural rubber and ensure the continued production of tyres and other essential items. In 1941, only 6,259 tons of synthetic rubber were made, compared with 775,000 tons of natural rubber. Yet, by 1946, the position had been

reversed with the production of 761,699 tons of synthetic rubber as against 277,597 tons of natural rubber. After the war, the output of the natural rubber industry subsequently recovered, so that by 1952, world-wide production stood at 1,785,000 tons, more than twice the amount of synthetics manufactured, 877,769 tons.

Today, the world's total annual rubber output is approximately 180,000 kilotonnes, made up of 40 per cent natural and 60 per cent synthetic, but only 15 per cent of natural rubber is produced by industrial plantations. The remainder is produced by small-scale subsistence farmers as a cash crop, 93 per cent in Asia, 5 per cent in Africa and 2 per cent in South America. An estimated 30 million people are reliant on the production of natural rubber for their livelihoods.

Despite the advent of synthetics, however, natural rubber remains an important constituent of modern-day tyres, being used alongside synthetic rubber in varying proportions according to the intended function of the finished product. For cars and light commercial vehicles, the mixture is typically 30-40 per cent natural and 60-70 per cent synthetic, while for trucks it is usually 80 per cent natural and 20 per cent synthetic. For tractors and earthmoving machines the proportion of natural rubber is even higher. A typical four-tonne earthmover tyre contains one tonne of natural rubber, the equivalent of the yield from five rubber trees collected over two decades.

For centuries, London has been the world's leading financial and commodity dealing centre and a premier international forum for the trading of natural rubber. So it was not surprising that, once established in South Kensington at the turn of the century, Michelin should take advantage of its proximity to the London market, to purchase additional supplies of this essential raw material, here in the United Kingdom.

In the period up to the Second World War, much of the company's requirement for natural rubber was provided either from its own large estates in French Indo-China and Indonesia, which had been planted in the 1920s, or on long-term contracts with other large estate owners in the region. Nevertheless, Michelin's London Rubber Department maintained a modest presence in the market to ensure an absolute continuity and flexibility of supply for all its factories world-wide, by buying-in extra supplies on the open market, as and when required.

From about 1931 until his retirement in 1957, the department's manager was a certain Mr J. L. Benezy, who combined this work with other financial functions at Fulham Road. He became a very

well known figure among the market dealers in the City, establishing for the company a lasting reputation for scrupulous observance of contracts – all struck, verbally, over the telephone. On one occasion during the Second World War when France was invaded and the factory at Stoke-on-Trent was cut off from the parent factory in Clermont, Mr Benezy was successful in diverting a ship from Singapore containing a cargo of rubber bound for Clermont, to Stoke.

When commercial activity began to increase after the war, however, Michelin established itself in Singapore where loose rubber, meeting the company's own exacting quality specifications, was purchased from local suppliers and delivered to independent warehouses, to be packed into bales ready for shipment to Europe.

By the late 1950s, the natural rubber plantations of the Far East could no longer meet the requirements of world markets requiring uninterrupted supplies for the manufacture of a multitude of products. Consequently, Michelin established extensive new company-owned plantations in Brazil and Nigeria to supplement those in Vietnam and Indonesia. Supplies from these new sources eventually replaced the rubber produced in the Far

Monsieur Bibendum brings a smile to the face of Her Majesty the Queen as she pauses at the Michelin stand during her tour of Expo 800. This was a major exhibition staged to show off Dundee's commerce and industry during the 800th anniversary of the city, in 1991.

Michelin's famous vintage bus, created in 1980, played a major part in Dundee's octocentenary celebrations, providing a courtesy service to and from the Expo 800 site.

Eastern plantations, which by the 1970s had either ceased production or were no longer operating under Michelin ownership.

Increasingly, as demand from Michelin's factories began to outstrip the 'in-house' supplies from its own plantations, greater recourse had to be made to the markets, both here and in the Far East. In those days, the rubber bought was, mostly, RSS1 (No. 1 ribbed smoked sheets) top quality, packed in bales of approximately 250lb and shipped by conventional steamers to Liverpool. From there, the consignments were collected by lorry and brought in to Stoke-on-Trent. Interestingly, the rubber shipped from Singapore had to be loaded into barges for transfer to ocean-going ships in the harbour, and this was done by gangs of sure-footed 'coolies', each carrying a 250lb bale on his shoulder, down a narrow plank from quay to barge! It was not until the 1960s that containerisation began to take over and a more mechanised form of transportation and delivery emerged.

Although the London Rubber Market was, slowly, having to cede its supremacy to Singapore, considerable profits/savings could still be made by 'playing' the two markets. Depending on their relative 'positions', a cable or fax would be received

from the Singapore office (a Michelin company called SMPT) listing its requirements, which the London Rubber Department – or Michelin (Rubber Purchasing) Ltd, as it became in 1974 – would then buy, in addition to its own needs. This enabled SMPT to stay out of the Singapore market and thus, force prices down. In its turn, this had an influence on the London market.

As with any commodity market, the supply of natural rubber was very sensitive to world events, particularly as the transport lead-time was many weeks long. The outbreak of the Korean War in 1950 resulted in extremely high prices, as did the closure of the Suez Canal in 1956. The latter was even more problematic as, until ships could be re-routed around the Cape, nothing arrived in Europe. However, despite having some thousands of tons marooned on the ships *SS Melampus, SS Agapenor* and *SS Sindh,* it was the proud boast of Michelin's rubber buyers that, by locating unsold tonnages held in UK and European warehouses, not one factory either in the UK or on the Continent was forced to cease production due to lack of rubber. Likewise, when the Panama Canal was closed temporarily, London was able to provide temporary aid for Michelin's American factories.

But as time wore on and Michelin's operations became more and more globalised and multinational, it was decided that all rubber buying should be centred on Singapore, and Michelin's long history of operating on the London commodity market came to an end in 1996.

Michelin and motorsport

As we have seen, in the early days of motoring the founders of the company, the Michelin brothers, were well to the forefront in promoting motorsport, even to the extent of participating in many of the first racing and trialing events, and in organising or sponsoring others.

However, in July 1913, they published an advertisement in *The Autocar* stating that 'Michelin no longer takes part in races… in order to curtail all useless expense. Races always demand the expenditure of time and energy, for which the customer pays. For us, races are now even more than useless. In the past we gained invaluable knowledge by taking part in them, but today they have nothing new to teach us. In the period during which we raced, we won 94 per cent of the races in which we participated. The enormous majority which we have over all our competitors is a better indication of the superiority of our products than any noisy manifestation'. So it was that Michelin's direct involvement in racing and rallying activities stopped for more than 45 years.

The increasing promotion and acceptance of the Michelin 'X' radial tyre throughout the late 1940s and 1950s demanded a change of policy, in order to reap the publicity benefits that can only come from success in major international competitions and especially rallies involving standard production cars. So, while not actually entering team cars under its own name, Michelin began to encourage the use of its products by motor manufacturers and sporting drivers taking

part in major international events, such as the Monte Carlo Rally, that were likely to produce favourable press reports and comment.

Sure enough, major national publicity in the British press ensued following Michelin's success with 'X' tyres in the January 1958 Monte Carlo Rally. X tyres equipped not only the winning car, a Renault Dauphine driven by Guy Monraisse and Jacques Feret, but also those in third and fourth positions. The following year, a works-entered team of Ford Zephyrs fitted with Michelin Xs won the team prize in the 1959 Tulip Rally. The Monte Carlo Rally has always held a special significance and appeal for British motorsport enthusiasts, as Michelin recognised by lending its support to competitors. For example, in February 1966 a Michelin service van from the Maidstone branch, manned by two UK employees, gave free tyre advice to all 37 British entrants in the rally as they passed through Dover.

Michelin also featured prominently in the annual Mobil Economy Runs staged throughout that era. In 1965 every class winner in that year's event was on 'X' tyres, while in 1973, 21 of the 40 crews taking part were using Michelin tyres. In fact, four out of the five class winners on the two-day event, which ended at Harrogate on 20 March, were running on ZX or XAS tyres. In the 1975 Total Economy Drive, five of the six class winners were on Michelin tyres. The three-day event was staged over a 950-mile course, finishing in Harrogate on 25 March.

By then, Michelin had been selling motorcycle tyres for racing in the United Kingdom for a number of years. Not surprisingly, however, the

One of the Michelin Pilot Team Ford Escort Cosworths, which became a common sight on the rally scene in the British Isles between 1993 and 1995.

Wayne Gardner, riding a Honda shod with Michelin tyres, wins the British Motor Cycle Grand Prix in 1992.

successes achieved on the Continent during 1974 increased the demand from British and Irish riders who had already used Michelin tyres or had heard of our successes in Europe. Michelin's Racing Service (technical advice and assistance and tyres for sale), was introduced in 1975 at main events in Great Britain, which produced a considerable increase in Michelin's fitments.

In July 1977, Michelin entered Formula One motor racing, with the world's first radial tyres expressly designed for motor racing, fitted on a Renault-Turbo in the British Grand Prix held at Silverstone. The following year's British race was another milestone for the company, when Carlos Reutemann won at Brands Hatch in his Michelin-shod Ferrari.

February 1978 saw Michelin's winning success in the Brazilian Grand Prix. In its edition of 11 February, *The Autocar* commented: 'There is something clean and healthy about a tyre company winning the Monte Carlo Rally and the Brazilian Grand Prix on the same weekend'. That was the start of a remarkable series of grand prix successes,

which continued until Michelin announced in 1984 that it would cease participating in Formula One. In 1981, the Northern Ireland born driver John Watson won the British Grand Prix in front of 85,000 spectators at Silverstone. He was driving an all-British McLaren running on Michelin tyres. The following year, Niki Lauda also won the British Grand Prix in a Marlboro McLaren, fitted with Michelin tyres. Michelin's 21st century performance in F1, following its re-entry into a sport which is a very different game than that of 25 years ago, is proving challenging and currently bodes well for a dominant position.

Meanwhile, on the rallying circuit, the good results went on and on. Michelin-shod cars filled four of the top eight places in the 1980 Lombard RAC Rally, generally reckoned to be the toughest in the world. The victor, Henri Toivonen, in a Talbot Sunbeam Lotus, was the youngest ever driver to win the event. This was the first time that Michelin had entered the RAC Rally with serious intent. In 1984, following wins at the 1000 Lakes and Sanremo rallies in a Michelin-shod Peugeot

205 T16, the Vatanen-Harryman duo made it a hat trick by winning the RAC Rally outright in November. In 1982, the Michelin-shod Opel Ascona 400, driven by Scotsman Jimmy McRae, won the Manx Rally and clinched the RAC Open Rally Championship for the second year running.

The MG Metro 6R4, a four-wheel-drive, mid-engined, six-cylinder two-seater car, running exclusively on Michelin competition tyres, was launched in 1984 while the following year, Michelin began a successful partnership with Renault in the R5 Turbo Championship. In 1987, the company sponsored all four TT Production Races on the Isle of Man, while in the Lombard RAC Rally the following year, seven out of the top ten cars came home on Michelins, including the winner. The 1990 event marked the end of an era for rallying in the British Isles when Michelin announced that it would be ceasing active participation in this form of motorsport in future, to concentrate on World Sports Car racing, having won 94 World Championship rallies since 1973. However, despite the reduction in full-support service enjoyed by

In 1992, Michelin opened its new Commercial Distribution Centre at Basildon, Essex – one of 12 such depots located at strategic points on the motorway network around the country. Quite a contrast to the typical depots of the late 1930s, only fifty-odd years earlier!

Michelin tyres were also the choice of sand yachting star Max Plummer who ranked as the sport's British Junior Champion in 1989. His yacht raced with two 1³/₄-inch Type Y Cyclomoteurs on the front and a single 4.50 A Comfort at the rear.

Lincoln (3 August), Sheffield (5 August). The Championship provided the perfect opportunity to promote Michelin's Hi-Lite range of competition tyres.

Undoubtedly, one of the most successful motorsport publicity campaigns in the company's history resulted from its partnership with Ford, launched in 1993. Motorsport enthusiasts from throughout the British Isles and Europe gathered around the Ford stand at the Autosports International exhibition in January to witness the unveiling of a new motorsport venture – the Michelin Pilot Team Ford. A new team of Ford Escort Cosworths was formed to carry the banner of both Ford and Michelin in the 1993 Mobil 1, Top Gear British Rally Championship. The two cars, in a striking blue and yellow livery designed in Michelin's UK publicity studio, were driven by Malcolm Wilson in Group A and a Group N version by Scotsman Robbie Head. This was the first major team sponsorship by Michelin for a motorsport programme in Britain. The eye-catching cars provided plenty of opportunity to gain maximum exposure for the company's new Pilot range of car tyres. The cars looked really stunning, securing them plenty of media coverage, and a place in rallying's history. A Pilot car was often used at product presentations, dealer events and for internal promotional purposes.

For the 1994 season, the team comprised two Group A Escort Cosworths, driven by Malcolm Wilson and Irishman Stephen Finlay. In addition to the British Championship, one car was entered in the Irish Tarmac Rally Championship. In 1995, the last year of the Pilot Team Ford, the cars were driven by various 'star' drivers such as François Delecour in the Vauxhall Rally of Wales, and Ari Vatanen in the Cumbrian Rally. Other cars, such as the Renault Mégane entered in 1999, continued Michelin's success in the British Rally Championship.

Previously, in 1993, Michelin had entered the British Touring Car Championship (BTCC), providing tyres for the official factory Renault 19 and Peugeot 405 teams. Each team comprised two cars. Later in this first season for Michelin, Ford Mondeos, BMWs and even a privateer all took the lead from a well-established company slogan and 'Switched to Michelin'!

Michelin supported Alfa Romeo, Ford, Peugeot and Renault plus some privateers in the 1994 BTCC season. Success was achieved early on in this most popular circuit racing series, and at the June Brands Hatch race, Michelin-shod cars were utterly dominant. By the end of the season, Michelin-tyred cars had won 14 of the 21 races, as well as taking 19 second places and 17 thirds – all in all, 50

drivers in previous years, Michelin-shod cars still came first and second in the 1991 RAC Rally!

Two-wheeled competition was not neglected either. In 1984, the new radial motorcycle tyre was used experimentally by a number of teams in various races, before its superiority was proven beyond doubt in the 1985 season. It proved to be an annus mirabilis in 1989 when Michelin riders achieved winning success in both the Isle of Man TT and the Shell British Motor Cycle Grand Prix events, the latter held at Donington. Later, in the 1993 season, there were many motorcycle successes, notably at the Isle of Man TT where Michelin occupied 12 podium places, more than all the other competitors put together.

In 1984 Michelin announced that it would support the Isle of Wight Classic, Britain's biggest professional cycle race. This led to the sponsorship, in 1988, of the professional City Centre Cycling Championship held in various venues: Glasgow (8 May), Northampton (19 June), Ipswich (23 June),

podium places from a possible 63. In the Privateers' section, Michelin recorded 17 wins from 21 starts. With rapid and ever-increasing success in the BTCC, even more teams chose Michelin's products for the 1995 season.

In the five years from 1993 to 1997, Michelin carried three drivers to the BTC Championship crown: 1994 Gabriele Tarquini, Alfa Romeo; 1995 John Cleland, Vauxhall Cavalier and in 1997, Alain Menu, Renault Laguna. Michelin's 100th BTCC race win, on 20 September 1998, was marked by the presentation of a cheque for £1,000 to winner James Thompson at the Silverstone race. The 100 wins recorded amounted to a total considerably higher than all the other tyre manufacturers' scores put together. Further success in the 1999 season meant that Michelin's dominance in the second half of the 1990s was such that the company won the exclusive rights to supply the entire BTCC grid with tyres for the three years 2000-02.

In 1997, racing driver Tim Sugden created a scholarship for budding motorsport stars. With support from Renault and Michelin, this became a partnered sponsorship leading to the opportunity for the winner to race in the Clio UK Cup Championship. This, like its in-house training schemes for youngsters, was an example of Michelin's support for people showing potential in an activity directly allied to its business. In 2002, the scholarship visited Ireland for the first time and 14 Ballymena factory employees succeeded in getting through to Round Two of the competition.

Although motorsport in the 21st century may be rather more sophisticated than that of the 19th in terms of its technology, its presentation and, most certainly, its prizes, it is still reliant upon the spirit of competition that comes from the meeting of friendly rivals. A century ago, Michelin was renowned for promoting and developing its products in races for two and four-wheel machines alike, held at events throughout Europe such as the Gordon Bennett Cup series, the precursors of F1 as we know it today. Over the ensuing 100 years, British and Irish competitors and vehicles have contributed a great deal to the development of mobility through their exploits, and Michelin has been proud to assist them along the way, whether at Brands Hatch circuit, through the forest tracks of Wales, or even on the tarmac of a typical city centre high street.

The port of Southampton acquired six new Finnish-made Valmet container handling machines in 1992 for its busy container terminal. Capable of moving 50-tonne loads at up to 28mph the carriers work up to 16 hours a day. With all eight wheels expected to cope with weights of up to 11 tonnes each, only Michelin tyres were judged fit for the job of keeping import and export freight moving.

1995–2005

Into the New Millennium

1995 The pneumatic automobile tyre is 100 years old.

The Space Shuttle lands on Michelin radial tyres. As sole supplier to NASA, Michelin makes special tyres able to withstand loads of about 146,000lb at landing speeds in excess of 250mph.

1996 The SMMT celebrates the centenary of the British motor industry.

Michelin's association with the London Rubber Commodity Market ends.

Michelin introduces an innovation in agriculture: the world's largest radial tyre for harvesting machinery. One metre in width it is able to carry very heavy loads (around 11 tonnes per wheel) at low inflation pressures to reduce pressure on the ground and avoid soil compaction.

1997 Michelin develops the revolutionary, vertically anchored tyre, ultimately designated as the PAX System.

1998 Monsieur Bibendum, the Michelin Man, celebrates his 100th anniversary.

Michelin develops the Delta Radial Construction concept, for high performance motorcycle tyres.

Michelin creates Challenge Bibendum, a global environmentally clean vehicle and sustainable mobility forum.

1999 Édouard Michelin becomes the head of the company.

Michelin introduces an ultra low-pressure tyre for earthmoving machines. It is 4 metres tall and capable of carrying up to 360 tonnes.

2000 Monsieur Bibendum is chosen as the world's best-loved and most widely recognised brand symbol by an international panel of design and advertising professionals.

All Michelin's UK commercial functions are regrouped at a new office development, Riverside, alongside the factory at Stoke-on-Trent.

2001 Michelin develops a new technology for aircraft tyres which enables Concorde to return to the skies.

Monsieur Bibendum returns to the Formula 1 motor racing scene.

After 74 years, November sees the end of all new tyre production at Stoke-on-Trent.

2002 François Michelin retires.

The steel cord production workshops at Stoke-on-Trent are closed.

Michelin opens a shared service centre in Manchester for European financial functions.

2003 Michelin awarded the EcoProduct of the Year for its Energy range of tyres at the Fleet Excellence Awards in London.

Fortune magazine rates Michelin as one of the top 50 most admired companies in the world.

2004 Michelin Travel Publications launches a new guide coupled with an annual award, 'Eating out in pubs' which features 500 of the best pubs to dine in throughout the British Isles.

Britain and France celebrate the 100th anniversary of the Entente Cordiale.

2005 The Michelin Tyre Company Ltd. celebrates its centenary.

According to the latest count from the DVLA, there are in the region of 31,207,000 vehicles on British roads including 26,240,000 private cars, 1,000,000 motorcycles and 3,967,000 assorted vans, lorries and other commercial and public transport vehicles. They are driven by approximately 31,500,000 drivers, 17,500,000 of them males and 14,000,000 females.

Thanks in no small part to the success of the steel-belt radial pneumatic tyre, individual mobility by motor car is now almost universal, just as André and Édouard Michelin had foreseen over a hundred years ago!

Tyres hired by the mile!

Naturally, the vast majority of Michelin's commercial vehicle tyres purchased in the UK are bought outright by the user, but even so, there exists a particular system of tyre use and payment pioneered by the company, where tyres are hired out on a usage basis throughout the bus and coach industry in the British Isles.

Introduced in the late 1920s, the Michelin Mileage Contract system means that those PSV operators subscribing to the scheme pay so much per mile for the tyres they use, while the actual tyres remain the property and sole responsibility of Michelin. This arrangement requires a comprehensive network of maintenance fitters, of course, to service the fleets of vehicles involved and, as such, a force of several hundred Michelin employees has been present in bus garages up and down the land for many years.

These fitters are expected to be able to recognise such things as mechanical vehicle defects, overloading, driver characteristics, and so forth. It is worth remembering that a tyre rendering 15,000 miles of service has revolved no fewer than 10,000,000 times, during which each and every part of the casing must flex the same number of times. This illustrates the importance of correct measuring and loading.

During the Second World War, the Mileage Contract Scheme's maintenance staff experienced a very heavy workload, in addition to their ARP and Home Guard duties. Many garages suffered damage from air raids, resulting in Michelin fitters working long hours alongside the staff of the client customers' premises in order to maintain vital national public transport services. Another difficulty was the introduction of synthetic rubber with all the initial complex problems that this technical development entailed.

Although the principle established over 75 years ago remains much the same today, the service has evolved and developed greatly, so that Michelin Fleet Solutions, the organisation responsible for this type of work, currently offers a considerably more sophisticated maintenance package for more than 30,000 vehicles which it services, now enhanced by the use of computerised statistics.

The distribution network expands and contracts

Since distribution represents the vital link between the producer and the customer, Michelin was keen to establish an efficient supply network from the very start of its presence in the British Isles. After using agents prior to 1904, the creation of the 'temporary depot', including transport, at Sussex Place marked the beginnings of the company's self-sufficiency. Once the Fulham Road premises were opened, a fleet of Renault vans was soon in evidence to show customers the strength of the operation. These vans worked in conjunction with official Michelin stockists, as they were called. The 1911 Michelin Guide to the British Isles devotes several pages to these stockists, describing the official publicity sign, the actual stock carried in terms of tyre sizes, and the firm's current conditions of sale, and location. A form which could be returned to Fulham Road was included with the guide stating that 'We ask our customers who wish to be kept informed of all our latest improvements which may interest them, to fill up the form given below. We shall be pleased to give free of charge all such information'. The first marketing campaign had begun!

Subsequent guides continued to show stockists and agents, using a friendly Bibendum head and an adjustable spanner respectively as symbols. After 1922, the air-cylinder symbol, indicating where Michelin air cylinders could be exchanged, was discontinued as the availability of compressed air at garages became more widespread.

Michelin's January 1920 price list shows the presence of two depots in addition to Fulham Road; these were located at 102-110 London Road, Manchester and 24-28 Berkeley Street, Glasgow. By December, Bristol (10 Welsh Back), Dublin (85-86 Middle Abbey Street) and Birmingham ('To be opened shortly') had been added to the list. All had similar dual telegraphic addresses, for example BIBENDUM, Bristol or PNEUMICLIN, Bristol, the latter being the form adopted for many years.

As sales grew, so did the network and by 1917 there were nine depots in addition to Fulham Road. However, the outbreak of the Second World War forced the closure of much of the network due to the scarcity of new tyres for the home market, and the lack of personnel, as a great many employees had volunteered (or were later called up) for active service. Surprisingly, few depots suffered as a result of the Blitz, even the premises in Liverpool escaped with the loss of a mere few windows. Despite heavy air raids on the cities of both Plymouth and Liverpool, not a single tyre was lost at the Michelin depots and they both remained open throughout the conflict.

The post-war years saw the distribution network grow with a vengeance. Sales were rising dramatically, thanks to products which were in great demand, notably the 'X' radial tyres. In 1950, the network numbered 21 branches (where orders were actually received) and depots (where tyres were

stored), scattered all over the British Isles.

Generally speaking, depots were attached to branches, with a branch manager being in charge of both. The branches and depots were also the base from which sales representatives operated. Not surprisingly, Fulham Road, serving the entire London area, had its work cut out to keep pace with the daily commercial demand. In 1954, a new five-cylinder, 100bhp 12-speed Foden truck was introduced to make the journey between Stoke-on-Trent and London several times each week, carrying tyres and tubes – the vehicle and its load representing a fully laden gross weight of up to 12 tons in those days!

From 1965 to 1977, the network numbered 38 depot and branches, the maximum number of locations ever, ultimately operating at a time when there were six UK factories, plus the commercial headquarters in Fulham Road. Such an organisation required a massive logistics operation to control the flow of production from the factories, the import of products not made in the UK but needed for the home market, the export of UK-made products to destinations throughout the world, and the supply of products to vehicle manufacturers and retail customers throughout the British Isles. Add to that the complexities involved

in supplying maps and guides to bookstores, and it can be appreciated why, by the 1970s, Michelin had developed an enviable expertise in transport, storage and distribution. Additionally, the company's expertise extended to designing and building storage premises, typically of 5,000m² in the 1980s, although some were increased by 50 per cent beyond that level.

Towards the end of the 20th century, however, the British road transport scene saw the arrival of specialist logistics operators. The use of these third party carriers, who were able to use their vehicles more efficiently, enabled distribution costs to be reduced dramatically. Previously, many vehicles in Michelin's own fleet would run seriously empty on their return journeys up and down the country. Trial exercises in operating with a mixture of company-owned vehicles and external companies led inevitably to the policy of contracting-out of the company's distribution operation to a third-party provider. This decision had the knock-on effect of reducing the need for storage premises and the network of depots gradually diminished to the point where, today, Michelin maintains only two major distribution centres in the British Isles. These are at Stoke-on-Trent and Basildon, where there is an 18,600m² company-owned warehouse.

This specially-developed ten-wheeled semi-trailer vehicle was new to Toleman's car transporter fleet of over 400 vehicles in 1990. It was designed to carry 12 executive-size cars – a load worth up to £250,000. Based at Brentwood in Essex, Toleman was transporting more than 900,000 cars a year, representing a retail value of almost £10 billion. Both the trailers and the Iveco tractor units were fitted with Michelins as standard.

Unipower (the company that bought Scammell from the Rover group), won a contract in 1991 to build what were then the largest civilian trucks ordered from a British manufacturer for many years. These Unipower S24 Contractor units weighing 45 tonnes were destined for oilfield support work in desert conditions and were specified to run on Michelin tyres.

Towards a cleaner environment

During the 1980s and early '90s, concerns about environmental issues were becoming more pressing, both nationally and internationally. Business organisations were put under the spotlight to determine the way in which their goods were being manufactured and transported, what happened to any waste products that were generated, and how their products performed in terms of their energy consumption and efficiency. These issues have always been of interest to Michelin and none more so than the question of recycling. Indeed, the re-use of tyre casings using retreading processes has been promoted by the company almost since the earliest days of motoring.

The Michelin Tyre Company's Repair Works, initially located at Barking in Essex, and subsequently incorporated in the Fulham Road building, was a service designed to prolong the life of a tyre wherever possible, thereby reducing the expenditure on new material. Retreading of truck tyre casings, in a process known today as REMIX©, has been in existence for almost 50 years and is now carried out at the Stoke-on-Trent site.

Michelin's introduction of the energy-efficient radial tyre in the 1940s, when compared to the crossply of the day, was a major step forward both in terms of fuel-saving and in the considerable extension of tyre life. In 1995, the company announced yet another important step on the road to reduced rolling resistance and hence, fuel efficiency, with the launch of the Energy range of tyres. The catch-phrase 'Driving down the cost of motoring' became the slogan for an advertising campaign which promoted the environmental benefits of the new tyre. Energy technology has been extended to other tyre ranges, notably for the transport sector where both fuel and tyre bills are at the top of the hauliers' lists in terms of operating costs.

On 12 November 1996, at an awards ceremony in London, René Zingraff, managing partner of the Michelin Group, received the AA Award for Energy Conservation from Sir George Young MP, the Secretary of State for Transport. The award recognised various benefits of the Energy range, not least that its ability to cut fuel consumption has helped to lessen the impact of motoring on the environment.

Beneficial tyre design in environmental terms is not limited to fuel efficiency and mileage however. It can reflect less obvious characteristics as in the case of Michelin's agricultural tyres. Michelin has won four prestigious Royal Agricultural Society of England Silver medals, in 1988, 1994, 2002 and

2004, for the performance of its agricultural tyres, tyres which can operate at single-figure inflation pressures and minimise soil compaction.

The factories have also contributed to improving their environmental performance, not only in terms of their production processes and the services which support them, but also in the physical environment around the sites.

Health & Safety issues

Just as health and safety matters have always assumed a very high priority in the affairs of the parent company in France, the same concerns were regarded as being of the greatest importance by the United Kingdom affiliate even in its earliest years, and remain so to this day. When the Stoke factory was being planned in 1926, provision was made for a surgery on site in anticipation of a large number of employees. The facility was built within the main tyre production workshop (Building No. 2) and comprised an area of 90m², largely separated into two distinct sections; one for men and the other for women. There were waiting and treatment areas, a drugs storeroom, a sterilisation unit, washing facilities and various other services. Details about the staffing of the surgery are sketchy, but it is believed that one nurse was permanently employed who was assisted by two temporary or occasional nurses, as the occasion demanded.

The first company doctor was Dr B. S. Bhandarkar who came from India. His was probably one of the first Asian families residing in the Stoke-on-Trent district and in the late 1920s, the young girls applying for administrative positions at the factory thought it most unusual to be interviewed by a coloured doctor. Like all the company doctors who have followed him over the years, Dr Bhandarkar was keen to promote good health and to educate employees about health matters. With this objective in mind, he participated in the MAC's lecture series programme and gave a talk on 'Diet and Fitness', as early as 1934.

Soon after the start of the war, in 1940, a new surgery building was erected between Buildings No. 4 and 13. Erected is perhaps not quite the right term, because it was half underground! In its new guise, it formed part of a decontamination centre, equipped with the needs of wartime very much in mind: anti-gas showers, emergency lighting sets etc. When post-war normality arrived, the contents were reviewed. Out went the air-raid precaution material and in came equipment more relevant to the needs of the day.

Once the house magazine *Bibendum* reappeared after the war, regular health topics were published to keep everyone aware of the facilities available and to promote good practice. Information came thick and fast: articles on corns, boils, teeth, the hygiene service available to women, the dangers of misuse of compressed air, etc. etc. Knowing how important it was to

Michelin tyres make a big contribution to British and Irish agriculture by helping farmers to obtain optimum productivity from their expensive machinery. When fitted on tractors these specialised low-pressure, steel-braced radials ensure that more power is transmitted to the ground, while on trailers, combines and other harvesting equipment they help to reduce soil compaction and hard-pan.

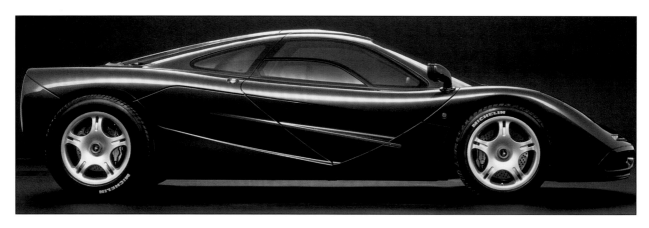

First seen in 1993, the McLaren F1 was the supercar par excellence and the ultimate in automobile engineering, design and technology. Capable of 230mph, it had a price tag of £540,000. Powered by a 6.1 litre V12 engine, producing 627bhp at 7,400rpm, it was equipped with Michelin FZ tyres specially designed and manufactured for McLaren.

provide some sort of medical cover for a round-the-clock, 24-hour production operation, the doctor of the day, Dr Hind, also encouraged the development of a first aid scheme throughout the workshops. Individuals, often volunteers, were given basic training and access to local first aid facilities. In November 1947 a film, First Aid in Factories, made and shown by Elastoplast, was presented to a large number of the first aid workers. An article published in *Bibendum* in 1947 indicated that 6,000 accidents were treated at the works infirmary in a year, although very few were serious, with fewer than 200 causing absence from work. Even so, the need and usefulness of such a medical facility was unquestionable.

In later years, employees had the opportunity to join a 12-week course, from which successful candidates would receive a first aid award from the St John Ambulance Association. The course members were not confined to those in the Medical Department itself as there were those from the site's security team as well as production workers and administrative staff.

Colds and influenza were just as problematical in the 1940s as they are today. With this is mind, and presumably with the practical thought of maintaining production plans, an ultra-violet ray lamp was purchased early in 1948, the installation of which was inaugurated with a popular, free winter sunshine course! Employees were regularly encouraged to use it as a means of preventing winter illnesses.

It was probably in August 1948 that the first approach was made to the company regarding the establishment of a blood donor service for the benefit of local hospitals. The idea was wholeheartedly accepted and it was on 17 November that year when 72 volunteer donors came to what was the first visit of a blood donor team to a factory in the Potteries. Then, like today, blood was always in demand and there was need of approximately 750 donors a week, according to the Blood Donor Service at the time.

That first session started a tradition which extended to other sites and has led to a steady flow of Michelin blood. The visit on 11 October 1950 solicited 112 volunteers and the Stoke service said: 'There are no arrangements in force for blood transfusion sessions at industrial establishments in Stoke-on-Trent other than those at the Michelin Tyre Company'. There was a steady growth in volunteers during the years of manufacturing expansion such that by 1972, 118 volunteers had attended at Burnley and 773 at Stoke. It was calculated that between 1964 and 1976, 15,500 pints of blood had been given by donors at Stoke.

Mass radiography became popular in the early 1950s and a unit came to Stoke factory in September 1952. It was a great success with 93 per cent of the workforce attending, making it the highest response in all industrial surveys of the unit at that time. The unit returned three times over the next six years achieving high levels of take-up on each occasion. Construction workers of Peter Lind & Co. were back on site in 1954 for production extensions and they too joined the radiography sessions.

The influence of the operation of the statutory occupational health service in France led Michelin's management to create a similar structure in the British Isles. As a result, for the first time, two new posts were made in 1958: a full-time doctor, Dr A. Childs, and a nursing sister fully trained in occupational health, Mrs M. Wright, to head the nursing team. The Medical Department now provided a full three-shift cover, but was still based in the old decontamination unit 'bunker'.

Medical professionals were by now regarding occupational health as a multi-disciplinary activity, involving not only doctors and nurses, but also occupational hygienists and ergonomists, and were looking much more at the control of the working environment. Michelin saw this as an important shift and itself began to look at working conditions with a view to tackling the hazards of noise, skin irritants, exposure to dust, fumes, chemicals and solvents, as well as accident prevention. The Medical Department worked closely with the Safety Department for its preventive programmes.

In 1963, a fully trained and experienced occupational physician, Dr C. Veys, was recruited to head the team and to complement the existing specialist part-time consultancy chest service then being provided by Dr M. Kennedy, who had replaced Dr Childs in 1961.

The impetus to improve conditions throughout the rubber industry was brought to a head when several coroners' inquests had brought to light cases of bladder tumours in rubber and cable workers. These cases related to the use of certain chemicals during the 1930s and 1940s. Serious harmful effects from exposure could take up to three decades to be revealed, so detailed research projects to define the affected workers and set up surveillance and screening procedures were undertaken. Michelin, out of all the members of the rubber processing industry in the British Isles, has been the only company to make a serious and thorough study of this issue. The Company considered it imperative that reassurances could be given to management, unions and employees that any past hazard had indeed abated and any other hazards can be excluded. This was successfully done with the results published internally and in scientific literature. In recognition of this and other work on

health and safety in the rubber industry, Charles Veys was awarded the OBE in 1990.

By the early 1970s, Michelin's UK workforce had expanded greatly. A new purpose-built Medical Department was opened at Stoke in 1973, with a staff of 20 providing 24-hour cover for accident, injury or illness occurring at the place of work. There was an x-ray service, physiotherapy, a sick visiting scheme as well as guidance and rehabilitation on placement and return to work.

Michelin's UK medical service was a unified one, fully supported by successive senior managers. In Northern Ireland a service was developed to cover both sites, with local part-time GPs and full-time nursing staff; likewise in Dundee and Aberdeen. Similar arrangements were made for Burnley too. Exchange visits between medical and nursing staff in all factories were made to ensure good liaison and to maintain a high standard. Strong links, increasingly from the 1980s, were also made with other Michelin groups and in addition to France, with Spain, Italy, Germany, Canada, USA, Brazil and Nigeria, and exchange visits and conferences were arranged.

Industrial safety and accident prevention issues have also been given top priority within the company from the start, latterly through area safety committees established in all production departments, as is illustrated by the case of safety spectacles. Drawing steel wire down to a very fine thread at speed inevitably has potential dangers. The area safety committee of the steel cord production department carried out investigations which led to a review that established the most suitable form of eye protection available. The committee's recommendations were swiftly

The Year of Bibendum was declared in 1998 in recognition of the centenary of the creation of the company's famous mascot. A new logo was introduced and all corporate publicity standards redefined. The vehicle here sports the new livery, complete with the anniversary logo and the Football World Cup symbol (Michelin was a sponsor of the 1998 World Cup).

implemented, resulting in a major reduction in eye injury in the department. An optician, working in conjunction with the Safety Department, provided a free eye-testing and fitting service for a compulsory safety glasses programme.

As a result of the Health & Safety at Work Act which came into force on 1 April 1975, the Health & Safety Commission was created, charged with the formation of policy, and comprising members of the TUC, the CBI and local authorities. Michelin had established good practice for some considerable time before the Act became law, with a structured safety committee organisation throughout the company. For the first time, all six manufacturing sites won British Safety Council Awards in June 1981.

The turn of the millennium saw a reduction of manufacturing facilities in the UK, at Stoke in particular. In response to this, the Medical Department, under an alliance with the consultancy group MPCG and its occupational physician, extended its role to provide advice and services to local businesses, local authorities and educational establishments in the area.

Rubber processing plants are potential danger zones and must be protected accordingly, so not surprisingly, a fire brigade with its own fire station manned by 27 firemen was maintained at Stoke from the very beginning. The first brigade chief was 'Captain' Sidney Pearce, who was also in charge of the works police, a security force which numbered 16 men and two women. A fire fighter since the age of 19, he had begun his career with the London Fire Brigade. Mr Pearce joined Michelin at Stoke in June 1927 and stayed until 1944, by which time the Factory Fire Brigade numbered 25 men, led by a chief officer and a deputy with the rank of second officer. All these men normally worked in departments across the site, but were ready for action at a moment's notice. Throughout the years of the Second World War the fire brigade assumed the additional responsibility of air-raid warning duties, although the Stoke factory was never subjected to attack.

Naturally, it was normal for the Michelin brigade to train with the City of Stoke-on-Trent Fire Brigade and joint exercises were held regularly to ensure the two organisations could work together effectively in the event of a major incident at the factory. One such exercise was Operation Fireman held in July 1958. Earlier, in July 1955 and again in January 1957, the Michelin fire brigade team had twice won the Dobson Cup, a contest for works brigades in the county, held in conjunction with

Many events took place during The Year of Bibendum, including a visit by Michelin employees to Blackpool – which included a ride on a special-liveried tram.

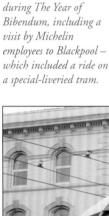

Michelin has supported the London Lord Mayor's Show for many years. Here, the company's float is seen passing St Paul's Cathedral in 1998. M Bibendum is standing proud alongside his anniversary cake, representing the character's centenary theme.

the City of Stoke-on-Trent Fire Brigade. During the Cold War years of the 1950s and '60s, the brigade formed part of the local Civil Defence organisation.

Today, Ballymena, Dundee and Stoke sites all have first-line fire teams and equipment capable of responding quickly to emergencies. They work closely with the Local Authority Emergency services in order to keep each other in constant touch with developments that can affect the safety of these major rubber-processing factories.

Michelin today

And so to the next 100 years. Michelin's presence in the British Isles at the start of the second century of its activities is as exciting and as challenging as it certainly was in 1905. Way back then, the fledgling company, albeit backed by the resources of a dynamic and innovative French parent, looked to establish itself as *the* tyre company of the 20th century. It came with a reputation for excellent products of the highest quality and the service to support them, characteristics that the British and Irish knew already through personal experience as customers, despite the difficulties which had been put in the company's way by competitors anxious to monopolise the home market.

Without the opportunity to benefit from Michelin's regular innovations in the field of mobility, our ability as nations to prosper would undoubtedly have been hampered. How long might it have taken others to introduce concepts such as detachable rims, twin tyres, low-pressure tyres and, most especially, steel-braced radials? This process of innovation is ceaseless and essential in order to satisfy the ever-demanding needs of customers. Michelin's international operation, spread across all continents, enables the company to benefit from the expertise and experience of its customers and its employees in a wide variety of ways. In this regard, Michelin Tyre PLC continues to play a positive and active part in the international company's life. The great British manufacturing base that had been established by the mid-1970s may have gone, but the company's commitment to a viable operation commensurate with the commercial environment of the 21st century is as strong as it has ever been.

Recent years have seen developments and advances on a wide number of fronts. Commercially, customers have reacted with enthusiasm and positive support on various issues. Rolls-Royce has taken a major step forward by equipping its latest Phantom model with Michelin's PAX System, giving this prestigious luxury car optimised run-flat performance combined with exceptional road holding and handling qualities.

Bibendum hot-air balloons were a major international attraction during The Year of Bibendum. Some of the largest balloons ever made, they were always guaranteed to bring a smile to people's faces, as here at the Bristol Balloon Festival in 1998.

In the agricultural market, the XeoBib tyre with its patented Ultraflex technology, is enabling farmers in the British Isles to use exceedingly low inflation pressures in tyres that have good endurance and long wear life. Michelin's CargoXBib tyre has also met a great response from the agricultural community and has gained the company another Royal Agricultural Society of England (RASE) Silver medal. Truck operators have taken to Michelin's latest technologies too. In 2004, Lancashire-based Coach House Antiques became the first UK operator to use the company's new Anti-Splash tyres, designed to reduce dramatically the projection of water created by tyres during wet-weather driving. Similarly, the X-One truck tyre, replacing traditional twin-tyre combinations, represents an important and promising development for the world of transport. Commonplace in North America, it is beginning to establish itself in Europe and will undoubtedly be the new standard in the future. Virgin Atlantic Airways has joined a growing list of airlines to put their trust in Michelin. Virgin's latest Airbus A340-600 aircraft will be fitted with NZG (near zero growth) radial technology tyres. Michelin's NZG technology

gained recognition for the advanced safety features which helped Concorde to take to the skies again in 2001.

Success has also been achieved on two extremes of the tyre market: two-wheel and earthmoving machines. The Hinckley-built 2005 Triumph Speed Triple motorcycle is to be fitted with Michelin Pilot Power tyres, and the 2004 earthmover sales performance for both the UK and Ireland show a significant improvement. The sales figures for the latest offering from Michelin's Travel Publications, 'Eating out in Pubs', is also impressive, so proving that the company can tackle any job, no matter how big, or how small!

On the British manufacturing side, the Dundee factory continues to produce car tyres in high volume, Ballymena factory produces truck tyres, a high percentage for the North American market, and Stoke factory retains a truck tyre retreading facility, supplying its output almost exclusively to the British and Irish markets. Michelin's fuel-efficient Energy range of tyres was named the EcoProduct of the Year at the Fleet Excellence Awards ceremony in London in 2003. Much development has gone into this range over the years, both for car and for truck tyres, and the Dundee factory has recently been chosen to produce them.

Throughout all the company's operations much attention is given to maintaining a healthy and safe working environment. This is especially true in manufacturing, where the potential risks are inherently greater. It was therefore a particularly proud moment for the Ballymena factory when it learnt this year that it was the safest plant in the Michelin world. In one million working hours since May 2004, there was not a single lost-time accident. This achievement is the result of the employees' willingness to address issues of safety, something which is ever-constant. Such willingness has extended in recent months to Michelin UK's Road Safety Steering Group, charged with establishing a comprehensive road safety policy for all Michelin drivers, while simultaneously raising awareness and minimising the risks that personnel face on the roads.

Other fundamental employee-related issues touch upon training and the way in which our employees react with their local communities. In March 2004, the Michelin Technical Training Centre at Ballymena held its official launch ceremony. It was opened by Jane Kennedy, the Northern Ireland Government Minister for Employment and Learning, who said that it was an excellent example of how to establish an important partnership between business and further education in the Province.

A second type of partnership, set up at

Ballymena, Dundee, Stoke-on-Trent and at Burnley in recent years, is the community enterprise support offered through Michelin Development Ltd. This support is seen as essential in promoting and encouraging the development and growth of small and medium enterprises.

A century of activity in the British Isles has seen a vast number of changes taking place. New ways of working, new technologies and new structures and companies have been constant features of life. As recently as during the last five years, Michelin UK has seen a substantial change in its British manufacturing organisation, the creation of Michelin Lifestyle Ltd, the transfer of all the major commercial functions in the British Isles to Stoke-on-Trent, and the setting-up of a European shared service centre at Manchester.

After 100 years of the formation of a British registered subsidiary, Michelin continues to develop in the British Isles. Its manufacturing activity may be less than it was some 25 years ago, but it is still the biggest tyre maker in these islands. Equally importantly, the company still retains the major commercial presence which it has enjoyed for many decades, thanks to the support of millions of customers over the years.

Michelin Tyre PLC remains a wholly owned subsidiary of the international Michelin Group, the world's largest tyre supplier. The Group's net sales in 2004 were €15.7 billion, an increase of 6 per cent on the previous year. The 2003 listing of The Global Tire Report, an annual publication by the American journal *Tire Business*, shows that Michelin has been the world's No. 1 tyre producer for three consecutive years, with a market share of just over 20 per cent. Today, the company operates 74 production sites in 19 countries and has a sales network covering 170 countries. New production facilities and strategic alliances with other manufacturers and commercial organisations continue to develop to the extent that the Group produces and markets a wide range of product brands. Each working day, the Michelin Group produces 770,000 tyres, 95,000 inner tubes, 4 million kilometres of steel cord, 46,500 steel wheels, and 60,000 maps and guides.

Moreover, Michelin is both a producer of consumer and capital goods for the replacement tyre market and an original equipment supplier to vehicle manufacturers. Unlike traditional equipment suppliers who focus their activities on a few major customers, Michelin generates 70 per cent of its business in the supply of all categories of replacement tyres. These sales are realised via different distribution networks which the company supplies or which are owned by the company, such as Euromaster in Europe.

As we look to Michelin's next 100 years in the British Isles, we can be sure that there will be many developments and changes in the company's organisation, just as there have been in the past 100 years. But one thing is certain, Michelin will continue to strive to ensure *a better way forward* for its customers and employees.

Retired company artist Ernie Sherry devised the Bibendum characters for a new footbridge over the River Trent at Hanford, Stoke-on-Trent, opened in 2002.

Index